African American Education

A REFERENCE HANDBOOK

CONTEMPORARY EDUCATION ISSUES

African American Education

A REFERENCE HANDBOOK

Cynthia L. Jackson

A B C ⬤ C L I O

Santa Barbara, California • Denver, Colorado • Oxford, England

"Historically Black Colleges and Universities: A National Treasure" is reprinted in the appendix with permission of Arthur E. Thomas and Robert L. Green

Library of Congress Cataloging-in-Publication Data

Jackson, Cynthia L.
  African American education: a reference handbook / Cynthia L. Jackson.
      p. cm. — (Contemporary education issues)
  Includes bibliographical references and index.
      ISBN 1-57607-269-X (hard : alk. paper) — ISBN 1-57607-566-4 (e-book)
      1. African Americans—Education—History—Handbooks, manuals, etc. I. Title. II. Series.
      LC2741.J33 2001
      370'89'96073—dc21   2001000347

This book is also available on the World Wide Web as an e-book.
Visit www.abc-clio.com for details.

07 06 05 04 03 02 01   10 9 8 7 6 5 4 3 2 1

ABC-CLIO, Inc.
130 Cremona Drive, P.O. Box 1911
Santa Barbara, California 93116-1911

This book is printed on acid-free paper ∞.
Manufactured in the United States of America

To Derrick, Cynthia, Courtney, and Kendall,
the future of my family, and to the future
of all black families. Envision your futures
and create your own paradigms.

❧ Contents

Preface   ***xi***

Chapter One: American and African American Education:
*   *A Framework*   *1*

Education in the United States   *1*
Who Controls Education?   *2*
  Governmental Control   *2*
  Regional Accreditation   *4*
Educational Opportunities   *5*
  The Coleman Report   *5*
  Affirmative Action   *6*
Education's Assault on Poverty   *7*
  Head Start Programs   *8*
  Elementary and Secondary Education Act
    of 1965, Title I   *8*
School Reform Movement   *9*
  National School Reform   *9*
  One State's Education Reform Response   *10*
Higher Education   *13*
  Higher Education Reform Movement   *14*
  One State's Higher Education Reform   *15*
African American Education: An Overview   *16*
  African American Opinions on African
    American Education   *16*
  Status and Condition of African American Education   *22*
  Postsecondary Educational Attainment of
    African Americans   *29*
  African American Public School Employment   *31*
Resource Interview with Douglas V. Davidson   *32*
References   *43*

Chapter Two: Chronology of African American Education 47

Chapter Three: African American Schooling 59

African American Schooling Experiences 60
Curriculum and Instruction 61

Curriculum 61
Two Curricula Models 62
Instruction 63

African American Students and Testing 64

Tests and Their Uses 64
The Bell Curve 65

Public School Resource Interviews 68

Edward M. Harris 69
Janice B. Henry 77

Schooling Options for African American Students 88
Schooling Options Resource Interviews 89

Vivien Davenport 89
Derrick L. Moité 101

Additional Schooling Options 104

African American Immersion Schools 104
Supplementary Programs 105

References 105

Chapter Four: Historically Black Colleges and Universities 107

HBCUs: An Overview 108
HBCUs Defined 109
Accomplishments and Challenges of HBCUs 128

Accomplishments 128
Challenges 129

HBCUs and Desegregation 131
Organizations Established to Assist HBCUs 134
National Association for Equal Opportunity in Higher Education 134
National HBCU Faculty Development Network 134

Office for the Advancement of Public Black Colleges   *134*
United Negro College Fund   *135*
White House Initiative on HBCUs   *135*
HBCU Resource Interviews   **136**

Arthur E. Thomas   *136*
Linette P. Fox   *147*
Two Programs Designed to Assist HBCUs   **156**
The Historically Minority Universities Bioscience
and Biotechnology Program Initiative   *157*
The Union Institute HBCU Initiative   *165*
HBCUs as Cultural and Historical Repositories   **171**
References   **171**

Chapter Five: *Legal Influences on African American*
Education   **173**

Presidential Executive Orders   **174**
U.S. Constitutional Amendments   **174**
Legislative Acts   **175**
Opinions of the U.S. Supreme Court   **177**
Conclusion   **197**
References   **200**

Chapter Six: *Organizations, Associations, Schools, and*
Government Agencies   **201**

Accrediting Organizations   **201**
Higher Education Advocacy Associations   **202**
Immersion Schools and Supplementary Programs   **203**
Museums   **203**
National Organizations   **204**
Organizations Established to Assist HBCUs   **206**
Panhellenic Organizations   **207**
Professional Associations   **208**
Research Centers   **209**

Chapter Seven: *Selected Print and Nonprint Resources*   **213**

Print Resources   **213**
Articles, Books, and Reports   *213*
Journals   *235*
Periodicals   *236*

Nonprint Resources *236*

    Internet *236*
    Television *237*
    Videos *238*

Appendix: Historically Black Colleges and Universities: An Irreplaceable National Treasure, Arthur E. Thomas and Robert L. Green *245*

Glossary *267*

Index *273*

About the Author *293*

❦ Preface

African American education is an interdisciplinary topic. A topic is interdisciplinary when it is essential for one to make connections among disciplines in order to understand the breadth and scope of the topic.

As an interdisciplinary topic, African American education must be examined through the lenses of several disciplines. Enlightenment on the implicit and explicit issues that comprise African American education requires delving into the historical and contemporary knowledge bases and theories of American law, history, economics, sociology, psychology, and political science—to name a few.

African American education is one cornerstone of a story of a people who want to realize the American doctrines of equality, equity, and quality of life. These doctrines are at the core of the sustainable development of African American individuals, the race, and the country. The doctrines of equality, equity, and quality in education are fundamental to the success of African Americans as well as all Americans. If made fully operational, these doctrines would mean access to an educational system that viewed African Americans as potential productive citizens. African Americans would be recognized for their contributions to society and developed for the good of the United States and its status in the world.

AFRICAN AMERICAN EDUCATION
AND THE INSTITUTION OF RACISM

What prevents these doctrines from being realized by African Americans? The answer to this question requires an examination of the American institution of racism. Racism is a complex institution steeped in history and tradition. Research on racism, its existence, and its effects continues to be the subject of studies in American history, law, economics, psychology, sociology, and education.

Racism in the United States is a social institution. For social institutions, there are established and prevailing formal and informal practices and behaviors that are part of the structure of the society. These practices assert people's predetermined societal roles based on their race. In the United States, racism is maintained based on a belief in the superiority of whites. In its operational form, racism is about power. It is the power of one racial group to restrict the economic and social development of individuals in other racial groups. For example, whites control the government, the economics, and the educational systems of the United States. Ultimately, racism marginalizes, trivializes, isolates, and rejects the existence, contributions, and full participation of particular groups of people in a society.

 . Understanding the issues and concerns in African American education requires acceptance of the premise that racism, as an institution, exists and is an active practice in the United States. Racism overtly and covertly dominates the collective psyche of African Americans. Racism also defines and determines the manner in which the three doctrines of equality, equity, and quality are exercised in terms of the education African Americans receive through America's education system. In turn, racism, to a great extent, frames their positions and roles in society.

African Americans achieve a sense of identity from their own experiences. As much as being African American is about being of African descent, it is about a state of mind. This state of mind reflects the unique experiences shared by African Americans—varied as they are—that set them apart from any other racial group in the United States. The development of this state of mind began in their resolve regarding the method and the purpose of their immigration to America. In 1619, twenty Africans disembarked from a Dutch boat in Jamestown, Virginia. These first Africans to colonial America were indentured servants. As indentured servants, like their white counterparts, they were to pay the cost of their passage and other expenses by providing labor for the colony. The period of indentured servitude was usually seven years. For about thirty years, when Africans' terms of indentured servitude expired, they were freed and were given land. Colony authorities realized that free labor boosted the economy of the colonies more than indentured servants did. By the early 1650s, the terms of African indentured servants began to be extended gradually, with fewer Africans being freed. In 1661, Virginia was the first colony to legalize the slavery of blacks. Since African Americans arrived in the "New World," non–African Americans have determined the perimeters and content of the education that is "appropriate" for African Americans. Generally, the education system has ignored and continues to ignore their history and culture, and their self-identified aspirations and values.

EDUCATION AND CULTURAL COMPATIBILITY

Education occurs inside and outside of the place called school. One's initial education occurs in the family and community. In these two settings, enculturation and socialization first occur. Children learn their history and the expected and accepted aspirations, values, and beliefs of their culture.

A substantial number of research studies have concluded that the relation between home and school is a significant factor in student achievement. Children tend to succeed in schools that reflect the culture and values of the communities in which they live. In spite of these findings, an increasing number of African American students attend schools that do not reinforce their family and community culture, values, aspirations, and beliefs.

Although the education by family and community continues, American children next enter institutions of formal education. Through formal education, instruction is given in the history, expectations, aspirations, values, and culture of American society. Far too many African Americans, including those who achieve advanced degrees, accomplished lifestyles, or both, find incompatibility between their early informal educational experiences and their subsequent formal educational experiences. Because most of the formal American education system does not reinforce African American principles of family and community, African Americans find themselves having to live and function with the dichotomy.

INTENT OF THE BOOK

This book is intended to provide readers with information and resources on three prevalent issues concerning the education of African Americans—schooling, higher education, and legal influences. The book covers historical and current events that shape the milieu in which African Americans are educated. Although an overview of African American education for more than 300 years is provided, primary emphasis is placed on the period from 1954 to the present, especially the past 20 years. The challenges of African American education are confronted. The book presents a black perspective of African American education. The approach taken enables the reader to focus specifically on African American social, economic, and educational status and attainment as well as institutions and events that shape, enrich, and define African American lives and education.

This book focuses on the following issues in African American education: precollege schooling, historically black colleges and universities, and legal actions. More specifically included are summary discussions on various aspects of the topic; resource materials; statistical data on the status and condition of African Americans; African American social, critical, and political thought; the influence of testing, curricula, and institutional approaches; the effects of desegregation and affirmative action; and more.

The last two chapters, Chapters 6 and 7, include selected print and nonprint resources. Also listed are scholarly books, articles, and reports as well as organizations, associations, and video and television resources.

The eight interviews in the book breathe life into the history, status, accomplishments, and challenges of African American education. The interviews are provided to edify the reader's understanding of the topic through the experiences and insights of black educators.

The majority of the quotes used in the book were not altered to reflect the "political correctness" of our time. The author believes it is essential to capture the thoughts as well as the language of the eras of the quotes. The views expressed in this book were chosen by the author and do not necessarily reflect those of the university at which she is employed. The views expressed by those whose interviews are contained in the book do not necessarily reflect the attitudes or the official position of their affiliations or institutions.

ACKNOWLEDGMENTS

This book is possible because of the support and assistance of several people. Numerous resources exist that could have been included in this book. Selecting the definitive resources in the field was not a task the author believed should be done by one person. Therefore, a panel of five individuals with expertise in diverse fields and professions related to African American education was surveyed to assist in selecting the resources included in the book. Their input was invaluable. The panel members' names, positions, and affiliations follow. The historically black colleges from which they received their baccalaureate degrees are included in parentheses, when applicable.

James D. Anderson is professor and head of the Department of Educational Policy Studies at the University of Illinois at Urbana-Champaign in Urbana, Illinois (Stillman College, Tuscaloosa, AL).

Evelyn J. Carroll is the retired chairperson of the Division of Education and the Department of Education at Spelman College in Atlanta, Georgia (University of Arkansas at Pine Bluff, formerly Arkansas A. M. and N. College).

Douglas V. Davidson is associate professor of sociology at Western Michigan University in Kalamazoo, Michigan (Tougaloo College, Tougaloo, Mississippi).

J. Stephen Dobbins is president of the Arts Consortium of Cincinnati, Ohio.

Edward L. Wingard is acting vice president for academic affairs at the Union Institute in Cincinnati, Ohio.

The time, energy, and openness of the eight interviewees are greatly appreciated. They are Douglas V. Davidson, Edward M. Harris, Janice B. Henry, Vivien Davenport, Derrick L. Moité, Arthur E. Thomas, Linette P. Fox, and Eleanor F. Nunn. In addition, the information shared through personal correspondence between the author and Raymond C. Pierce of the Office of Civil Rights in the U.S. Department of Education was extremely valuable.

I am indebted to my father, the late William S. Jackson; my mother, Mary S. Jackson; and my sister, E. Camille Moité, for their consistent encouragement in everything I do.

A special thanks is extended to John E. Hall, deputy managing editor of the *Sun-Sentinel* newspaper in Fort Lauderdale, Florida, for his archival and technical assistance. In addition, the author acknowledges Danny Weil for providing the opportunity to write this book and the editors at ABC-CLIO for making it a reality.

Chapter One

❧ American and African American Education: A Framework

To understand the status, conditions, and issues in African American education and place it in the proper context, one must be familiar with aspects of the American education system. The first half of this chapter provides an overview of American education. Summaries are presented on the topics of American educational ideology, jurisdiction, opportunity, school reform, and higher education.

The second half of the chapter makes the link between African American education and American education. This section opens with quotes on social, political, and critical thought on African American education from selected African Americans. Statistical data, primarily obtained through the U.S. Census Bureau and U.S. Department of Education, are presented. The data are provided to illustrate the current condition and status of African American education. A resource interview with Dr. Douglas V. Davidson, a sociologist, provides a sociological analysis of the statistical data and an overview of African American education and its reliance on the American education system and American society.

EDUCATION IN THE UNITED STATES

The United States is a country with the ideology of universal education. The universal education system, financed through public funding, provides free schooling for its juvenile citizens in prekindergarten through twelfth grade. In most states, attendance is compulsory until children reach the age of sixteen.

The ideology of universal education is based upon the premise that a democratic society must have an educated citizenry because educated citizens can be productive and can make knowledgeable decisions about issues affecting the country. At the core of this publicly supported, universal education system are the doctrines of equality, equity, and quality. Frequently, these doctrines are discussed and addressed as discrete entities. However, they are mutually reciprocal and hierarchical.

Level 1, at the base of the hierarchy, is equality in education. Equality occurs when the same number of resources is available to all schools within a school district. For example, all school libraries have the same number of books.

Level 2 is educational equity. Equity in education is the manner in which fairness or impartiality is exercised to ensure that all students in the school have access to educational opportunities that will enable them to develop their potential. For example, all schools in a school district have the same number of library books but the majority of the books in one school are outdated or are not educationally beneficial for the students in the school. Then equality is occurring but equity is not.

Level 3, the highest level, is quality in education. Quality is synonymous in this context with excellence. In many ways, excellence is more abstract than concrete, and dependent on individual perceptions and interpretations. For the purpose of education, excellence is codified through educational standards. The standards are the measures of the ascribed inputs and outputs of the education system. Written educational standards, and the attributes of instructional personnel and student outcomes, are the primary measures used to determine excellence. Educational standards are the guidelines for determining the curriculum and the measures of student achievement. Standards are derived from the educational goals the states, and to some extent the federal government, have established. These standards are written on the presumption that equality and equity exist in the education system. To continue the example of library books, each school library has the most appropriate books for its students.

Teachers, administrators, and other education professionals implement the educational standards. Education quality is dependent upon competent instructional professionals who are expected to possess and demonstrate professional training and to exercise professional judgment in an equal and equitable manner.

WHO CONTROLS EDUCATION?

Governmental Control

Education, an institution vital to the future of the nation, falls under the jurisdiction of the states. Because it is the primary responsibility and concern of states, education focuses on the demands of the state, specifically, and the needs of the nation, generally.

States' span of control in education includes certifying professional staff; determining the curriculum and its content; measuring student achievement and outcomes; creating and regulating student health services, guidance and counseling services, and breakfast and lunch programs; determining the scope of extracurricular activities; distributing monetary and human resources; and maintaining educational facilities. This list is by no means exhaustive.

Each state decentralizes its authority by distributing control over certain decisions to individual school districts. School districts are required to operate within the provisions of the state constitution and statutes but may, through the authority of their individual school boards, select resources to implement the state's curriculum. These resources include textbooks, library resources, instructional methods, instructional resources, instructional and noninstructional staff, and funds. Decisions on resource disbursement are considered necessary to meet the needs of districts' students and the communities they serve.

There are over 15,000 public school districts in the United States. Each district forms its own interpretations of the doctrines of equality, equity, and quality. In turn, the school districts develop operational regulations, procedures, and practices based on their interpretation of the doctrines.

With this hierarchical decentralization, two questions might come to mind: What is included in the national curriculum? and How does the national curriculum guide what is included in the states' curricula? A national curriculum does not exist. However, national expectations are identified and generally agreed upon. It is expected that graduates of schooling in the United States should be at a functional level in reading, writing, and computations. This functional level is perceived as being directly related to the ability of citizens to be productive and socially and politically informed. As the United States becomes more technological, a higher functional level is required of citizens. Therefore, the functional level is on a sliding scale.

While it can appear that states have total autonomy concerning education, this perception is not accurate. States must operate within the framework of the U.S. Constitution. When state laws and practices violate the provisions of the Constitution, the federal government can intervene. The Constitution does not directly address education, so access to public education is not in and of itself a right protected by the Constitution. Education is a state right. Yet education is considered to be incorporated in the constitutional phrase "to provide for the general welfare." The "general welfare" is interpreted by most to include the protection of citizens' right to access the states' education system. As such, it is an obligation of the federal government to ensure that the state right to an education is protected for all of its citizens, for the good of the country.

Federal intervention in education most often occurs in the areas of civil rights and school finance. U.S. Supreme Court decisions, executive orders, and congressional enactments are the means by which the federal government most frequently uses its influence in education. Chapter 5 contains a discussion of federal and state legal decisions and their influence on African American education.

Regional Accreditation

The United States may be the only country that has a completely decentralized education system. Instead of a national authority, such as a ministry of education, six regional accrediting agencies are recognized by the U.S. Department of Education. These agencies exist to appraise the quality of education offered by elementary, secondary, and postsecondary institutions in the states. They are the closest the United States comes to having an entity for national quality control of education. Higher education schools that are not accredited by the regional accrediting agency for their state are not eligible to participate in federal grant and assistance programs.

As outlined by the Office of Postsecondary Education in the U.S. Department of Education, the accrediting procedures are:

1. Standards are developed collaboratively by the accrediting agency and the educational institutions.
2. Self-studies are conducted by the institutions. There are in-depth evaluations of how well the institutions are meeting the established standards.
3. On-site evaluations are conducted by a team that is selected by the accrediting agency.
4. The names of the institutions that are accredited by their regional agency are published.
5. Reevaluation of the institutions is conducted periodically by the accrediting agency.

The fifty states, the District of Columbia, and the U.S. territories are divided among the six regional accrediting agencies. While the schools are assessed by their respective regional agencies, an accredited institution is recognized by schools in the regions of other accrediting agencies. This mutual recognition is important for admission to institutions, and, in many instances, employment at institutions across regional areas. The six regional institutional accrediting agencies follow. Accrediting agencies' directory information is provided in Chapter 6.

> *Middle States Association of College and Schools*
>   Accrediting Areas: Delaware, the District of Columbia, Maryland, New Jersey, New York, Pennsylvania, Puerto Rico, the U.S. Virgin Islands
> *New England Association of Schools and Colleges*
>   Accrediting Areas: Connecticut, Maine, Massachusetts, New Hampshire, Rhode Island, Vermont
> *North Central Association of Colleges and Schools*
>   Accrediting Areas: Arizona, Arkansas, Colorado, Illinois, Indiana, Iowa, Kansas, Michigan, Minnesota, Missouri, Nebraska, New Mexico, North Dakota, Ohio, Oklahoma, South Dakota, West Virginia, Wisconsin, Wyoming, Navajo Nation
> *Northwest Association of Schools and Colleges*
>   Accrediting Areas: Alaska, Idaho, Montana, Nevada, Oregon, Utah, Washington
> *Southern Association of College and Schools*
>   Accrediting Areas: Alabama, Florida, Georgia, Kentucky, Louisiana, Mississippi, North Carolina, South Carolina, Tennessee, Texas, Virginia
> *Western Association of Schools and Colleges*
>   Accrediting Areas: California, Hawaii, U.S. territories of Guam and American Samoa, Republic of Palau, Federated States of Micronesia, Commonwealth of the Northern Marianna Islands, Republic of the Marshall Islands.

EDUCATIONAL OPPORTUNITIES

Life, liberty, and the pursuit of happiness are achieved by individual Americans to a wide and varying degree. One factor that contributes to achieving these three constitutional rights is one's economic opportunities and circumstances. In the United States, economic opportunities are generally related to educational attainment, which is in turn dependent on the accessibility of educational opportunities.

The Coleman Report

Sociologist James Coleman's book *Equality of Educational Opportunity* was first published in 1966. Commonly known as the Coleman Report, it became benchmark research on opportunity in education. Coleman found that the factors that contributed most significantly to the academic achievement of students were their family social status and the social status of the families of classmates.

The study results completely contradicted what had previously been considered necessary for quality education. According to Coleman's findings, class size, instructional personnel salaries, educational resources, funding, and curricular methods had no direct influence on learning. Coleman's findings weakened the premise, and somewhat the support, of the Elementary and Secondary Education Act of 1965's Title I early in its implementation. Title I, which is discussed in more detail later in this chapter, was enacted to decrease class size, provide remedial education, increase personnel salaries, and increase funding for education. The U.S. Commission on Civil Rights used Coleman's findings as the catalyst for introducing busing as a common practice for school desegregation.

Affirmative Action

The concept of affirmative action was introduced in 1941, in President Franklin D. Roosevelt's Executive Order 8802. In 1965, President Lyndon B. Johnson first used the phrase "affirmative action," in Executive Order 11246. This legislation is detailed in Chapter 5.

Affirmative action's origins are in employment. Executive Order 11246 required "contractors," or organizations receiving federal funding, to agree to "not discriminate against any employee or applicant for employment because of race, color, religion, sex, or national origin" during the duration of the contract with the federal government. The underlying social principle of affirmative action is to redress the discriminatory practices in employment by agencies that receive federal money.

Educational institutions that accept federal contracts have to abide by the provisions in the executive order. In postsecondary institutions, the relationship between admissions and affirmative action is evident in the practice of colleges and universities who are receiving federal funding to subsidize student tuition. Colleges are required to practice affirmative action in admission in order to receive federal funds.

At the center of the current debate on affirmative action is the issue of reverse discrimination. Claims of reverse discrimination are based on the concept that unqualified individuals, primarily people of color, are, because of race, receiving preference in admissions over qualified individuals—whites and, more specifically, males. The concept of reverse discrimination first came to the U.S. Supreme Court in the 1979 case *Regents of the University of California v. Bakke.* A discussion of the Bakke case can be found in Chapter 5.

EDUCATION'S ASSAULT ON POVERTY

Poverty crosses all racial groups. In the 1960s, the plight of the poor took center stage in social policy and social action in the United States. President Lyndon Johnson declared a "War on Poverty." His declaration sparked a flurry of governmental and nongovernmental activities to address this societal dilemma. Michael Harrington's 1962 book, *The Other America: Poverty in the United States,* heralded an era of awakening for the majority of Americans. All was not well in the country. Too many children, America's future, were living in poverty.

The U.S. Bureau of the Census reported that in 1960 22 percent of the U.S. population lived below the poverty level. The National Center for Education Statistics reported in *The Condition of Education 1996* that 27 percent of all children lived in poverty in 1960. Governmental and nongovernmental agencies from across the country focused human resources and funding to combating poverty. Poverty, they realized, has a direct relation to educational achievement and subsequent attainment of education. Research concluded that poverty negatively affected children's physiological, educational, and psychological potential and their possibility of future productivity. In 1998, 13.5 million children, or approximately 19 percent of all children in the United States, were living in poverty (Children's Defense Fund website 1999). This percentage had fluctuated between 17 and 22 percent since 1975.

One of the fronts in the war on poverty was education. Two federal education programs were established in 1965 and continue to operate. One is the Office for Economic Opportunity's Head Start Program and the other is the Elementary and Secondary Act of 1965, Title I. Both of these programs were expected to even the educational playing field for America's children living in poverty.

These well-intentioned programs with their ambitious missions were not without their critics and detractors. Admitting that poverty existed and the level at which it existed was not easy for many Americans. To declare a war on poverty meant accepting that poverty existed and was not going to go away with the wave of a wand. America had to attack this problem because it lessened the potential pool of human capital. These new programs meant potential changes in the social, economic, and political traditions of the nation.

Head Start Programs

Head Start began in 1965. Its purpose is to strengthen the school and learning readiness of preschool children (ages three through five) whose combined family income is below the federal index of poverty. Initiated in the Office of Economic Opportunity, the Head Start Bureau is now part of the Administration of Children and Family of the Department of Health and Human Services.

Head Start is a comprehensive program designed to provide services that enhance the intellectual, social, and emotional growth of children who live below the poverty level. Its services are in education, health, social services, and nutrition. To strengthen and sustain the benefits of the services for the children, families receive social service assistance. Parent and community involvement are fundamental to Head Start programs.

Since Head Start's inception, the Children's Defense Fund reports, it has served 15 million children. In 1997, 40 percent of all eligible children participated. Head Start links education to the communities of the children served by operating in schools, community agencies, and religious institutions. In 1995, 5,000 Head Start programs operated in public schools, 2,000 in churches, 1,800 in governments buildings, 1,000 in community centers, and 1,000 in public housing (Children's Defense Fund website 1999).

The Head Start Bureau (1999) reported an enrollment of 822,316 children during the 1997–1998 academic year. Nationally, 1,513 local public agencies, private nonprofit organizations, and school systems were awarded Head Start funds. There are 48,004 Head Start classrooms and 15,872 Head Start centers. Thirteen percent of the children enrolled have learning or physical disabilities. Eighty-eight percent of Head Start teachers have credentials to teach in early childhood education classrooms. The 668 home-based components serve 42,743 children. Twenty-nine percent of the parents who are employed by Head Start have children who are former or current Head Start participants. Over 808,147 parents volunteer in local Head Start programs.

Elementary and Secondary Education Act of 1965, Title I

The Elementary and Secondary Education Act (ESEA) of 1965 was enacted to ensure equity and quality in education for students. It was reauthorized in 1994 as the Improving America's Schools Act. Under the Excellence for All Children Act of 1999, President William Jefferson Clinton proposed the reauthorization of ESEA. The Excellence for All Children

Act of 1999 emphasizes high standards, instructional staff quality, accountability, and a safe school environment. The reauthorization was not passed by both houses of Congress in 2000.

The largest funded component of ESEA is Title I. Title I programs provide compensatory education for children whose combined family income is at or below the poverty level. Most of the educational activities are remedial in nature. Title I was designed to close the achievement gap between economically advantaged and disadvantaged children. Through Title I, funding increased to "poverty impacted" schools. The purpose of Title I was to provide remedial programs, primarily in reading and arithmetic, for disadvantaged students.

According to the U.S. Department of Education, as of 2000 approximately 14,000 school districts received Title I funding. Of the funding, 90 to 93 percent was spent by school districts on instructional resources (USDE website 1999). Not all schools that are eligible for Title I receive Title I funding. The 1994 ESEA authorization attempted to rectify this by increasing the funding for Title I.

SCHOOL REFORM MOVEMENT

National School Reform

The 1980s were the beginning of the push for widespread educational reform and change. The impetus for change can emanate from inside or outside of a system. Much of the force for educational reform emanated from outside the system. The four forces for change in education were: (1) shifts in the demographics of schools, (2) increased use of technology as an instructional and management tool, (3) the practice of revisiting and redirecting the focus on educator professionalism, and (4) changes worldwide.

During the 1980s and 1990s, in response to the four forces listed above, broad changes were made in the education process at the state and school district levels. The primary focus was on students completing the "correct" subjects, new standards for outcomes, increased testing, more mathematics, and more rigorous graduation requirements. Several educators, including Clark and Astuto (1994), Hilliard (1995), and Wise (1988), viewed and continue to view the changes as being nonresponsive, in whole or in part, to the four forces that created the need for education reform.

The documented catalyst for change was the 1983 publication *A Nation at Risk: The Imperative for Educational Reform,* a study by the

National Commission on Excellence in Education, which was established by U.S. Secretary of Education Terrel H. Bell. The commission reported that education in the United States was inadequate and characterized it as "mediocre" and "noncompetitive." It concluded that the poor quality of the education system put the country in peril.

The Commission gathered testimony from educators and community representatives. The testimony revealed that: (1) When compared to the student achievement scores of other industrialized countries, U.S. students came in last. (2) Test scores generally in the basic skills of reading, writing, and computation had declined. (3) Critical thinking skills, such as inference, persuasion, evaluation, and synthesis, were not at the expected level for high school graduates. The Commission's alarm was compounded when it considered the increased use of and demand for technology in American workplaces and homes. Technology would require new job skills, ways of working, and intellectual agility.

Based on its findings, the Commission made six recommendations:

1. Increase high school graduation requirements.
2. Increase testing to measure achievement.
3. Establish more rigorous admissions requirements to college.
4. Spend more time on teaching the basics. If necessary have a longer school day or year.
5. Improve preparation of teachers.
6. Increase accountability of educators and elected officials in school outcomes.

These recommendations sparked school reform nationally. States and school districts redirected their resources to address the recommendations. School reform was to entail a major restructuring of the education process. Yet education reform had little to do with restructuring and more to do with expanding what already existed. School reform was more likely to focus on school operations, logistics, programs, and procedures. The human factors of education—students and teachers—tended to be considered primarily by outcome measures—test scores, standards, and grades.

One State's Education Reform Response

The Florida Statewide Assessment Program serves as an example of the type of systematic, periodic assessment programs that were instituted by states in response to the call for school reform. The program is administered through the Florida Department of Education and calls for accountability in the public schools.

Florida's assessment program was established in 1971. Until 1984, the program consisted primarily of the High School Competency Test. After 1984, five additional tests were added to measure various aspects of student academic achievement. In addition, state tests were added to determine whether individuals were qualified to be teachers and administrators in Florida.

Florida Student Assessment Program

The Florida student assessment program consists of six tests. These tests are administered to students enrolled in public elementary and secondary schools in Florida:

1. High School Competency Test—This test is administered to eleventh-grade students. Students are to demonstrate proficiency in basic skills in communications and mathematics. Passing both sections is required for high school graduation.
2. College-Level Academic Skills Test—This is an achievement test to measure students' communication and mathematics skills at the college level. The skills were identified by faculties at community colleges and state universities. To enroll in public postsecondary institutions, students must pass this test.
3. Grade Ten Assessment Test—This achievement test measures "higher order" skills and replaced the minimal skill tests for this grade.
4. Florida Writing Assessment Program—Through this test, students' writing proficiency is evaluated. In a determined time period, students are to develop a composition on an assigned topic. The test is administered in the fourth, eighth, and tenth grades.
5. Florida College Entry-Level Placement Test—This test measures basic computation and communication skills for students who plan to pursue a degree in a public community college or university. The results are used to determine the appropriate academic level for entering college students.
6. Florida's Comprehensive Assessment Test—This achievement test was developed to measure students' ability to meet state "benchmark" standards. The reading portion of the test is administered to second-, fourth-, eighth-, and tenth-grade

students. Fifth-, eighth-, and tenth-grade students are administered the mathematics section.

In addition to the six state-administered tests, students can be assessed through norm-referenced tests, which compare individual and group scores to those of a norm group. The Florida Department of Education does not administer these tests. School districts in the state can select the tests they want to administer. Since the test results are not interchangeable, it is not possible to compare school districts unless they are using the same tests. Generally, the tests are administered in kindergarten through grade eight. Test results for fourth and eighth grades are reported to the Florida Department of Education. School districts have used the following nationally norm-referenced tests:

- California Achievement Test Form A
- California Achievement Test Forms E and F
- Comprehensive Test of Basic Skills Forms A and B
- Comprehensive Test of Basic Skills Forms U and V
- Iowa Test of Basic Skills Form K
- Comprehensive Assessment Program National Achievement Test Form 3
- Stanford Achievement Test Form E and F
- Stanford Achievement Test Forms J, K, and L

Florida Professional Assessment Program

The Florida professional assessment program consists of two examinations for teaching and administrative employees. The two professional examinations were instituted during the mid-1980s.

1. Florida Teacher Certification Examination—This test assesses the comprehension, writing, and computation skills of prospective new teachers to the state. Prospective teachers are required to pass the three test sections to obtain a Florida teaching certificate.
2. Florida Educational Leadership Exam—To obtain administrator state certification, individuals are required to pass three subtests: (1) Leadership, Management, and Personnel; (2) Communications; (3) Curriculum, Finance, Law, and Technology.

HIGHER EDUCATION

Higher, or postsecondary, education in the United States was designed originally to prepare the scholars and researchers of the nation. Individuals were being prepared to conduct the necessary research and development (R&D) in industry, government, and universities. Increasingly, more practicing professionals were required to pursue graduate degrees to remain competitive in their fields. For example, in many states teachers are required to obtain their master's degrees within their first three to five years of teaching. In the late 1970s through the mid-1980s, the number of master's of business administration (MBA) degrees tripled. An increasing number of people were completing postsecondary degrees and remaining practicing professionals.

Changes in the U.S. and world markets are directly related to what is considered minimal education. As the United States moved from an agrarian society to an industrial society, a high school diploma was considered minimal for skilled positions. Then, as it began to move from an industrial society to a technological society, a college degree was considered minimal for skilled positions.

At one time universities and colleges were sheltered from outside intervention. External influence escalated during the early 1960s as postsecondary institutions became increasingly involved in political and social issues, and as they received more public funding. Once a haven from the influences of society, higher education is now expected to take the leadership role to train specialists, practitioners, and researchers for the good of society.

There are five levels of postsecondary degrees. Associate degrees provide the option to receive training for an immediate career, or to explore areas for possible further study. Baccalaureate degrees are at the rudimentary level for developing a focused field of study. Master's and graduate professional degrees are generally field specific, providing training for practicing a profession. Professional degrees include medicine, law, and dentistry, among others. Doctoral degrees are the highest degrees that can be attained. There are two types of doctorates. While individuals with both types of doctorates are employed at universities, it is the nature of their studies for the degree that makes the distinction between the two types. Doctorates for a specific discipline, such as the Doctor of Education (Ed.D.) or the Doctor of Psychology (Psy.D.) are considered practitioner degrees. Individuals with these degrees focus their studies on the specific discipline of the degree. The culminating product of their studies is a major project for practical use in the discipline. The Doctor of Philosophy (Ph.D.) is a research-based degree.

While persons with these degrees identify a specific discipline in which they will focus their studies, their studies are broadened to encompass theories and research from related disciplines. The culminating project for the Ph.D. is a dissertation. The dissertation is a research-based project that contributes new knowledge, creates new theory, or expands on existing theory in the identified discipline.

In the post–World War II era there was an unparalleled growth in college enrollment. This growth was due in large part to the Servicemen's Readjustment Act of 1944, or the GI Bill. Ninety days of service was worth a free year of higher education, with a cap of forty-eight months. By 1947, 49 percent of college students were veterans. College enrollment continued to increase until the 1970s.

The launching of Sputnik by the Soviet Union in 1957 created a furor in the United States for honing its technological and scientific talent pool. During this period, the number of Ph.D. degrees increased annually. Between 1958 and 1973, the number increased from 8,773 to 34,000.

Higher Education Reform Movement

In the 1980s, higher education was put under the microscope. Mandates and recommendations for higher education reform were imposed. The fact that outside forces, such as federal funding and federal and state legislation, were calling for reform in higher education was unusual and shocking. For the most part, until the 1980s, postsecondary institutions were allowed to operate undisturbed by outside intervention. Increased change in higher education mandated by state departments of education and legislatures made it necessary for postsecondary institutions to begin to examine their effectiveness and their contributions to the nation.

To Strengthen Quality in Higher Education was published by the American Council on Education (ACE) in 1982. The National Commission on Higher Education Issues conducted the study and made recommendations for reform in higher education. The recommendations concerned the role of institutions' boards of trustees, methods of recruiting and selecting administrators, the importance of college students demonstrating mastery of basic skills, mandates for professional continuing education, the needs of adult learners, and faculty tenure and merit salaries.

Large amounts of money are devoted to higher education by state and federal governments each year. Funding from these sources is accompanied by specific regulations that are to be followed in order for funding to continue. As public funding to higher education increased, so did the level of outside intervention regarding the missions, goals, objectives, policies, and practices of higher education institutions. With increased social demands and more fields of specialization, institutions of higher education became dependent on external funding. Much of this funding was from governmental agencies.

When an institution accepts funds it ostensibly accepts the funding agency's purposes, requirements, and regulations, even if these factors are in conflict with the institution's philosophy, mission, and culture. External funding requires institutions' compliance with and accountability to external agencies. Acceptance of funding can have programmatic, instructional, and organizational implications. These funding realities increase the influence of federal and state departments of education, special interest groups, and legislative mandates in higher education institutions.

One State's Higher Education Reform

An example of higher education's response to state mandates occurred in Ohio in the 1980s. The description of the mandate that follows is from a research study the author conducted.

"The Standards for Colleges and Universities Preparing Teachers," also known as Teacher Education Redesign, or Redesign, was adopted in 1975 by the state of Ohio. By July 1980, Redesign programs were to be fully implemented by the forty-eight Ohio institutions that certify teachers.

The standards were written in response to increasing evidence that students preparing to be teachers in a changing society needed a broader educational background in order to do the job. The teacher education faculty at the forty-eight universities and colleges involved were to redesign the governance, organization, and programs of teacher education.

A unique aspect of Redesign was the funding arrangement. Unlike many change efforts, which provide seed money for initiation and implementation, the institutions involved in Teacher Education Redesign were to continue to receive funding from the Ohio Department of Education even after the program was incorporated into the institutions.

The new standards required an integration of five areas that were considered of concern to all pre-service teachers regardless of content area or level of concentration: reading, human relations, discipline, cultural pluralism, and analysis and evaluation through the use of diagnostic instruments. The standards also required that all institutions work closely with schools in the community, conduct follow-up studies of graduates, provide teacher education student services (i.e., admissions, counseling, placement, follow-up), establish an advisory committee for curriculum design and evaluation that was representative of the areas of concern, and provide field experiences for the students no later than the beginning of the sophomore year.

The intention of Teacher Education Redesign was to develop a program that was comprehensive enough to adapt to the needs of all pre-service teachers, enabling them to address the changing and varying needs of students. It became obvious that the Redesign program, in order to meet this challenge, was to be no small undertaking. The Teacher Education Redesign program meant a total restructuring of the colleges' and universities' goals, programs, and instructional techniques. The restructuring also meant changes in hiring practices and in the roles and relationships among faculty members. Until Redesign, university faculty members' work environment and interaction had been predominately independent, individualized, and field specific. Redesign created the need for collaboration and cooperation among faculty members (Jackson 1982, 4–5). The level of restructuring was dependent on the size of the institution. The larger the institution, the more Redesign looked like business as usual. For the most part, the larger institutions did not make changes to their teacher education programs.

AFRICAN AMERICAN EDUCATION: AN OVERVIEW

African American Opinions on African American Education

The philosophical tenets of proponents of African American education are emancipation and recognition. Emancipation means economic, social, and political empowerment and freedom. Recognition refers to the contributions African Americans have made and continue to make nationally and globally.

The writings of a number of African American scholars, researchers, practitioners, and activists express a variety of views on how to bring about emancipation and recognition through education. Their ideas range from assimilation to nationalism, from identifying issues to examining and responding to issues, from social thought and criticism to practical methods and applications. The following quotations represent the historical and contemporary opinions of selected African American writers about African American education and the pursuit of equality, equity, and quality.

For all quoted, and those who are not quoted, it is important to recognize that their thoughts are not monolithic. Yet they agree on one common principle: that education is directly related to African Americans' being prepared to fully participate in and advance society. Quotations are used to honor the writers' thoughts and their unique voices and to illustrate their convictions and passions for a better quality of life for African Americans. Readers are encouraged to access the articles and books to further evaluate and analyze the ideas that are presented by the writers.

> Let us have an education, that shall practically develop our thinking faculties and manhood; and then, and not until then, shall we be able to vie with our oppressors, go where we may. We as heretofore, have been on the extreme; either no qualification at all, or a Collegiate education. We jumped too far; taking a leap from the deepest abyss to the highest summit; rising from the ridiculous to the sublime; without medium or intermission. Let our young women have an education; let their minds be well informed; well stored with useful information and practical proficiency. . . . They must be *useful.* (Martin R. Delany, 1852, *The Condition, Elevation, Emigration, and Destiny of the Colored People of the United States,* 91)

> The Negro race, like all races, is going to be saved by its exceptional men. The problem of education, then, among Negroes must first of all deal with the Talented Tenth; it is the problem of developing the Best of this race that they may guide the Mass away from the contamination and death of the Worst, in their own and other races. . . . Intelligence, broad sympathy, knowledge of the world that was and is, and of the relation of men to it—this is the curriculum of that Higher Education which must underlie true life. On this foundation we may build bread winning, skill of hand and quickness of brain. . . . Education and work are the levers to uplift a people. Work alone will not do it unless inspired by the right ideals and guided by intelligence. (W.E.B. DuBois, 1903, *The Talented Tenth,* 518, 533)

> One of the chief hindrances to the progress of Negro education . . . is the fact that the Negro colleges in which so many of the teachers are prepared have not realized the importance of convincing the Southern white people that education makes the same improvement in the Negro that it does in the white man; makes him so much more useful in his labour, so much better a citizen, and so much more dependable in all the relations of life, that it is worth while to spend the money to give him an education. (Booker T. Washington, 1911, *The Mistakes and the Future of Negro Education,* 439)

> Negroes have no control over their education and have little voice in their own affairs pertaining thereto. . . . The education of the Negroes,

then, the most important thing in the uplift of the Negroes, is almost entirely in the hands of those who have enslaved them and now segregate them. . . . The present system under the control of the whites trains the Negro to be white and at the same time convinces him of the impropriety or the impossibility of becoming white. . . . Real education means to inspire people to live more abundantly, to learn to begin with life as they find it and make it better. (Carter G. Woodson, 1933, *The Mis-Education of the Negro,* 22, 23, 29)

American schools were to seek to develop better health, give a command of the fundamental processes, develop vocational efficiency, create worthy home members, build better citizens, teach worthy uses of leisure time, and refine ethical character. . . . It is impossible to conceive of any future status of the Negro, or any social configuration of the American State, in which it will not be desirable to cultivate these qualities where Negro children are concerned. . . . Schools for Negro children . . . must function as coordinate elements of a unified system, and not in utter isolation from the world of action and social change. (Horace Mann Bond, [1934], 1966, *The Education of the Negro in the American Social Order,* 8, 9)

It must be borne in mind that the first lesson in Humanities is to make a people aware of their contribution to civilization; and the second lesson is to teach them about other civilizations. . . . The erroneous world opinion that the African Continent has made no contribution to civilization, and that its people are naturally backward . . . is the misrepresentation that has become the basis of race prejudice. . . . I bring this information to the attention of the world, so that . . . all races and creeds might know the truth and free themselves from those prejudices which have corrupted human relations; . . . and the people of African origin might be emancipated from their serfdom of inferiority complex, and enter upon a new era of freedom, in which they would feel like free men, with full human rights and privileges. (George G. M. James, 1954, *Stolen Legacy,* 7, 8)

I kept close to the top of the class [in] scholastic standing. . . . One day, just about when . . . we would enter high school the next year . . . I happened to be alone in the classroom with Mr. Ostrowski, my English teacher, [a] white man. . . . I had gotten some of my best marks under him, and he had always made me feel that he liked me. . . . I doubt that he meant any harm. It was just in his nature as an American white man. I was one of his top students, one of the school's top students—but all he could see for me was the kind of future "in your place" that almost all white people see for black people. He told me, "Malcolm, you ought to be thinking about a career. Have you been giving it thought?" . . . I told him, "Well, yes, sir, I've been thinking I'd like to be a lawyer." . . . Mr. Ostrowski looked surprised. . . . "Malcolm, one of life's first needs is for us to be realistic. . . . We all here like you, you know that. But you've got to be realistic about being a nigger. A lawyer—that's no realistic goal for a nigger. You need to think about something you *can* do. You're good with your hands—making things. . . . Why don't you plan on carpentry?" . . . Mr. Ostrowski's advice to others in my class—all of them white . . . try something new, he had encouraged. . . . I realized that whatever I wasn't, I *was* smarter than nearly all of those white kids. But apparently I was still not intelligent enough, in their eyes, to become whatever *I* wanted to be. (Malcolm X, [1964] 1999, *The Autobiography of Malcolm X*, 37–38)

Northern and Southern educators . . . committed themselves to the task of determining whether or not millions of Negro Americans could be trained to function effectively as a caste in a society that would otherwise be democratic, and whether or not they could be made to remain satisfied with their condition. . . . The entire system of opportunities for upward mobility within the black caste depended upon the extent to which the traditional needs of whites to discriminate against the Negroes would be revived. What could be the most troublesome problem of all was the inescapable possibility that the experiment would make the Negroes dissatisfied with their caste assignment rather than strengthen their satisfaction with it. . . . There was always the ever-present risk that the Negro's need for racial equality would once again assert itself. (Henry Allen Bullock, 1967, *A History of Negro Education in the South: 1619 to the Present*, 167, 168)

Three components are ideal for a curriculum for Black children: (1) Political/cultural (ideology); (2) Pedagogical relevance (method); (3) Academic rigor (content). . . . An alternative curricular model for Afro-American children must have at its foundation an accurate historical and political analysis of the situation of Black people in America and in the world. . . . An alternative curricular model will . . . suggest ideas for changing the way Black children are treated in the educate process. . . . The third component of an alternative curricular model is academic rigor. . . . A curriculum for Black children must imbue Black children with the skills and exposures that are necessary to perform well. (Janice E. Hale-Benson, 1986, *Black Children: Their Roots, Culture, and Learning Styles*, 152, 157)

The education of blacks in the South reveals that various contending
forces sought either to repress the development of black education or
to shape it in ways that contradicted blacks' interests in intellectual development. The educational outcomes demonstrate that blacks got
some but not much of what they wanted. They entered emancipation
with fairly definite ideas about how to integrate education into their
broader struggle for freedom and prosperity, but they were largely unable to shape their future in accordance with their social vision.
(James D. Anderson, 1988, *The Education of Blacks in the South,
1860–1935*, 285)

I have been disturbed by the lack of direction and confidence that
plague many African American children. I believe it is because they are
not culturally centered and empowered in their classrooms. One of the
principal aspects of empowerment is respect. Students are empowered
when information is presented in such a way that they can walk out of
the classroom feeling that they are part of the information. . . . Lacking
reinforcement in their own historical experiences, they become psychologically crippled, hobbling along in the margins of the European
experiences of most of the curriculum. (Molefi Kete Asante, 1991/1992,
"Afrocentric Curriculum," *Educational Leadership*, 29)

The multicultural education movement emerged out of Western democratic ideals. One of its major aims is to close the gap between the
Western democratic ideals of equality and justice and societal practices
that contradict those ideals, such as discrimination based on race, gender, and social-class. . . . The major goals . . . are full inclusion of the
victimized groups into Western institutions and a reform of these institutions so that their practices are more consistent with their democratic ideals. . . . Multicultural education is designed to reduce race,
class, and gender divisions in the United States and the world. (James
A. Banks, 1991/1992, "Multicultural Education: For Freedom's Sake,"
Educational Leadership, 32, 35)

In higher education, a period of boundless expansion and optimism
has moved into one of retrenchment . . . , which is reflected in a dilu-
tion of higher education's commitment to Blacks. . . . Any attempt to
address the problems faced by African-American college students without considering the broader context of issues confronting Blacks as a
discriminated minority in America is doomed to fail, for the experiences of Black students in higher education are in part products of
larger systemic problems. (Walter R. Allen, 1992, "The Color of Success:

African-American College Student Outcomes at Predominantly White and Historically Black Public Colleges and Institutions," *Harvard Educational Review*, 27)

I have long suspected a particular culprit—a culprit that can undermine black achievement as effectively as a lock on a schoolhouse door. The culprit I see is stigma, the endemic devaluation many blacks face in our society and schools. This status is its own condition of life, different from class, money, culture. It is capable . . . of "breaking the claim" that one's human attributes have on people. I believe that its connection to school achievement among black Americans has been vastly underappreciated. (Claude M. Steel, 1992, "Race and the Schooling of Black Americans," *Atlantic Monthly*, 69)

Every human being requires a knowledge of self as part of the proper cultivation of the divinity that is in them. . . . When we see the curriculum as an outgrowth of self, then we can identify with the curriculum, giving us an incentive to learn. . . . If America believes in pluralism, a new system of education must be developed that gives all human beings their proper due. . . . The fundamental philosophies of Western civilization are rooted in white supremacy. You can't bring a black child into that kind of educational environment and produce a child who loves and respects itself. (Minister Louis Farrakhan, 1993, *A Torchlight for America*, 49, 51)

School changed utterly with racial integration. Gone was the messianic zeal to transform our minds and beings that had characterized teachers and their pedagogical practices in our all-black schools. Knowledge was suddenly about information only. It had no relation to how one lived, behaved. It was no longer connected to antiracist struggle. . . . When we entered racist, desegregated, white schools we left a world where teachers believed that to educate black children rightly would require a political commitment. Now, we were mainly taught by white teachers whose lessons reinforced racist stereotypes. For black children, education was no longer about the practice of freedom. (bell hooks, 1994, *Teaching to Transgress: Education as the Practice of Freedom*, 3)

Educators have had a difficult time accepting the existence of varieties of culture and style. Many Americans have had a kind of ideological commitment to the notion of the nation as a "melting pot," as both an ideal and a reality. Some have a very hard time simultaneously managing the ideas of democracy on the one hand and cultural pluralism on the other hand. Yet, there is no conflict between the two concepts. In fact, one test of a democracy may well be the degree to which it provides an environment within which . . . cultural pluralism can exist. (Asa G. Hilliard, III, 1995, *The Maroon within Us*, 170–172)

Despite our necessary efforts to provide access to Standard English, such access will not make any of our students more intelligent. It will not teach them math or science or geography—or, for that matter, compassion, courage, or responsibility. Let us not become so overly concerned with the language form that we ignore academic and moral content. Access to the standard language may be necessary, but it is definitely not sufficient to provide intelligent, competent caretakers of the future. (Lisa Delpit, 1998, *What Should Teacher Do? Ebonics and Culturally Responsive Instruction*, 26)

Implicit in the demand for desegregation were several assumptions. Desegregation would increase opportunities for blacks. . . . Desegregated educational institutions would promote greater racial harmony and understanding among young people from different ethnic communities, which in turn would promote residential integration. Affirmative-action policies . . . would gradually increase the number of African Americans . . . in administrative and managerial positions. It seemed evident that as African Americans escaped the ghetto and were more broadly distributed across the social-class structure and institutions of society, racial tensions and bigotry would decline in significance. As blacks were more thoroughly integrated into the economic system, it was thought, the basis for racial confrontation would diminish. This thesis was fundamentally flawed. . . . Desegregation did not benefit the entire black community uniformly. (Manning Marable, 1998, *Black Leadership*, 150)

Status and Condition of African American Education

All things being equal, the ideology of universal education is a rational and empowering concept. The philosophy of universal education could create opportunities for all citizens to develop and nurture their potential. Citizens would be able to select from among opportunities that would provide avenues for them to attain the level of education most suited to them and their aspirations. Yet not all things are equal.

African Americans, including those who attain high levels of education, obtain an education in a system that thwarts their opportunities, stunts their potential, and has preconceived notions of their abilities. It is under these circumstances that African Americans acquire the knowledge, attributes, and skills needed to participate in America's society.

African American Population

In 1998, blacks made up 12.7 percent of the U.S. population. Fifteen percent of the black population was children under the age of 18 years. In 1999, nationally, 85.4 percent of African Americans lived in metropolitan areas. Of those, 54.5 percent lived in urban areas, the inner city.

In 1996, African Americans accounted for 16.9 percent of the public school population, grades one through twelve. The percentage of African Americans composing the public school population increased by 1.4 percent between 1970 and 1996. An increasing number of black students in these grades, 9.1 percent in 1996, were enrolled in private schools. The private school enrollment was up from 7.2 percent in 1990, and down from 11.1 percent in 1994.

In 1959, 55.1 percent of the African American population lived below the poverty level. By 1997, 26.5 percent lived below the poverty level. In 1959, 54.9 percent of African American children under the age of 18 years lived below the poverty level. By 1997, that figure had fallen to 36.8 percent. In 1997, black children between the ages of three and four years comprised 36.1 percent of the Head Start population, indicating an increased involvement in positive activities. Despite these encouraging statistics, the percentage of African American children under the age of six who live in poverty remains higher than any other age group, and any other racial and ethnic groups.

African American Academic Achievement

The academic achievement of African Americans sends a mixed message. While in some instances there is evidence of gaining ground, the significance of the gained ground should be viewed with a cautious eye. In the preschool years there is little disparity between black and white students' test scores (Steele 1992). Some would attribute this to preschool programs such as Head Start. However, beginning in first grade and most noticeable by fourth grade, an achievement gap, as measured by national normed-reference tests, can be observed throughout African American students' academic careers. The disparity occurs regardless of the socioeconomic level of African Americans.

The College Board's Advanced Placement (AP) Program is considered one measure of high achievement. The examinations of the program measure high school students' college-level knowledge in thirty

Table1.1.

Percentage of African American Students Using Computers at Home and School by Current Grades 1–12, 1984, 1989, 1993, and 1997

Year	Grades 1–6		Grades 7–12	
	School	*Home*	*School*	*Home*
1984	15.1	5.1	18.4	4.9
1989	34.3	6.0	36.5	8.5
1993	54.1	8.3	50.5	10.2
1997	70.1	19.3	74.2	22.3

Source: U.S. Department of Education, *The Condition of Education* 1999.

courses, such as American history and calculus. By participating in the program and passing the course examinations, students can receive college credit. Between 1986 and 1996, twenty thousand African American twelfth-graders took AP examinations. Yet the College Board reported in 1999 that African Americans participating in the AP program "are less likely to . . . receive college credit." In other words, after participating in the AP program, many blacks' scores on AP examinations do not meet the goals of the AP program.\

Participation and success in America's technological society requires computer literacy. Increasing facility with computers is becoming an indicator of potential academic success. Computer literacy is one of the few academic skills that is not abstract. Obtaining computer literacy is dependent upon students' early access to computers and the opportunity to use them. Table 1.1 presents African American students' exposure to computers in grades one through twelve. Clearly, much of the exposure occurs in schools. This is not surprising when one considers the percentage of African Americans who live below the poverty level and the cost of computers. Most African American students' exposure to computers is through Title I programs.|

Generally, computer use for mathematics instruction is for one of four purposes: demonstration of new topics, drill and practice, playing learning games, or simulations and applications. These instructional methods are hierarchical in nature. The demonstration of new topics employs instructional methods, which introduce a new skill or concept to students. Drill and practice consists of repetitive rote instructional methods to reinforce a student's understanding and development of a skill or concept. Learning games are used to demonstrate a student's mastery of a skill or concept. Simulations and applications are used when a student has mastered a skill or concept and can engage in independent activities to demonstrate higher level thinking and conceptualization of the skill or

concept. Higher level thinking and conceptualization skills include comparing and contrasting, critiquing, synthesizing, analyzing, evaluating,
and creating. Fourth-grade African American students' use of computers
for mathematics is primarily for two purposes: for drill and practice 30.2
percent of the time, and for learning games 34.4 percent of the time.
While the use of computers for mathematics instruction for whites is also
concentrated in these two areas, they use it more for learning games (40.3
percent) than for drill and practice (26.6 percent).

By eighth grade, the majority, or 25.9 percent, of African American students' mathematics computer experience is for drill and practice. White students' computer experiences are divided almost equally
among drill and practice, 14.1 percent; playing learning games, 12.4 percent; and simulations and applications, 13.9 percent. African American
students have fewer opportunities to expand their computer experiences beyond drill and practice.

African American Students' Selected Precollege Experiences

For over twenty-five years, African American students have continued to
experience overrepresentation in special education, disproportionate
suspensions and expulsions, and a higher dropout rate. These three experiences remove a significant number of African American students
from the general school population conditionally, temporarily, or permanently. Removal from the general school population lessens these
students' access to educational opportunities and future productive
participation in American society. These experiences contribute to the
value, or lack of value, that so many African American students place on
school (Steinberg, Dornbusch, and Brown 1992; Graham 1994; Taylor
1994; Voelkl 1999).

Special Education. Special education is a high-profile issue in the
education of African Americans. African American students are overrepresented in three special education classifications: learning disability, mental retardation, and emotional disturbance. The number of
African Americans placed in special education increased 13.2 percent
between 1980 and 1990. For whites, the number increased 6 percent
during the same period.

Data from the 1994 U.S. Department of Education Office of Civil
Rights Elementary and Secondary School Compliance Reports for
race/ethnicity assist in illustrating the overrepresentation. Approximately
10 percent of all African American students enrolled in public schools
were placed in one of the three classifications mentioned earlier. Nationally, 5.7 percent were classified as having a learning disability, 2.6 percent

were classified as mentally retarded, and 1.1 percent were classified as emotionally disturbed. Nationally, the proportion of African Americans placed in programs for mental retardation is four times greater than that of all other racial and ethnic groups combined. Wagner argues that the overrepresentation of African Americans in special education is a result of socioeconomic conditions more than race (1995). Low-income students are more likely to be placed in special education than middle- and upper-income students.

The overrepresentation of African American students in special education became a concern of the U.S. Congress immediately after the reports. Recognizing that by the year 2000 people of color would represent one-third of the national population and that the population of children of color in public schools was increasing, Congress attributed this overrepresentation to "mislabeling" of students. Mislabeling meant that they were identified and labeled for special education incorrectly. In the reauthorization of the Individual and Disabilities Education Act (IDEA) of 1997, Congress noted that while African American students comprised 16 percent of the public school population, they made up 21 percent of the total special education enrollment. In an amendment to the reauthorization of IDEA, Congress noted that African American students who lived in poverty were 2.3 times more likely than the average African American student to be identified by teachers as being mentally retarded.

To address the concerns of overrepresentation in special education, in the 1998–1999 academic year Congress began requiring all states to submit reports on the special education pupil count by race. It was anticipated that such a reporting system would enable monitoring of the overrepresentation.

Disciplinary Actions. Learning cannot occur in an environment where students and school staff are concerned about their safety. Violence, disruption, and vandalism create unsafe and unstable school climates and environments. In the 1980s, public concern for the safety of students in American schools reached a crisis level. Disruptive student behavior was considered threatening to the stability and perhaps the existence of public education. No one foresaw the school massacres of white students killing peers and teachers that would occur in the late 1990s. At the end of the twentieth century, American schools no longer represented the safe havens that they had been viewed as for decades.

Disruptive student behavior interrupts the learning environment. The behavior of disruptive students must be addressed. On these two points, most would agree. It is not the addressing of the behavior that is of concern. Of concern is the way in which disruptive behavior is perceived and addressed, and the uneven manner in which black students are seen in this context.

School staffs have instituted a number of practices to prevent, control, and reduce disruptive student behavior within schools. These practices include, but are not limited to, detention, suspension, and expulsion. All of these forms of punishment remove students from the general school population and, in the case of the latter two, from the school.

Disciplinary actions taken against African American students are the focus of a great deal of debate and research. It is in the instances of suspension and expulsion that African American students are disproportionately represented. African American students are suspended two to three times more than white students. In addition, African American males are suspended and expelled at a higher rate than any other group of students. Tardiness, unexcused absences, and fighting, usually with other children, are most often the reasons for suspension and expulsion of black students.

Carter and Jackson's (1982) analysis of the 1973 data from the Office of Civil Rights found that schools in New York City, Houston, Cleveland, Memphis, and Dallas suspended over 50 percent of their students of color. Yet in each city blacks represented less than 40 percent of the total student population. These percentages equated to approximately 1 million suspensions or twenty-two thousand school days missed.

In the twenty-five years between 1973 and 1998, the data reflect that African American students continued to be suspended and expelled at a higher rate than all other racial and ethnic groups. The National Coalition of Advocates for Students (1998) reports that in Colorado, where African American students represent 5 percent of the state school population, they account for 12 percent of school expulsions. In Florida, African American students in grades six through twelve are more likely to be suspended and expelled than their white counterparts. African Americans are 40 percent of the student population in Michigan and account for 64 percent of expulsions. These states' data are not the exception. They are the rule, nationally. In addition, nationally, the majority of those suspended or expelled are African American males. McFadden, March, and Price (1992), Polite (1994), and Rodriguez (1997) have studied the relationship between the disparity of disciplinary actions applied to African American students and the value these students place on schools.

Is it possible that African American students, and more specifically African American males, display disproportionate misbehavior? The Office of Civil Rights and other research, including Bennett and Harris (1982) and Skiba and Peterson (1999a), are consistent in responding,

"No." The disproportionality is credited to the existence of a double standard in disciplinary response.

In the late 1980s, several school districts established "zero tolerance" policies. "Zero tolerance policies mandate predetermined and immediate consequences for various infractions of public school discipline codes. They generally result in suspensions and expulsion from school, sometimes regardless of the circumstances or without due process procedures" (Mobilization for Equality 1998, 1). It is interesting to note that the origin of the term "zero tolerance" is in the U.S. Department of Defense.

Many school personnel see the Gun-Free Schools Act of 1994 as national approval of school districts' zero tolerance policies. The blending of the policies and the legislation in the minds of school personnel is creating new conditions for African Americans, especially African American males, to experience increasingly disproportionate rates of suspension and expulsion. Some educators, advocates for children, parents, and communities are questioning the real intent and observed exercise of zero tolerance policies (Vail 1995; Zirkel 1997; Claiborne 1999; Johnston 1999; Skiba and Peterson 1999a; Skiba and Peterson 1999b).

Grade Retention and Dropouts. Students who are not promoted to the next grade, that is, who are retained, have been judged by their teachers not to have mastered the academic or social skills, or both, necessary to be successful at the next grade level. Retention is intended to be a positive school practice, giving students additional time to master skills that are necessary for future success in school. In far too many instances, the converse has occurred for African American students. Retention is translated into not only failure in school but failure as a person. This lessens students' self-esteem and tends to shorten their academic career. The National Center for Education Statistics reports that students who are retained are more likely to drop out of school (1995).

In 1995, 18.7 percent of African American students were retained in one or more grades. The highest percentage of retention was in kindergarten through third grades. Seven percent of African American students were retained at the beginning of their education (National Center for Education Statistics website).

Dropouts are students who leave school before completing the requirements to receive a high school diploma. Generally, students drop out in tenth, eleventh, or twelfth grade. There have been many students in the annals of American education who left school before obtaining a high school diploma. Dropouts became a concern during the industrial era of the United States. With the Russian launch of Sputnik in 1957, students' early exit from the school system became an issue on the American education agenda. It was during this period of American education that a high school diploma became the norm rather than the exception.

The dropout rate for African Americans decreased between 1970 and 1997 from 22.2 percent to 11.2 percent. In spite of the decrease, over 693,000 African American students exited school without receiving a high school diploma. The dropout rate of African American students classified as special education students is 31.2 percent.

In 1996, 22 percent of black dropouts were employed. This is in contrast to 45 percent of white dropouts who were employed. In addition, 42 percent of black high school graduates and 69 percent of white high school graduates were employed.

Postsecondary Educational Attainment of African Americans

In the thirty-eight years between 1960 and 1998, the percentage of African Americans receiving high school diplomas increased approximately 60 percent. By 1998, 76 percent of African Americans 25 years and older had completed four years of high school or more. In spite of the increase in high school graduations, only 14.7 percent of African Americans had completed four or more years of college.

In 1997, 39.3 percent of African Americans between the ages of 18 and 24 were enrolled in college. Those enrolled were more likely to be enrolled in two-year colleges than four-year colleges. Approximately 15 percent of African Americans who completed an associate's degree transferred to a four-year college.

Overall, as shown in Table 1.2, the percentage of African Americans receiving bachelor's, master's, and doctorate degrees in the humanities and social and behavioral sciences increased between 1989 and 1994, and degrees conferred in the natural sciences remained constant. The percentage of bachelor's degrees conferred in computer sciences and engineering decreased by 2.3 percent, and the percentage of degrees conferred in technical/professional fields of study decreased by 2.4 percent. At the master's level, there was a slight increase of conferred degrees in computer sciences and engineering, and a similar decrease in technical/professional majors. Computer science and engineering had the greatest increase of all fields of study at the doctoral level, and the technical/professional fields of study had the greatest decrease, 4.5 percent.

African Americans have made gains in educational attainment at the postsecondary level. It is expected that employment opportunities increase with the increased level of conferred degrees. In 1997, 87 percent of blacks with bachelor's degrees were employed and 95 percent of

Table 1.2.

Percentage of Bachelor's, Master's, and Doctorate Degrees Conferred to Blacks by Majors, 1989 and 1994

	Bachelor's		Master's		Doctorate	
	1989	1994	1989	1994	1989	1994
Percentage of Blacks' Conferred Degrees to All Races	5.8	7.3	5.1	6.4	3.8	4.4
Percentage of Blacks' Conferred Degrees by Majors						
Humanities and Social and Behavioral Sciences	28.2	32.8	11.0	12.1	31.9	34.3
Humanities	12.0	13.9	5.2	5.7	11.4	16.5
Behavioral Sciences	16.1	18.9	5.7	6.3	20.4	17.8
Natural Sciences	5.9	5.9	1.8	1.8	8.8	8.3
Life Sciences	3.3	3.6	.8	.6	5.2	4.5
Physical Sciences	1.2	1.1	.5	.6	2.8	3.3
Mathematics	1.3	1.2	.4	.5	.7	.5
Computer Sciences and Engineering	9.9	7.6	4.4	4.8	2.6	5.0
Computer and Information Sciences	4.3	2.9	1.4	1.7	.1	.7
Engineering	5.5	4.6	2.9	3.1	2.5	4.3
Technical/Professional	55.9	53.5	82.6	81.1	56.6	52.1
Education	7.3	7.5	37.6	32.8	42.6	37.5
Business Management	26.0	24.3	21.7	23.7	1.7	2.7
Health Services	6.8	5.8	6.0	6.8	3.8	4.2
Other Technical/ Professional*	15.7	15.8	17.1	17.7	8.3	7.6

Source: U.S. Department of Education, *The Condition of Education* 1997.
*For Master's mostly Public Administration; for Doctorate mostly Agriculture and Natural Resources

whites were employed. The unemployment percentage of black males with college degrees was 7.4 percent and for white males 1.6 percent.

Higher levels of educational attainment are also associated with higher levels of income. While African Americans' incomes do increase with an increase in their level of educational attainment, African Americans' incomes do not equal those of whites with an equal level of educational attainment. This is illustrated in Table 1.3.

Blacks and whites with the same level of educational attainment and doing similar jobs are not paid at the same level. Ironically, the disparity is greatest at the highest level of educational attainment. Income differences create a dual class system. Economically, for example, the black middle class is not equivalent to the white middle class.

Table 1.3.

Educational Attainment and Mean Income, 1975 and 1997

Educational Attainment	Year	Black Income	White Income
No High School Degree	1975	$ 5,406	$ 6,438
	1997	13,185	16,596
High School Degree	1975	6,281	8,005
	1997	18,980	23,618
Some College	1975	7,212	8,525
	1997	22,899	26,906
College	1975	9,473	12,597
	1997	32,062	41,439
Advanced Degree	1975	12,333	16,920
	1997	42,791	65,058

Source: U.S. Bureau of the Census, Internet Release, December 10, 1998.

African American Public School Employment

The positions held by professional staff in public schools dictate the span of influence they have on policies and practices. Policy decisions made by administrators and instructional practices of teachers have a great deal of bearing on the educational success of the youth for whom these professionals are responsible. Teachers have the greatest influence on the academic achievement and self-esteem of youth as well as the manner in which equality, equity, and quality are exercised.

Table 1.4 shows that between 1982 and 1996 the percentage of African American school officials and principals has increased, and the percentage of African American teachers has decreased. However, most African Americans employed in public schools are not in instructional positions.

Between 1977 and 1994, there was a 14.5 percent decrease in African Americans majoring in education at the baccalaureate level. At a time when the number of African American youth attending public schools is increasing, the number of African American teachers is decreasing. African American teachers serve as role models who can have a positive effect on African American students' success. With fewer African American teachers, the lack of opportunities for African American students to come in contact with role models during their early formative academic careers creates a dismal prognosis for their success.

In national data for the 1993–1994 school year, there were 2,217,000 whites and 188,000 blacks teaching full-time. Yet African American teachers had a higher percentage of full-time teaching experience and advanced degrees. Approximately 71 percent of African American teachers had ten to twenty or more years of full-time teaching

Table1.4.

Percentage of Black Public School Employees, 1982 and 1996

Occupation	1982	1996
All Occupations	14.0	13.6
Officials and Administrators	7.3	10.6
Principals and Assistant Principals	12.2	14.8
Elementary Teachers	12.2	9.8
Secondary Teachers	9.4	9.1
Teacher Aides	20.9	21.3
Clerical and Secretarial Staff	9.0	11.2
Service Workers	21.6	23.8

Source: U.S. Bureau of the Census, *Statistical Abstract of the United States* 1999.

experience, and 29.3 percent had between one and nine years of full-time teaching experience. Approximately 65 percent of full-time white teachers had ten to twenty or more years of teaching experience; 34.9 percent had one to nine years of experience. The percentages of African American full-time teachers having master's, education specialist, and doctorate degrees were 44.6 percent, 5.4 percent, and 0.9 percent, respectively. The percentages of white full-time teachers having master's, education specialist, and doctorate degrees were 42.5 percent, 4.4 percent, and 0.7 percent.

A continued decrease in African American teachers will mean that African American students in public schools will have a greater possibility of being taught by individuals who are not like them, are less experienced teachers, and are less educated.

RESOURCE INTERVIEW WITH
DOUGLAS V. DAVIDSON

Douglas V. Davidson is originally from Hattiesburg, Mississippi, but lived most of his childhood in Oxford, Mississippi. His family moved to Davenport, Iowa, when he was twelve, and later to rural southwestern Michigan.

Davidson received his bachelor's degree from Tougaloo College in Tougaloo, Mississippi, which is a historically black private college. His master of science degree is from Illinois Institute of Technology, and he received his doctor of philosophy degree from the University of California at Berkeley. All of his degrees are in sociology. In addition to sociology, Davidson's areas of expertise are black studies, urban studies, pan-Africanism, sociology of education, multicultural studies, sociology of colonialism, and third world development.

Currently, Davidson is associate professor in sociology at Western Michigan University. His previous positions include: professor in the black studies department at City College of New York, assistant to the university administrator charged with overseeing the development of the ethnic studies department at the University of California at Berkeley, associate professor in the School of Social Work at Atlanta University, director of black studies and lecturer in sociology at the University of Massachusetts–Boston, chair of the black studies department and assistant professor at Amherst College, and assistant professor of the black studies department at the University of North Carolina at Charlotte. He is a member of the National Advisory Board for the African Heritage Studies Association, a former member of the National Council of Black Studies, and an associate of the now-defunct Institute of the Black World—a Pan-African Research and Studies Center.

The author had the opportunity to talk with Douglas Davidson about the sociology of American and African American education. The conversation follows.

How does sociology assist in understanding U.S. education?

As a sociologist, I teach students that education is one of the primary institutions for socializing children. Indeed, many observers would argue that it has replaced the family and parents as the primary socializing agent. As an agent of socialization, it teaches the language, history, values, and norms of behavior of the larger society. In essence, it has the responsibility of training an individual to become a responsible, loyal citizen; how to become an accepted and effective member of the larger society. Sociologists argue that for a society to maintain itself as a stable, harmonious, effective collective over time, it must have effective socialization institutions which reproduce like-minded people for each new generation.

In addition to its overt, primary function of teaching or transmitting socially and intellectually necessary knowledge to the next generation, it also teaches socially required and acceptable behavior which is what people call the hidden curriculum. That is obeying orders, sitting in your chair, performing in the way that teachers expect you to perform, satisfying the teachers' requirements to regurgitate to them the information they gave the students. These are excellent ways of preparing people to take orders in the work place and to do as they are told. They are trained not to question or challenge the status quo.

Education is talked about as teaching people about the history and culture of the nation state of which they are a part. In addition, education is a way of preparing people to function effectively in the broader political economy of the country.

How does sociology assist in understanding the education of African Americans?

For African Americans, the education system has in many ways done what Carter G. Woodson said in his 1933 classic study, *The Mis-Education of the Negro*. Education in America has taught African Americans to understand the ideals, the values, and the norms of white society. It has taught African Americans what white society expects as appropriate normative behavior. It has not taught African Americans anything about themselves or their experience as a people in this particular society.

Essentially, African Americans learned the same general set of criteria, the same kind of propaganda that is taught from kindergarten through twelfth grade, regarding how America was founded and what are the important values in America. We have acquired this information as if all Americans are the same. It does not recognize the differences among blacks, whites, Native Americans, Mexican Americans, to name a few. The fact that in American education everybody is perceived as being just American is what many people refer to as the brainwashing function of the United States educational system.

The education system worked very effectively to help white immigrant populations transform themselves into what is considered mainstream, working, and middle class Americans. It was expected to transform people of color in a similar manner. Black Americans were expected to become loyal, unquestioning, uncritical, colorblind mainstream Americans. Except, there is a contradiction. African Americans were being taught about all of this equality while they were physically segregated.

Racism is a reality in the daily lives of African Americans and in their communities. In many ways, it is unavoidable. But there is nothing in the educational system that explains that racism or that accounts for why they are the unique victims of it in so many ways.

Young black people in the education system are in some ways almost intuitively critical of the system. Their experiences are invisible in the curriculum. They are invisible in the education system. In some ways, the curriculum is a lie in relation to their reality. It is almost as though they are going to school to study fiction. Everything they are reading is true for certain people, but it is mostly not true for them. They know it is fiction because they are living a different life as soon as they walk out of the school building. Sometimes they recognize differences within the context of the school building. They look around and see there is nobody in those rooms but other black people reflecting the segregated school system and the segregated neighborhoods. They look at their school buildings, which are in deplorable conditions. They have a sense that something is wrong.

What teachers are compelled to teach them in a sense is a lie and black students are being miseducated. They are being educated to believe something that is not real. If they accept the fiction, it is a form of self-negation. Acceptance means they make themselves invisible.

What is the origin of black studies?

Black studies grew out of historical concerns about the invisibility of African Americans in United States history. Carter G. Woodson started Black History Week; it later became Black History Month. Its purpose was to try to replace, to correct, some of this invisibility of black people in the larger United States culture and society. His introduction of Black History Month was a way of celebrating the accomplishments, the achievements, and the contributions of black people. It was an effort to compel the nation to acknowledge blacks in ways that it has refused to do. It was designed to acknowledge, to illuminate, the black presence in American society and culture.

Black studies was also an effort to fill the knowledge gap, the glaring omission, and to extend Woodson's vision. Black students can go to school, learn United States history, and never learn anything about themselves. The role of blacks in American history, literature, science, politics, economics, and music was not being taught. Black studies was concerned about trying to make the black experience in this country visible. To begin to educate young people along two tracks.

There is something called United States history which in many ways has worked to the advantage of whites, because it is about them. Then there is something called black history, which parallels United States history, but the black experiences are very different from the experiences that are being taught as characteristic of white people. Black studies' core curriculum explains the realities of black people, and their relationships and their experiences in this country with white people. It explains how that relationship has worked to our disadvantage. It explains how the black struggle is a very different struggle than the struggle of white immigrant groups as they adapted and adjusted to the white Anglo-Saxon dominated culture.

You had an opportunity to review the statistics that are presented earlier in this chapter. As an African American sociologist, how do you interpret those data in relation to the status and condition of African American education?

The data indicate two very almost contradictory trends. It shows that on the one hand African American performance in many ways is improving according to standardized measures. African Americans are graduating from high school in higher numbers. They are doing better in some ways, although there is still a gap between how they perform on standardized tests and how white students perform. In that sense, the statistics can be interpreted as "things are getting better." And, in some ways, they probably are. At the same time, the gap still remains and there is evidence that it is widening again. The data indicate that black young people who are graduating from high school are in some ways a bit more competitive in their ability to enroll in postsecondary institutions and continue their education. More than African Americans were twenty or thirty years ago.

On the other hand, knowledge is changing and expanding rapidly. Technology's role in both knowledge dissemination and the content of knowledge is increasing. Differences in scores, or the gap, reflects the fact that African Americans are not getting access to as much of that technology as they need. They are dependent upon the schools for access to computers and the knowledge of computer applications. They do not have computers nearly as much in the home as white families. Thus, they are dependent upon the educational system to provide them with the access, the introduction to, and the application of this new technology much more than white students.

Let me give you an example of how computer exposure benefits white students. Increasingly, major universities require students to come to the college or university with computers in hand. White students are able to comply. For black students coming out of predominantly black high schools in the inner cities, many families probably cannot afford to send their students to school with computers. Nor are black students ready to use it at the same level because they have not had as much exposure to computers. Black students do not have it in the home. The students do not have the chance to set it up, to play with it, to be creative with it and to use it in its full extent.

White students have had computers since sixth, seventh, or eighth grade, or earlier. These students have been playing with them in the home and school, and doing special summer projects. However, black students do not have that kind of exposure. They are going to be disadvantaged. I think that currently this lack of exposure and experience contributes to the difference between what African Americans are able to do with a high school education versus what whites are able to do with a high school education.

The number of blacks entering the field of education and the number of African American teachers in public schools are decreasing. At the same time, an increasing number of black students are entering public schools. What are your thoughts on this?

School desegregation in the South eliminated many black teachers and black administrators. Our numbers have declined precipitously ever since then.

Requirements for receiving a degree in education are more rigorous. After students receive their degrees, the National Teacher Examination or state examinations are required. Some black young people have completed the education courses, received their degrees, but have not been able to pass the National Teacher Examination or the state examinations. Therefore, they are not able to be certified. I think that many black college students are beginning to wonder if the hurdles are worth it.

College students do not begin taking education courses until their junior year. They have to major in a discipline, and then take the education courses. Then they have to take state certification courses. Then they have to pass the National Teacher Examination or state examinations. I think that many of our young people have discovered the rewards for completing all of this have not been very high. They have discovered that they can go into other areas and probably make more money with fewer headaches.

In addition, the kinds of expectations that people now have for teachers have increased. The bureaucratic work is more demanding. The role of teacher as a surrogate mother, father, friend, counselor, mentor, and community relations person can be overwhelming. Everybody wants the school system to solve all problems. If students do not perform well on standardized achievement examinations, then the teachers are blamed. I think many young black people see it as an impossible job. The rewards that come with being a teacher and the fact the profession itself is undergoing significant transformations has made teaching a less desirable professional choice for many African Americans. Additionally, when young African Americans see that a professional athlete, truck driver, movie star, construction worker, or other skilled laborers earn higher salaries than a teacher, they are being logical to ask: "It is worth it?"

The values in the American society are skewed. We think it is acceptable that a football or basketball coach earns more than the university president. The poor faculty members are not even in the ballpark! The society expects the people who are most responsible for the future success of their children to work for what the blues singer Albert King called "chump change." There is something sick in that formula. Once the society becomes more balanced, sane in its value system, possibly more African Americans will be attracted to teaching as a profession.

How do you interpret James Coleman's findings in Equality of Educational Opportunity?

Essentially, Coleman discovered that if you mix low-achieving students in a classroom with high-achieving students, the low achievers would rise to the higher level in terms of their achievement. Equally as important, these achievement phenomena occurred in schools where the socioeconomic status was mixed, not the racial composition of the student body. That is, low-income students attending schools with a significant percentage of students from middle-income families or above achieve at significantly higher levels than low-income students attending schools with other low-income students. The students who have the lowest achievement scores, in all likelihood, are going to be from lower socioeconomic backgrounds. If a school is located in an impoverished community, and the student body is reflective of the families in that community, then that is probably where the lowest scores, the greatest gaps, are going to occur.

Theoretically, low-income black students did not have to be bused to upper-income white communities, although that is what happened. They could have been bused to upper-income black communities. That would have taken away the race variable to deal with.

Coleman's finding was that the middle-income students had to be in the majority. I think the percentage was seventy percent to thirty percent. By the middle class being in the majority, essentially, the school's culture would reflect middle-class culture, discipline, and values.

How do you describe the culture, the climate, and the environment of the precollege educational setting in which African Americans obtain an education, historically and currently?

Historically, the public school system was designed by white people for white people to achieve a certain type of end. They were very worried about bringing in immigrants from Eastern and Western Europe who did not speak English and were unfamiliar with United States history and culture.

The public school system was designed to socialize those young people into being American citizens. Public school education was designed to reorient European immigrants from their original national backgrounds as well as their ethnic identity. It was to transform them so their commitment to the United States superseded their commitment to their ethnic group or to the national backgrounds from which they came. The public school system was designed to achieve this end.

When blacks entered the public school system, the purpose of our education was to transform us from our slave heritage. Ultimately it was to allow us to come to know United States history and United States culture from the perspective of white Anglo-Saxon Protestant Americans. The school system, even in the segregated variety, was to be white in its perspective and in the curriculum. We were being taught the same thing that the white students were being taught in their schools. The only difference is that our teachers were black and the student body was completely black.

I can remember going to elementary school in Mississippi and reading the old cast-off books from the white school system. When I got older, through my own studying, I discovered that the curriculum in the black schools was a watered down version of the curriculum in the white schools. The black superintendent of the school had to take directions from the white superintendent. The white superintendent was in charge of what was taught in both school systems. Therefore, it was certain that the black students were taught what was taught in the white schools. There could be very little variation. Black history week/month was maybe the only time black schools could talk about people like Frederick Douglass or W. E. B. DuBois or Mary McLeod Bethune. I do not even remember us talking about DuBois that month. We talked a little about Frederick Douglass and we heard a lot about Booker T. Washington and Mary McLeod Bethune. However, we received a black version of white education.

We were being taught by people who sometimes had completed only eighth or ninth grade. However, they could teach kindergarten for black children. We were being taught by people who often only had a high school education or had just started college. My ex–mother-in-law was a positive, outstanding teacher in her own way. She started teaching school to black students when she completed the ninth grade. She finished high school, began teaching, and went to college during the summers for years before she got her bachelor's degree. Nevertheless, she was an elementary school teacher. Teaching somewhere between first and third grades all of those years.

I am talking about the 1950s, 1960s, and earlier. During segregation, if black teachers were in the system and still going to school every summer to work towards the bachelor's degree, the white administrator would allow them to teach. That is a component of segregation that many people do not know and understand. Students in the white schools were being taught by a person who had completed college. Black students were going to a black school and in all likelihood were being taught by people who may not have completed college. Even in the 1960s. Think about the qualitative differences in terms of what people are exposed to as college graduates versus having completed high school, or eighth grade. You can see another dimension to how we were getting behind in the educational system. This was particularly true in the segregated South. I sometimes stop and reflect on that. They could teach us only as much as they knew about reading, writing, and arithmetic.

When the schools desegregated in the South, black teachers were told that they were not really prepared to be teachers. They had to get a master's degree before they would be prepared to be in an integrated school. The system requirements changed immediately, and the whites knew exactly what they were doing. I see this as an acknowledgment of how blacks were mis- and undereducated intentionally and systematically. I think many people missed the meaning of the requirements. A large number of black teachers and black administrators had to leave the school system.

The education blacks were receiving was meeting the needs of whites. We were being educated to participate in the economy at the level where whites felt black people ought to participate. We were never supposed to be competitive with white people in the first place. Because of the educational practices in the South, when blacks moved North, we were routinely retained a grade or two. We were not up to par.

After desegregation, the two school systems merged. There was now one system, imposing these new standards. Not only did black teachers have to have bachelor's degrees, but they had to have master's degrees, also.

Many of the black teachers who had college degrees received their degrees from predominately black colleges, state and private. The whites in charge of the school system told the blacks that the ones that went to the state schools really were not prepared to teach white children. At the time, very few black postsecondary institutions offered master's degree programs. This meant that the majority of black teachers had to enroll in predominately white universities. White universities in the South were segregated, for the most part. Black teachers had to go North. This meant that they taught during the school year and each summer would go North until they completed their master's degrees. This could take five to six years.

The master's program in the post-desegregation era included certification requirements. Essentially, blacks getting the master's degree meant that they were being prepared to teach white students.

After school desegregation, for the first time many African American children were introduced to classroom settings where a white person was in charge with his/her standard teacher credentials and teaching the white "normative" curriculum. Generally, the white teachers are doing it very grudgingly, and they are very uncomfortable with black students in the classroom. Black students were introduced to new standards by people who probably did not have a commitment to whether they learned.

In the statistics earlier in this chapter, it shows that as of 1994 black teachers in public schools now have higher degrees than the whites who are teaching. How would you explain that?

It suggests to me that the double standard still exists. There is still that little cloud over African Americans that says we have to prove to ourselves and whites that we can perform as well as whites and that we have the expertise and the skills to do the job. I think that covertly there is a higher set of standards and qualifications for blacks. I do not think African American teachers can feel secure in what they are doing unless they keep going to school, and getting more and more credits. Even now, they have to constantly demonstrate that they are staying abreast, and are up to date in terms of what is happening in whatever areas they are teaching. It is a repeat of the old saying, "Blacks have to work twice as hard to get what whites get for half the work, and half the effort."

The income differentials in Table 1.3 illustrate the higher exceptions for blacks. A white with no high school degree makes almost as much as blacks with a twelfth-grade education. A white with a twelfth-grade education makes more than a black with some college. A white with a college degree makes as much as a black with an advanced degree. We have to have more education to demonstrate that we are eligible and to get the job. Many whites still do not believe that we are as smart as they are, that we are as intelligent as they are. We have to overachieve in order to do what they get under just normal routine situations.

What is your assessment of the anti–affirmative action movement in higher education?

It is a complicated issue. It is hard to identify who is the real enemy and what is the real intent. People supporting anti–affirmative action such as Ward Connerly [a black member of the University of California Board of Regents] believe we do not need affirmative action anymore. To their way of thinking, affirmative action has done everything that we needed for it to do. They seem to be taking the line that all people now have an equal opportunity to achieve and the playing field has been leveled at the level of opportunity.

To me it is a backwards assumption. The assumption is that all school systems and all schools are roughly equal. No matter which school people attend, regardless of their color, class, and background, school systems have the ability to make everybody equal in terms of their competitive abilities. That assumption obviously contradicts most of the statistics and research.

This assumption does not explain that while the gaps have been closing some, we know that the gap still exists. That blacks still have a two-to-one dropout rate. There are still people graduating from high school reading on the fifth-, sixth-, and seventh-grade levels. There are still problems with functional illiteracy in many minority communities. The problem of literacy has not been solved. Yet the playing field has been leveled in terms of these people having an equal opportunity. That is crazy.

What is scary about reversing affirmative action is that at some time during the twenty-first century, people of color are going to become the majority population. Essentially, this has happened in California. It could happen in Florida soon. It may already be true in South Carolina; we do not know. We do know that people of color being the majority is going to become a reality. If we reverse affirmative action, we are returning to the concept of merit. Given the history of nonwhite people and their educational experiences in this country eventually a system of liberal apartheid or meritocratic apartheid is going to be created.

If affirmative action is dismantled then we are saying everybody starts at a level playing field. We know that this is a lie, an inaccuracy, a falsehood. A situation will be created where the people who have the highest scores, who have become the top achievers, who just happen to be white, will continue to rule everything. However, it will be said that it is not racism, because everyone has the same equal opportunity. The only problem is that the rest of us have not quite caught up. They will reason that it does not matter if the suburban school systems are spending three to four times more money than inner-city schools are spending per student. We can discount class background, and not take into account that a large percentage of the population cannot afford exclusive, private, educational training and teaching. Why? Because the playing field is level. It is just unfortunate that there are families who are not middle class or above, and you do not live in the suburbs, and you do not have access to the kinds of resources that those schools have. But, that is really no one's fault. There is nothing we can do about that. Students in the inner-city public school system, I guess the line would go, have the same opportunity even though their schools are probably not going to be up to par with the suburban schools.

The argument that Ward Connerly and his colleagues are making is going to be devastating. If affirmative action is reversed, it will be devastating to the opportunities of the next generation, or two, of young black people and other youth of color. The communities affected by this reversal have to take the position that they want the same level of resources spent on inner-city, predominantly nonwhite schools that is spent on suburban, predominantly white, schools. Only then can we talk about leveling the playing field.

Any final comments?

I want to say something about the charter schools and what they might represent as alternative to public schools for inner-city people. I think they are highly controversial. Whether they address the special educational problems of blacks and other nonwhite communities remains to be seen.

Charter schools are going to have to be monitored very closely to see how well they provide the kind of education that nonwhites need. For example, I know a black woman who opened a charter school. She is a very religious person and wants her school to reflect a religious and morals orientation. Now that may be fine. However, I am wondering if within that context are they doing the other kinds of things that need to be done to prepare the children to be competitive. Are they providing the necessary computer skills, math training, and science instruction for those young people to be able to be more successfully competent in high school and postsecondary education? I wonder what is the dominant orientation and practice in the school. Is it on teaching young people how to behave? This is very important. However, there are other things these young people need and will be expected to know.

What worries me about the whole charter school movement is that some people are organizing the schools around personal value orientations and agendas. Will these schools help to remove the gap? Will charter schools confront the real problems that need to be resolved concerning black young people? These problems are reading skills, math skills, reading scores, math scores, science scores, and the fear of science and math. In order for young black people to be competitive, and given the current economy as well as the future directions of the economy, black students must have these kinds of skills.

Finally, few charter schools are talking about multiculturalism and the introduction of the histories and cultures of nonwhite people as a part of their curricula. To me, these are the types of questions that need to be raised, answered, and monitored as charter schools become more numerous.

REFERENCES

Allen, Walter R. 1992. "The Color of Success: African-American College Student Outcomes at Predominantly White and Historically Black Public Colleges and Universities." *Harvard Educational Review* 62, no. 1: 26–43.

Anderson, James D. 1988. *The Education of Blacks in the South, 1860–1935.* Chapel Hill: University of North Carolina Press.

Asante, Molefi Kete. 1991/1992. "Afrocentric Curriculum." *Educational Leadership* 49: 28–31.

Banks, James A. 1991/1992. "Multicultural Education: For Freedom's Sake." *Educational Leadership* 49: 32–35.

Bennett, Christine, and J. John Harris III. 1982. "A Study of the Causes of Disproportionality in Suspensions and Expulsions of Male and Black Students:

Part One—Characteristics of Disruptive and Non-Disruptive Students." Pp. 49–74 in *Student Discipline: Legal, Empirical and Education Perspective*. Edited by J. John Harris III and Christine Bennett. Bloomington: Indiana University Press.

Bond, Horace Mann. [1934] 1966. *The Education of the Negro in the American Social Order*. Reprint. New York: Octagon Books, Inc.

Bullock, Henry Allen. 1967. *A History of Negro Education in the South: From 1619 to the Present*. Cambridge, MA: Harvard University Press.

Carter, David G., and Cynthia L. Jackson. 1982. "Student Discrimination, Disproportionality and the Law." Pp. 37–48 in *Student Discipline: Legal, Empirical and Education Perspective*. Edited by J. John Harris III and Christine Bennett. Bloomington: Indiana University Press.

Children's Defense Fund. 1999. *Key Facts: Essential Information on Child Care, Early Education, and School Age Care—Overview*. Washington, DC: Children's Defense Fund. http://www.childrensdefense.org/.

Claiborne, William. 1999. "Study: Racial Disparity in School Discipline." *Washington Post* (December 17), A3.

Clark, David L., and Terry A. Astuto. 1994. "Redirecting Reform: Challenges to Popular Assumptions about Teachers and Students." *Phi Delta Kappan* 75: 512–520.

Coleman, James S. [1966]. 1979. *Equality of Educational Opportunity*. New York: Arno Press.

Delany, Martin R. 1966. "The Condition, Elevation, Emigration, and the Destiny of the Colored People of the United States." Pp. 37–101 in *Negro Social and Political Thought, 1850–1920: Representative Texts*. Edited by Howard Brotz. New York: Basic Books, Inc.

Delpit, Lisa. 1998. "What Should Teacher Do? Ebonics and Culturally Responsive Instruction." Pp. 17–26 in *The Real Ebonics Debate*. Edited by Theresa Perry and Lisa Delpit. Boston: Beacon Press.

DuBois, W. E. B. 1966. "The Talented Tenth." Pp. 518–533 in *Negro Social and Political Thought, 1850–1920: Representative Texts*. Edited by Howard Brotz. New York: Basic Books.

Farrakhan, Louis. 1993. *A Torchlight for America*. Chicago: FCN Publishing Co.

Graham, Sandra. 1994. "Motivation in African Americans." *Review of Educational Research* 64, no. 1: 55–118.

Gun-Free Schools Act of 1994. *Elementary and Secondary Act, Part F—Gun Possession, Sec. 14601. Gun-Free Requirements*.

Hale-Benson, Janice H. 1986. *Black Children: Their Roots, Culture, and Learning Styles*. Rev. ed. Baltimore, MD: Johns Hopkins University Press.

Harrington, Michael. [1962] 1997. *The Other America: Poverty in the United States*. Reprint. Portland, OR: Book News, Inc.

Head Start Bureau, Administration of Children and Families, United States Department of Health and Human Services. 1999. http://www2.acf.dhhs.gov/programs/hsb.

Hilliard, Asa G., III. 1995. *The Maroon within Us*. Baltimore, MD: Black Classic Press.

hooks, bell. 1994. *Teaching to Transgress: Education as the Practice of Freedom*. New York: Routledge.

Jackson, Cynthia L. 1982. "A Study of the Relationship between Administrators' Characteristics and the Implementation of Mandated Change in Higher Education in Ohio." Ph.D. diss., Ohio State University (UMI No. 8222104).

James, George G. M. [1954] 1989. *Stolen Legacy*. Reprint. New York: United Brother Communications Systems.

Johnson, Robert C. 1999. "Decatur Furor Sparks Wider Policy Debate." *Education Week* 19, no. 4: 1, 4.

Malcolm X. [1964] 1999. *The Autobiography of Malcolm X*. As told to Alex Haley. New York: Ballantine Books.

Marable, Manning. 1998. *Black Leadership*. New York: Columbia University Press.

McFadden, Anna C., George E. Marsh, and Barrie Price. 1992. "A Study of Race and Gender Bias in the Punishment of Handicapped School Students." *Urban Review* 24: 239–251.

"Mobilization for Equity." 1998. The National Coalition of Advocates for Students. http://www.ncas1.org/.

National Center of Education Statistics. 1995. "Dropout Rates in the United States: Grade Retention." Washington, DC: ED Pub.

National Commission of Higher Education Issues. 1982. *To Strengthen Quality in Higher Education*. Washington, DC: American Council on Education.

National Commission on Excellence in Education. *A Nation at Risk: The Imperative for Educational Reform*. Washington, DC: GPO, 1983.

Polite, Vernon C. 1994. "The Method in the Madness: African American Males, Avoidance Schooling, and Chaos Theory." *Journal of Negro Education* 64, no. 4: 588–601.

Rodriguez, Jorge. 1997. *"At-Risk": A Measure of School Failure in American Education*. ERIC Document Reproduction Service No. ED 412220.

Skiba, Russ, and Reece Peterson. 1999. "The Dark Side of Zero Tolerance: Can Punishment Lead to Safe Schools?" *Phi Delta Kappan* 80: 372–376.

———. 1999. "Zap Zero Tolerance." *Education Digest* 64, no. 8: 24–30.

Steele, Claude M. 1992. "Race and the Schooling of Black Americans." *Atlantic Monthly* 269, no. 4: 68–78.

Steinberg, Laurence, Sanford M. Dornbusch, and Bradford B. Brown. 1992. "Ethnic Differences in Adolescent Achievement: An Ecological Perspective." *American Psychologist* 47, no. 6: 723–729.

Taylor, Ronald D. 1994. "Explaining the School Performance of African-American Adolescents." *Journal of Research on Adolescence* 4, no. 1: 21–44.

United States Bureau of the Census. *Current Population Report.* On Census Internet sites. http://www.census.gov/population/www/index.html.

———. 1999. *Statistical Abstract of the United States: 1999.* Washington, DC: Government Printing Office.

United States Department of Education. 1994. *Elementary and Secondary School Compliance Report.* Office of Civil Rights: Ed Pubs.

United States Department of Education, National Center for Education Statistics. 1995. *Grade Retention.* National Center for Education Statistics. http://nces.ed.gov/pubs/dp95/97473-5.html.

———. 1996. *The Condition of Education 1996.* National Center for Education Statistics. http://nces.ed.gov/pubsold/ce96/c9644a01.

———. 1997. *The Condition of Education 1997.* Washington, DC: ED Pubs.

———. 1999. *The Condition of Education 1999.* Washington, DC: ED Pubs.

———. 1999. Department of Education. http://www.ed.gov/.

Vail, Kathleen R. 1995. "Ground Zero: Dealing with Students Who Bring Guns to School." *American School Board Journal* 182: 36–38.

Voelkl, Kristin E., John W. Welte, and William F. Wieczorek. 1999. "Schooling and Delinquency among White and African American Adolescents." *Urban Education* 34, no. 1: 69–88.

Wagner, M. 1995. *The Contributions of Poverty and Ethnic Background to the Participation of Secondary School Students in Special Education.* Menlo Park, CA: SRI International.

Washington, Booker T. 1966. "The Mistakes and the Future of Negro Education." Pp. 434–445 in *Negro Social and Political Thought, 1850–1920: Representative Texts.* Edited by Howard Brotz. New York: Basic Books, Inc.

Wise, Arthur E. 1988. "The Two Conflicting Trends in School Reform: Legislated Learning Revisited." *Phi Delta Kappan* 69: 328–332.

Woodson, Carter G. [1933] 1991. *The Mis-Education of the Negro.* Reprint. Philadelphia: Hamik's Publications.

Zirkel, Perry. 1997. "Zero for Tolerance?" *Phi Delta Kappan* 79: 89–90.

Chapter Two

☙ Chronology of African American Education

African Americans' educational journey is a unique one. They belong to the only immigrant group to have been legally denied access to education. Their milestones in attempting to achieve educational equality, equity, and quality remain the benchmarks for determining the progress being made in the education of people of color, generally. This chronology highlights the pilgrimage.

1619   Twenty African indentured servants disembark in the colony of Jamestown, Virginia.

1661   Slavery is legalized in the Virginia colony with other southern colonies following suit. Teaching slaves to read and write is considered illegal. Educating slaves is determined to be a deterrent to slavery.

1773   Phillis Wheatley's book of poems, *Poems on Various Subjects Religious and Moral,* is published in England. The book is evidence that some slaves are being taught to read and write. Wheatley is a slave in Boston, Massachusetts.

1774   The Abolitionist Society establishes a school for African American children in Philadelphia.

1787   The first African Free School is founded in New York City by the Manumission Society.

1790   Free blacks in Charleston, South Carolina, establish a school. Ninety-two percent of blacks in the United States are slaves.

1808   John Chavis, a free black, opens a school in Raleigh, North

1808 *(cont.)*	Carolina. Whites are taught during the day. Free blacks and slaves are taught at night. Beginning in 1831, white authorities in Raleigh forbid him to teach the black students.
1810	Charleston School for Free Negroes is founded in South Carolina.
1824	The seven African Free Schools in New York City are funded by the city. Free education for all black children in New York City is available.
1829–1849	Ohio excludes African Americans from public schools.
1833	Sarah Harris, a free black, applies and is accepted as a nonresident student at Prudence Crandall's boarding school in Canterbury, Connecticut. When most of the parents withdraw their daughters, Crandall opens a school specifically for African American females.
1834	South Carolina passes a law prohibiting teaching any African American children, free or slave.

White students at Oberlin College in Ohio are asked if black and female students should be admitted. When the students vote yes, Oberlin becomes the first college in the west to enroll African Americans and women. |
1837	Cheyney University of Pennsylvania is founded. It is the first institution of higher learning, primarily high school, for African Americans in the United States.
1839	Connecticut passes a law that makes it illegal to establish schools for blacks. Sarah Harris closes her private school for African American females.
1849	Sarah C. Roberts sues the city of Boston for discriminatory practices in its schools when a black child is refused admission. The case is lost.
1854	Lincoln University in Pennsylvania is founded. It is the first historically black institution founded specifically for college-level instruction.

1855 Massachusetts's legislature passes a law to prohibit the exclusion of a person from a public school because of race, color, or religion.

    Berea College in Kentucky is established and admits blacks. In 1904, Berea College is forbidden by Kentucky state law to continue to admit blacks. It begins to admit blacks again in 1954.

1856 Wilberforce University in Ohio is founded by the African Methodist Episcopalian (AME) Church. Richard Allen, a free black, founded the AME Church in 1799.

1857 The Dred Scott decision of the U.S. Supreme Court concludes that the U.S. Constitution does not allow slaves to become U.S. citizens and legalizes slavery in all territories.

1861 During the Civil War, teachers (African American and white) are sent from the North to the South to teach African American supporters of the Union Armies and those who are in the "liberated areas within the Union lines." In addition, schools for African Americans open in Hampton, Virginia; Port Royal, South Carolina; New Bern, North Carolina; and Lawrence, Kansas.

1862 The Morrill Act of 1862, passed by the U.S. Congress, provides federal funds for land-grant institutions of higher education for white students.

1865 The Thirteenth Amendment to the U.S. Constitution abolishes slavery.

    The U.S. Bureau of Refugees, Freedman, and Abandoned Lands, known as the Freedman Bureau, is established by Congress. It assists newly freed slaves with food, medicine, jobs, contracts, legal matters, and education. It participates in establishing over 4,000 schools for African Americans.

    Shaw University in Raleigh, North Carolina, is founded. It becomes the oldest black postsecondary institution in the South. It is the first black institution to have a medical school.

One out of ten newly freed slaves can read and write.

1865–1875   Twenty-four private black colleges open.

1866   Former Confederate states instate "black codes." The codes maintain the racial status quo before the Emancipation Proclamation and the Thirteenth Amendment.

1867   Howard University is founded when a charter is granted by the U.S. government to educate African Americans.

George Foster Peabody establishes a fund of $2 million to aid in educating black and white youth in "the more destitute portions of the Southern and Southwestern states."

1868   The Fourteenth Amendment gives blacks citizenship and "equal protection under the laws."

1870   The Freedman Bureau is abolished.

The Fifteenth Amendment gives blacks the right to vote.

Twenty-one percent of newly freed blacks are literate.

1871   Alcorn College is founded in Mississippi. It is the first African American land-grant college.

1876   Meharry Medical College in Tennessee is founded to educate health professionals for blacks. One-third of all black practicing physicians and dentists graduate from Meharry.

1880   Forty-five percent of blacks in the South are literate. Nationally, 30 percent of the black population is literate.

1890   The Morrill Act of 1890 is passed by the U.S. Congress. States with segregated higher education systems are required to provide land-grant institutions for both systems.

1895   Booker T. Washington's "Atlanta Compromise" speech stresses vocational education for blacks.

1896   The U.S. Supreme Court, in the *Plessy v. Ferguson* decision, upholds that states have constitutional authority to provide separate but equal accommodations for blacks.

1897   Alexander Crummel founds the American Negro Academy in Washington, D.C. The academy develops and disseminates African American arts and sciences.

1900   Fifty-five percent of the black population is literate.

Approximately 2,600 blacks have postsecondary credentials.

1901   W. E. B. DuBois, author of *The Souls of Black Folks* (1903), presents the concept of the "talented tenth."

1902   Palmer Memorial Institute is founded by Charlotte Hawkins Brown, a former slave. Located in Sedalia, North Carolina, Palmer is a preparatory day and boarding school for blacks. The school closes in 1971.

1907   Alain Locke is the first black Rhodes Scholar.

1909   The National Association for the Advancement of Colored People (NAACP) is founded. It is a civil rights organization whose mission is "to ensure the political, educational, social, and economic equality of minority group citizens of the United States." There are currently over 2,200 branches in all states, the District of Columbia, Japan, and Germany.

1910   The National Urban League is founded as a nonprofit, community-based organization. It is a social service and civil rights organization. The league has 115 affiliates in 34 states and the District of Columbia to advocate African American social and economic equality.

1915   Carter G. Woodson initiates the Association for the Study of Negro Life and History. Its name is changed to the Association for the Study of Afro-American Life and History in 1972. Publication of *The Journal of Negro History* begins in 1916.

1927   Seventy-seven black colleges and universities are operating, with a total enrollment of 14,000.

1929   Atlanta University is established as the first African American institution solely for graduate and professional education.

1932   *The Journal of Negro Education* is founded at Howard University. *The Journal* publishes research that identifies and defines the problems and issues in African American education.

1933   Carter G. Woodson's *The Mis-Education of the Negro* is published.

1935   The NAACP wins a suit against the University of Maryland law school and African Americans are admitted.

1944   The United Negro College Fund (UNCF) is incorporated. Conceived by Frederick D. Patterson, president of Tuskegee Institute, it is a consortium of 39 private, regionally accredited, four-year Historically Black Colleges and Universities (HBCUs). UNCF's purpose is to enhance the quality of education of HBCU students, provide scholarships, and raise operating funds and provide technical assistance for member institutions.

1950s   Seventy-five million dollars of public funds each year go to Southern educational institutions that do not admit African Americans.

1950   Kenneth Clark, an African American psychologist, conducts the now famous "doll" study. He finds that black children prefer to play with white dolls rather than black dolls and attributes this to the poor self-image black children have of themselves and their race. The findings of this study are cited in the 1954 *Brown* decision. In 1955, the study is published under the title *Prejudice and Your Child.*

1954   Thurgood Marshall, Special Council of the NAACP, provides the legal leadership for the defendant that results in a unanimous ruling by the U.S. Supreme Court in *Brown v. Board of Education, Topeka, Kansas.* The Supreme Court justices conclude that racial segregation in public schools violates the Fourteenth Amendment of the U.S. Constitution. President Lyndon B. Johnson appoints Marshall as Supreme Court justice in 1965.

1956   Autherine Lucy, a black woman, is admitted to the University of Alabama. After three attempts to matriculate in February of that year, the university trustees on a technicality permanently expell her. A decade later blacks matriculate.

1957   President Dwight D. Eisenhower sends federal troops to Little Rock, Arkansas, to enforce the law when Governor Orval Faubus refuses to desegregate Central High School.

1960s   Black Studies is defined as an academic field of study.

1960   Sixty-five percent of black students in college attend historically black colleges.

A National Education Association (NEA) study finds that 30,000 black teachers have lost their jobs since 1954. The job loss was in seventeen southern and border states. The loss of jobs is attributed to desegregation and discrimination.

1961   Charlayne Hunter-Gault and Hamilton Holmes matriculate at the University of Georgia, following a court order.

1962   All of the formerly all-white high schools in Little Rock, Arkansas, are desegregated. Elementary schools remain segregated.

The U.S. Circuit Court of Appeals orders the Mississippi board of higher education to admit African American James Meredith or be held in contempt. He matriculates at the University of Mississippi after 12,000 National Guard are sent to the campus to protect him.

1963   Alabama Governor George Wallace literally blocks the front doors of the University of Alabama to prevent two black students from matriculating. U.S. President John Kennedy orders the Alabama National Guard to facilitate the matriculation of the two students.

1964   Affirmative action policies are instituted based on the Civil Rights Act of 1964.

The Department of Health, Education, and Welfare (HEW) notifies the Prince George's County school district in Maryland that it is to follow HEW guidelines to eliminate all-black schools.

1965   President Lyndon B. Johnson signs Executive Order 11246 supporting affirmative action policies and practices.

Head Start programs begin as an initiative in the Office of Economic Opportunity. The programs are designed to address the educational, health and nutrition, and social service needs of low-income children, specifically, and their families, generally.

1966   Sociologist James Coleman's study *Equality of Education Opportunity,* popularly known as the "Coleman Report," is published. Based on the findings of the study, mandatory busing becomes the primary solution to the problem of ending school segregation. Tracking, the permanent placement of students in a program of study based on test scores and teacher judgments, becomes a common practice that frequently resegregates black students who are bused.

1969   The National Association for Equal Opportunity in Higher Education (NAFEO) is founded. It serves to address the interests of 118 historically and predominately black colleges and universities, primarily as a public policy advocate.

1970s   Twenty years after the 1954 *Brown* decision, there is more segregation in northern schools than in southern schools.

Thirty-four percent of black students in college attend black colleges.

1974   The Boston public school district is ordered by a federal court to desegregate. Protests and violence erupt at South Boston High School, while desegregation in the rest of the school district proceeds without incident.

1975   A class action suit, *Ayers v. Waller,* subsequently known as

Ayers v. Fordice, is filed against the state of Mississippi by the Black Mississippians' Council on Higher Education asking that the state enforce Title VI of the Civil Rights Act of 1964. When the U.S. Department of Health, Education, and Welfare (HEW) files suit, the suit is named *United States v. Fordice.* In the 1992 decision, the U.S. Supreme Court orders the state of Mississippi to dismantle its dual system in higher education. The Court decision includes the possible closing or the merger of institutions. The ruling is seen by many as putting public historically black colleges and universities in jeopardy.

1980s   Schools are more racially segregated than in 1954 because of "white flight," where whites move from areas of a city to avoid black neighbors and school desegregation.

Twenty-five percent of black students in college attend historically black colleges and universities.

1980   President Jimmy Carter, through executive order 12232, establishes the White House Initiative on HBCUs. It is to provide a systematic process to help HBCUs access federally funded programs. Executive orders are renewed by all subsequent U.S. presidents until the end of the century.

1981   President Ronald Reagan calls for a 25 percent cut in federal funds to education. The cutbacks decrease funding to poor students and are detrimental to the future of many black colleges.

1987   The American Council on Education in Washington, D.C., establishes the Office of Minorities in Higher Education.

1994   Fifteen percent of black students in college attend historically black colleges. This is the plateau in the declining enrollment of HBCUs.

1994–1999 Federal court orders release public school districts from having to continue to implement their desegregation plans. Many of those released have been leading the long-term legal and desegregation plan disputes about the attempt to achieve desegregation during the 1970s and

1980s. Some of the cities involved are Charlotte, North Carolina; Nashville, Tennessee; Oklahoma City, Oklahoma; Denver, Colorado; Wilmington, Delaware; and Cleveland, Ohio. The final rulings conclude that the vestiges of intentional segregation in public schools no longer exist.

1996   Spelman College's capital campaign reaches $114 million. This is the largest in the history of HBCUs.

Twenty percent of black students enrolled in college attend historically black colleges.

Ward Connerly places the Civil Rights Initiative (Proposition 209), an anti–affirmative action proposal, on statewide ballots in California, and later in Washington and Florida. He is a black California businessman and a member of the University of California Board of Regents.

California voters pass Proposition 209 with 54 percent of the votes. It amends the state's constitution to disallow affirmative action.

1997   Black student enrollment in California's higher education system decreases. The American Council on Education reports a 48 percent decrease in African American enrollment between 1997 and 1998.

1998   Civil Rights Initiative 200, an anti–affirmative action proposal, passes in the state of Washington with support from 58 percent of the voters. However, it is not an amendment to the state's constitution. Therefore, it is unclear whether the Civil Rights Initiative 200 supercedes existing state laws on affirmative action. The state's Asian American governor, Gary Locke, as well as executives of leading corporations in the state, opposes the initiative.

1999   Florida Governor Jeb Bush's One Florida Initiative is proposed as an alternative to Connerly's Civil Rights Initiative. The One Florida Initiative is similar to Texas's Ten Percent Law, which was signed into law by Texas Governor George W. Bush in 1997. The Ten Percent Law requires public postsecondary institutions to admit all Texas students who are in the top 10 percent of their high school classes, regardless of test scores.

The Florida Supreme Court refuses to hold hearings before March 2000 on Ward Connerly's anti–affirmative action proposal, which he pursues despite Governor Bush's One Florida Initiative. Connerly wants to have the Civil Rights Initiative proposal on a statewide ballot in 2000.

The American Council on Education files three amicus briefs in two federal courts. The briefs reaffirm the need for affirmative action and "race-conscious" admissions policies in higher education.

2000   Two African American Florida state legislators, Senator Kendrick Meek of Miami and Representative Tony Hill of Jacksonville, stage a sit-in in the office of Florida Governor Bush to protest his One Florida Initiative. The sit-in ends when the Florida Board of Regents agrees to postpone voting on the initiative and hold public meetings across the state. In February, the Florida Board of Regents approves the One Florida Initiative. In March, over 10,000 march in Tallahassee to protest the One Florida Initiative. In May it is announced that the earliest Ward Connerly's Civil Rights Initiative can be on a Florida statewide ballot is 2002.

Chapter Three

●◆ African American Schooling

Schools are open, social systems. Schools may be defined as systems because they are made up of an arrangement of tasks and individuals that collectively create an organization. As open systems, they are influenced by their external and internal environments. External environments include state boards of education and their policies and regulations, federal and state legislation, citizens, and parents. Their internal environments include curriculum, instructional practices, strategies and methods, assessment decisions, administrative and instructional staff, and students. Schools are social systems because their ability to achieve their purpose is dependent on the manner of the interactions of people.

A school environment is composed of its climate and its culture. School climate is an intangible sense or feeling that people have about the atmosphere of the school. Do people feel they belong, or do they feel alienated? Is there a sense of trust or distrust among the individuals in the school? Is there ease or tension in interactions?

School culture is composed of the behaviors, values, and assumptions that people make about each other and their roles in the school. Embedded in school culture are: (1) the ways in which authority is used, (2) the interactions between the school, parents, and the community in which the students live, and (3) the curricula content and instructional styles.

Schools, therefore, encompass more than educational regulations and procedures, curriculum, instruction, and assessment. Student achievement and attainment is also dependent on the environment, climate, and culture of the school in which learning is to occur. Schooling, then, is the interplay of all of these factors coupled with the manner in which the doctrines of equality, equity, and quality are exercised. In this book, schooling focuses on precollege education—prekindergarten through twelfth grade.

This chapter focuses on the precollege education of African Americans—public and private. The chapter begins with an overview of the schooling experiences of most African American children in public schools. This overview is followed by summary discussions on the education inputs of curriculum and instruction, and the outcome measures of assessment or testing as they relate to African American education. Interviews with an African American principal and teacher provide professional insights. Through their interviews they share their experiences and observations of the schooling of African American youth.

The black private school options chosen by some African American parents is discussed. An interview with the head of an independent black school is included. An African American father shares the reasons why he and his wife chose an African American independent schooling experience for their child. Additional alternative African American schooling experiences are explored.

AFRICAN AMERICAN SCHOOLING EXPERIENCES

Schooling is one of the most crucial experiences for children. It contributes to their social and psychological development as well as their educational achievement and future educational attainment and lifestyle.

For a large percentage of African American children, early schooling experiences minimize the value of the children and lack a nurturing, supportive environment that takes them into consideration. The dismantling of the link between family, school, and community as a result of desegregation stripped African American children of the support system that is vital to them and their academic success. School desegregation did not provide equality, equity, and quality in the schooling of African American children as promised.

Many African Americans have lost faith in and developed a distrust of the schooling process. They believe that the success of African American children in public schools is contingent on the children acquiescing to white culture and losing vestiges of themselves. These attitudes are supported by the majority of the research on the public school experiences of most black students.

Most frequently, research and observations conclude that the public schooling of African American children systematically requires them to forfeit their cultural ties, demeans their self-esteem, and has them relinquish their diverse forms of expression. This is attributed, in large part, to the reality and experience gulf between white teachers and black students.

In several years of classroom observation in a number of schools across the country, the author has witnessed the subtle and overt messages teachers, particularly white teachers, give African American students, consciously or unconsciously: conditional praise, such as "very good, but . . ."; rewording African American students' correct responses and not doing the same with white students; placing African American students at the back of the classroom or the end of the line; avoiding being in the proximity of African American children; and the troubled look or frown when addressing African American students. There is a belief by many in schools that African American students, especially males, tend to be hostile, belligerent, and verbally and physically aggressive, particularly in comparison to their white counterparts. African American students who are in desegregated schools are resegregated through tracking, placement in special education, and disciplinary practices. These types of experiences are familiar and daily occurrences for far too many African American students in public schools.

CURRICULUM AND INSTRUCTION

Curriculum

Curriculum is the sum total of knowledge to be acquired through the education process. It is delineated by a set of courses and skills that are provided. The curriculum represents the core of students' expected learning experiences. Simply put, the curriculum reveals what will be taught. The emphasis of the curriculum decisions determines who is taught, what is taught, and how information and knowledge are imparted.

Curricula may appear to be impartial and apolitical. Yet that is far from accurate. Curricula are the interpretation of state education laws. As such, curricula are policies. They are developed to assure adherence to, administration of, and implementation of state laws. Therefore, curricula are neither impartial nor apolitical.

Curricula are not formulated, developed, or implemented in a vacuum. Curricula decisions at the state, district, school, and classroom levels are made in a political environment. Based on available resources (human, monetary, and time), decisions are made about what is taught and what is not taught as well as who is taught and who is not taught. What may appear to be purely professional decisions are, in actuality, political acts.

It is the curricular decisions or political acts that proclaim which knowledge, culture, and people are valued in the American educational system and society. Through curricular decisions, students learn their importance or lack of importance in society. The results of curricular decisions in American education are seen by African Americans and other people of color as exclusive rather than inclusive. Because of the exclusion, there is a call for balance in the ethnocentric formulation, development, and implementation of the decisions.

Two Curricula Models

Afrocentric and multicultural education are two examples of curricula models that are designed to redress the ethnic imbalance in the American curriculum. An advocate of each model describes it.

Afrocentric Curriculum

The Afrocentric curriculum is a paradigm designed to amend the cultural imbalance in American school curricula for people of African descent.

Molefi Kete Asante defines the Afrocentric curriculum in "The Afrocentric Idea in Education." He writes,

> *Afrocentricity* is a frame of reference wherein phenomena are viewed from the perspective of the African person. The Afrocentric approach seeks in every situation the appropriate centrality of the African person. In education this means that teachers provide students the opportunity to study the world and its people, concepts, and history from an African world view. . . . African American students come to see themselves not merely as seekers of knowledge but as integral participants in it. Because all content areas are adaptable to an Afrocentric approach, African American students can be made to see themselves as centered in the reality of any discipline. . . . Afrocentricity does not condone ethnocentric valorization at the expense of degrading other groups' perspectives. (*Journal of Negro Education* 1991, 171, 172)

Multicultural Education Curriculum

A multicultural education curriculum is a model designed to include all ethnic and cultural constructs in the school curriculum. Carl A. Grant described multicultural education in "Reflections on the Promise of *Brown* and Multicultural Education."

> A curriculum that is multicultural begins with the academic needs and interests of the students. It highlights the history and contributions of all Americans and is infused throughout the entire kindergarten

through twelfth-grade program. It also highlights who we are as Americans and how that identity is represented throughout the world. Students are taught about oppression and social equality based on race, class, gender, and disability. Some curriculum concepts are organized around current social issues, including racism, classism, and sexism, and offer discussions about how these and other oppressive dynamics operate in school to produce knowledge and self-identity. Concepts are taught in a manner that includes the experiences and perspectives of several different ethnic groups and uses students' life experiences as a starting point for analyzing oppression. Also, the curriculum includes discussions about the relationship between knowledge and power and how both are acquired. (*Teachers College Record* 1995, 719)

Instruction

Imagine an American teacher deciding to teach in another country. The teacher does not become knowledgeable about the history and culture of the country and the people. Nor does the teacher understand how the history and culture influence behavior and learning styles, the social dynamics between and among the communities in which the children live, the experiences of the children, and their schooling. The lack of this type of insight puts the teacher and the children at a disadvantage. The teacher's improper instructional approaches create a high probability that he/she will fail as a teacher and the students' academic success and achievement will be marginalized, unless with this knowledge, the American teacher recognizes the need to modify his or her American teaching style, and in all likelihood develop and employ a different repertoire of teaching styles and strategies.

This scenario exemplifies what is at the heart of the matter on instructional style and education of African American children. The matter is compounded when teachers are indifferent to African American children and have low expectations of their ability to learn and be academically successful.

— Linked to instructional style is the organizational design of instruction. The academic tracking of African American children is tangible evidence of how equality, equity, and quality are exercised in a school.

Tracking is sometimes used synonymously with ability grouping. In this book, the two terms are not synonymous. The educational practice of ability grouping has a long history in American education. Based on skill development and achievement as measured by test scores and teacher judgment, students are grouped for instruction. The premise of ability grouping is that teachers can more effectively provide instruction to students who are approximately similar in the mastery of requisite skills. In the elementary schools, most ability groups are formed for reading and mathematics. In the high schools, ability groupings are based on the level of the courses students take. At its most effective, ability grouping recognizes the variance in students' proficiency in different subjects. For example, it is conceivable that a student could be in the "advanced" group for reading and the "below average" group for math. It is possible that students could move between ability groups as they develop academically.

Tracking, on the other hand, is the permanent placement of students in a program of study based on students' perceived ability to learn generally. Once students are tested, and judged by teachers to possess a certain learning ability, all of their subjects are at the level of one track. Tracking begins at the elementary level. The practice of tracking does not recognize the varying ability of students among subjects, nor the maturation of students.

The practice of tracking has been a formidable issue in African American education since the *Brown v. Board of Education* decision in 1954. Repeatedly, research studies find black students are overrepresented in the lowest academic tracks. Court reviews and decisions on school districts' desegregation plans raise issues, frequently, about this overrepresentation. Yet the practice of tracking does not decrease, nor does the overrepresentation of blacks in lower levels. Tracking resegregates African American students in supposedly desegregated schools and perpetuates the self-fulfilling prophecy that black students are inferior.

Teachers conduct instruction for tracked students based on a preconceived notion of the students' abilities. The social and physical distance between most African American students and white teachers generates stereotypes and reinforces teachers' low expectations and complacent attitudes toward black students. Black students' placement in a track labels them and determines their future educational opportunities and attainment.

AFRICAN AMERICAN STUDENTS AND TESTING

Tests and Their Uses

Tracking and testing go hand in hand. Based on test scores and the interpretation of those test scores, students are placed in an academic track. Between kindergarten and twelfth grade students are administered a battery of tests. Intelligence quotient (IQ) tests purport to measure the cognitive endowment of students. Achievement tests claim to measure the academic accomplishments of students. Ability tests are intended to determine the academic aptitude of students. Competency tests aim to measure the students' readiness for new skills or an advanced level of skills.

Tests are considered culturally biased when students of color are excluded from or minimally represented in the norming group, when the tests do not reflect the cultural characteristics of the students of color to whom the tests are administered, or both. Intelligence tests and achievement tests more frequently come under attack as being culturally biased. As an example, consider that until 1972, African American students were not part of the norming group for the "Stanford-Binet Intelligence Test." In spite of later inclusion of African American students in the norming group, few changes occurred in the test format and items. Heavy reliance on standardized test scores and the interpretation of those scores as the primary determinant of students' aptitudes and abilities results in disproportionate numbers of blacks being permanently placed in the lowest academic track. Horace Mann Bond wrote in 1966,

> Almost from the beginning of the use of standardized tests in American education, these instruments were regarded as infallible measures of the innate "intelligence" of children and adults. . . . Later, educators and the general public began to see in them marvelously efficient constructions by which the social class and environmental background of the child might be accurately measured, yielding evidence, not as to the innate capacity of the child, but of the degree to which the child approximated standard class performance, or varied from that norm. . . . This concept is important to the education of [black] children because since the invention of standardized tests they have been made the particular butt of facile racialistic interpretations of the scores such children make in comparison with other children. (1966, 475)

The Bell Curve

Educational anthropologists have conducted international comparative studies on IQ test scores and grades of dominant groups and groups targeted for discrimination. Their studies reveal that the dominant groups always surpass the discriminated groups in IQ test scores and grades. This occurs with the Koreans in Japan (Lee 1991), the Aborigines in Australia (Klich 1988), the Maoris in New Zealand (Barrington 1991), and the Irish in England (Benson 1995).

Collectively, African Americans are shown to score consistently lower than whites on standardized tests. Extensive research has been conducted on the "gap" in black and white test scores. The research conclusions range from attributing the gap to the cultural bias of standardized tests to asserting that blacks are innately intellectually inferior to whites. The former conclusion is discussed earlier in this section. The latter conclusion is grounded in a line of research that is designed to prove the genetic, hereditary inadequacy of blacks and other people of color.

Currently, this line of research is known as the "bell curve." The researchers, and those who support and accept their research as fact, seem to believe that if it is studied enough by highly credentialed individuals at what are considered prestigious white institutions, and findings are presented frequently enough, then the assumptions are true. Proponents of equal education for blacks compare this approach to Hitler's propaganda about the superiority of the Aryan race, and argue that it does not lend itself to a productive discussion about the education of African Americans. Yet, having said that, it is necessary to know the genesis, history, and continued inquiry of this research. Following is a summary of the actors and their roles in this debate.

The "bell curve" and the controversy surrounding it is the most recent manifestation of a long history of debate over quantifying intelligence in order to justify racism. As previously mentioned, racism is about power, and one way to justify and retain power is to assert intellectual superiority, and support that assertion through "research." Eugenics is grounded in the authors' own political, economic, and social need to prove superiority.

Primarily, this research originates in the fields of psychology and education. Frequently, it is coupled with genetics. Charles Darwin, an English naturalist, in 1859 published his theory of evolution. His book, *Origins of the Species: The Preservation of Favored Races in the Struggle for Life,* is the seminal study for the subsequent research. Darwin was obsessed with proving the intellectual inferiority of people of African descent. His work was predicated on his belief that blacks could never be intellectual equals to whites. Thus, according to Darwin, blacks could not compete for survival with whites. He claimed that evolution was based on natural selection or survival of the fittest, and that blacks are the "missing link" between apes and humankind (meaning whites). (Darwin's works appear on the website of David Duke, former Imperial Wizard of the Ku Klux Klan.)

Influenced by Darwin's work, in 1869 Francis Galton, an English scientist, published *Hereditary Genius: An Inquiry into Its Laws and Consequences.* He concluded that intelligence is hereditary. In 1883, he coined the term "eugenics." Eugenics is considered a science. Its purpose is to improve the mental and physical attributes of humans by controlling the factors that influence heredity. To accomplish this, eugenics would control the selection of those who procreate.

It is important to note that eugenics is not singular in its focus on those of African descent. The focus of the "science" is directed toward all people of color, Jews, and Eastern Europeans. The focus on Eastern Europeans was most prevalent during the nineteenth century in the United States. Eugenics is grounded in the conviction that Western Europeans are superior to all. Devotees of eugenics have shaped and attempt to continue to shape education, educational assessment, psychology, and social issues.

\ Who are some of the eugenicists? One is Charles Spearman, an English statistician, who in 1904 identified the "g-factor," which means "general intelligence." The g-factor is supposed to demonstrate the accuracy of IQ tests and predict future success in life. Another is Alfred Binet, a French psychologist, who in 1905 developed the first IQ test for children, based on children in Paris. Lewis Terman, a psychology professor at Stanford University, in 1916 brought the Binet test to the United States. Finding that the test did not yield the same results in the United States as it did in France, he revised the test. His revisions resulted in the Stanford-Binet test. Arthur Jensen, professor emeritus of Educational Psychology at the University of California–Berkeley, avers in his work that blacks are intellectually inferior to whites.\ He does not consider himself a racist. Rather he sees himself a realist. Jensen's work first received recognition in 1969. He continued his line of reasoning for over thirty years. In 1998 he published *The G-Factor: The Science of Mental Ability.* The late William Shockley, an engineering and mathematical science professor at Stanford University, in the 1970s and 1980s promoted a plan for the government to pay welfare recipients to be sterilized. Robert Gordon, a sociologist at Johns Hopkins University, has contended since 1976 that efforts to improve education have not changed the fact that blacks have lower IQ scores than whites. He claims that lower IQ scores attribute to black criminality. \

The late Richard Herrnstein, the Edgar Pierce Professor of Psychology at Harvard University, and Charles Murray, a Bradley Fellow at the American Enterprise Institute, published *The Bell Curve: Intelligence and Class Structure in American Life* in 1994. In *The Bell Curve,* they cite most of the eugenicists named here along with others. Herrnstein and Murray link their premise of inherited cognitive abilities to the economy of the United States. They maintain that there should be concern about the substantial differences in cognitive abilities because they are related directly to the future economic status of and social conditions in the United States.\Linda Gottfredson, a professor of educational studies at the University of Delaware, has expressed a concern with what she considers to be the number of blacks with low IQs who are professionals. She had a feature article in *Scientific American* in 1998. The article, titled "The General Intelligence Factor," supports the efficacy of the g-factor.

The primary funder of eugenics research is the Pioneer Fund, an ultraconservative organization founded in the late 1930s and based in New York City. Its founder was a sympathizer with Nazi Germany. Charles Lane cites the original and current purpose of the Pioneer Fund as being for "race betterment, with special reference to the people of the United States" (1995, 128). The race to which the fund refers is the white race.

There appears to be a correlation between the timing of publication of these studies and the progress of African Americans. Jensen's article, "How Much Can We Boost IQ and Scholastic Achievement?" in *The Harvard Educational Review* in 1969, and its subsequent publication in 1973 in *Psychology Today,* appeared just as the Civil Rights Movement reached its peak and legislation and court decisions mandated equality for blacks. Herrnstein and Murray's *Bell Curve* came at a time when blacks were making their greatest strides in America's society and many were calling for economic reparations.

Demographic research shows that the number of people of color in the United States is increasing and the number of whites is decreasing. It is projected that by 2020, people of color will outnumber whites. The work of contemporary eugenicists is built on their fear and insecurity, and that of like-minded whites. Their angst is centered on the real probability that, simply because of racial demographic size, they will lose the control and power that they have had for centuries in the United States. However, the number of people that view eugenics as scientific is decreasing, and an increasing number of people are becoming vocal against this type of research.

PUBLIC SCHOOL RESOURCE INTERVIEWS

Interviews with an African American principal and an African American teacher follow. Both are public school district employees. They share their observations and concerns regarding the American education system and the schooling experiences of African Americans in public schools.

Edward M. Harris

Edward Harris is a native of Boynton Beach, Florida. He received his associate degree in General Education from Palm Beach Community College. His baccalaureate degree is from Florida Atlantic University, with majors in mathematics and physical education. His master's degree in mathematics education is from Nova University in Fort Lauderdale, Florida. His education specialist degree is from Barry University in Miami with concentrations in elementary education and Montessori education. Harris enrolled in the Ph.D. degree program at The Union Institute in Cincinnati. His doctoral field of study is educational leadership with an emphasis in at-risk African American and Hispanic students.

Harris has a Florida Teacher's Certificate in mathematics and physical education, and a Florida Principal's Certificate. He has over twenty-seven years of experience as a professional educator. Nine of those years he has served as principal of Northboro Elementary School in Palm Beach County School District.

Harris's other professional experiences include serving as an adjunct professor for the American Academy of Distance Education Training in Miami. He serves as an adjunct professor for Redlands College's on-line program, which is based in El Reno, Oklahoma. In addition, he has served as a part-time instructor of mathematics, college algebra, and methods of teaching mathematics in elementary and secondary schools. He has served as an assistant and head football coach, an athletic director, and head track coach. He was recognized for his success in these positions in 1999 when he was inducted into the Palm Beach County Sports Hall of Fame.

The author's conversation with Edward Harris follows.

As a principal, what do you consider the primary issues in the pre-college American education system?

Five aspects of American education concern me. My first concern is the lack of equitable and adequate funding of schools. I tend to look at situations from a mathematical standpoint. Therefore, I always like people to define equality or equal when they are talking about education. In mathematics, equal means balance. What someone does to one side of an equation, one must do to the other side; therefore, both sides of the equation are balanced.

In education, an equal amount of too little is not enough. Does "equal" educational opportunity mean the same level of funding for all students, or must some students and localities be afforded extra resources to put them on equal footing with others in their quest for educational success? Why should and how can low-income communities be helped to provide adequate facilities and programs for educating their children? People make trade-offs when educational dollars are limited. Sometimes the trade-offs exist as choices between educational equity and educational excellence. Some people believe that efforts to promote educational excellence will swamp the poor, the weak, and the minority-group students. Others argue that money spent on equalization could be put to better use capitalizing on the strengths of outstanding students, such as the gifted.

Another challenge for the states is to decide how to recognize the cost differences inherent in educating some groups of students. States have considerable experience in providing funding for programs such as special education and bilingual education. Yet there is less experience in adjusting funding for cost-of-living differences among communities. Because the cost of education is typically higher in urban schools than in non-urban schools, equal levels of funding actually puts urban schools at a disadvantage. They cannot purchase the same amount of educational goods as their suburban and rural counterparts with the same amount of money. This exacerbates the problem of working with higher proportions of at-risk students.

My second concern is American cultural diversity. I have a major concern about saying everything is equal when some teachers overlook and ignore certain students because they are not what teachers expect. Yes, it concerns me deeply when teachers prejudge students by the color of their skin, or students' dress or hairstyle. Therefore, it is extremely important for great educators to make sure that students are being treated fairly. I think it is more important to be fair than it is to be equal.

I have seen many changes in education. When I first started teaching, we were more concerned about teaching children regardless of race, creed, or color. Now there are laws that seem to emphasize addressing the needs of immigrant students over the needs of American born students, at least that seems to be the case in Florida.

Providing equal educational opportunity in the classroom is complicated. That is because of continuing prejudice and discrimination in the broader society. Discrimination—differential treatment associated with labels—gives rise to conflict. People too often report and interpret information about groups as though all members conform to some mythical image of sameness. In turn, these reports and interpretations drive educational actions.

Cultural differences can become apparent in something as simple as not knowing or not having experience with guiding educational conversations in the classrooms. For example, while observing a teacher, I noted the following:

Ms. White is teaching her first-graders how to tell time. She points to a clock, telling her students "It's ten o'clock because the big hand is on the twelve and the little hand is on the ten."

"What time is it?" she asks the students. Many of the white children raised their hands, eager to answer. The black students sat silently. A few gave her a puzzled look.

Ms. White concludes that many of her black students do not know the answer, and she silently makes a note to herself to revisit the concept with them later.

In the African American children's families, such questions were posed only when someone genuinely needs to know the answer. "What is she asking us for?" Some of the black children stated later. "She just told us it was ten o'clock!"

Aspects of classroom life that are subject to misunderstandings between teachers and students include verbal communication, patterns of participating and listening, body language and movement, uses of signs and symbols (clothing, jewelry, and emblems), modes of relaxing and of paying attention, conceptions of time, social values, peer interaction patterns, values concerning what is worth knowing, and many other areas.

What can teachers do to ensure that cultural differences between them and their students do not have negative effects on student learning and achievement? Knowing students' backgrounds and giving culturally appropriate responses to students is an important first step.

The third concern is parent involvement. Parent involvement is critical. When I started teaching in the early 1970s parents from all ethnic groups were supportive, for the most part, and were aware of the importance for students of color to progress. Today, there is inadequate involvement of parents. Collaborative approaches must involve parents to succeed. Children's futures are inextricably linked to their parents. When parents take an interest in their children's progress, when parents hold high but reasonable expectation for their children's performance and support children by meeting their basic needs, good things happen. I have observed the following benefits: students' school attendance improves, their self-esteem and achievement spirals upward, and their long-term prospects for living successful, productive lives increase.

The push for parent involvement is occurring everywhere. Involving parents in their children's education seems to be a part of every educator's job description. As part of the Improving American's Schools Act, Title 1, local schools and districts are required to adopt three types of parent-involvement strategies. These strategies include: (1) parents being involved in the development of school policies, (2) forming school-parent compacts to raise students' academic performance, and (3) establishing school-parent partnerships to work on collaborative improvement projects.

Traditional wisdom says children are more likely to succeed in school when their parents are involved in their education. Some research shows the connection between parent involvement and children learning. Research findings conclude that parents who are invited by teachers to participate in school-based activities tend to feel more positive about helping their children learn, increase their interactions with children at home, and give teachers high ratings.

During my tenure as a principal, I have discovered a significant number of teachers who think it's a waste of time trying to involve poor, single, and undereducated parents. Some teachers believe parents do not care about their children's success in school. I find that teachers who go out of their way to make connections with parents are often successful in getting them involved, even though it may be in limited ways. Reaching out to every child's parents amounts to an act of faith on the part of teachers and principals. In terms of raising student achievement, such faith is well placed.

My fourth concern is technology in American education. Everyone today is jumping on the education technology bandwagon. I think if we are not careful, in American education we will progress in some ways and digress in other ways. For example, middle class and upper income students have computers in their homes. They are proficient with the technology. Students from lower socioeconomic levels do not have computers. This is an important and distinct disadvantage. In this information age, low socioeconomic students are not playing on a level playing field.

My final concern is the role of politics in American education. I believe politics have gotten in the way of education. More focus is put on politics rather than focusing on the needs of children and working with parents. Testing is part of the politics. Research shows that poor students do not perform as well as wealthy students. Thus schools that have a large number of poor families consistently score lower on standardized tests.

The A-Plus Plan in Florida is an example of politics in education and the lack of fairness in education. At an early age, children are put under stressful situations and have demands put on them with testing. Schools are graded based on their scores on the Florida Comprehensive Assessment Test (FCAT). In addition to the FCAT test, students must take a nationally normed or standardized test. An "A" school receives $100,000 from the state. Unfortunately, the schools which did not get an

"A" grade are usually the schools with low-income students. Low-income students are doing the best they can, but do not get anything. Schools' successes are measured by test scores rather than what they are actually doing and achieving.

The schools that are rated "D" and "F" receive less funding. The schools that are rated "A" are predominantly nonminority and in wealthy neighborhoods. Hence, the rich keep getting richer and the poor get poorer.

Let me put it this way. The waves look beautiful while surfing, because you are above the water, but the waves do not drown you. The undercurrents are what drown a person. The undercurrents in education are the changes that occur for reasons that are not disclosed fully. The undercurrents are the politics and the professional racism.

What are your concerns and observations on the education of African American students?

When making a case for education, education spending, and the plight of the African American children, I frequently point to connections between education and success in life, and between lack of education and failure. I would prefer to pay to help a child learn how to read than house an illiterate felon at three or four times the cost!

In 1954, Thurgood Marshall of the NAACP argued the famous landmark case of *Brown v. Board of Education.* In this case, the Supreme Court ruled that segregation of students by race is unconstitutional and that education is a right that must be available to all Americans on equal terms. Martin Luther King, Jr., and others led the nationwide civil rights movement into the 1960s. Nevertheless, it was not until 1964 when President Lyndon B. Johnson signed the Civil Rights Bill that it was affirmed that integration was to be fully implemented.

The economic, political, social, and educational conditions of African Americans have improved over the years. Although the physical separation of African American students is not legally sanctioned today as it was before *Brown v. Board of Education,* some people argue that public schools are becoming resegregated by economic and demographic factors, particularly in the cities.

Today, many African Americans remain at the lower end of the economic scale, have more health problems, have shorter life expectancy, and are statistically more prone to youth unemployment, teenage pregnancy, drug use, and violence.

A basic link exists between poverty and learning. Low-income communities mean underfunded school districts and poorer schools on virtually every index of quality. High-poverty schools exhibit diminished capacities to create educational opportunities for students. Current trends indicate students in high-poverty schools have test scores markedly lower than their counterparts in more affluent schools.

As a principal, I see my role as being fair to all regardless of ethnicity. However, as an African American, I have to look at and focus on black children because they are in my blood. I do not allow myself to overlook our children. I see black children and want them to do better than I have done, and better than they are doing.

My first concern for black students is to build their confidence levels. I have been in integrated situations where someone had to help me, mentor me. Because someone helped me then I need to help someone else. As an African American, if I do not make a significant difference in the lives and education of African American children, then I have failed. I tell African American children that if I had listened to certain people years ago, I do not think I would be a principal today.

I make every effort to make sure our students are given fair treatment in education. I make sure that our students can say that they are appreciated and important. When black students tell me that they feel that a teacher does not like them, I tell them, "You are not here to be liked. You are here for respect. The teacher does not have to like you. They have to respect you and see that you get an education." I emphasize this to all African Americans students, especially to the males.

Not all African American children are going to be professional athletes. I feel that we have to channel them. If athletics gets them started down the right path, fine. But athletics, academics, and attitude have to go hand in hand.

Once they believe in themselves, then you have to help them visualize. They have to visualize what they can be, and we have to help them do this when they are young. I never expected to be in an elementary school. I have come to recognize and appreciate the importance of these early years in the academic, social, and psychological development of African American children.

I try to get African American students to understand the struggle that blacks have gone through, so they understand the current struggles. Black students today need to be taught the history. However, they do not want to hear it. We used to call it the "olden days" when our parents talked to us. Black children today need to hear about the "olden days." They need to know that there are great African Americans who are gifted. They need to understand and appreciate the fact that these people were not given the opportunities that black students have today. Yet, in spite of the obstacles, they excelled. They need to know that there are everyday African Americans in their communities who can tell them of our history and help them.

Too many people tell or act as though African American students cannot learn, cannot achieve, and cannot succeed. We have to counter those statements and actions. We have to let African American children know that they can learn and are expected to learn. Like all ethnic groups, some learn at a slower pace, some learn through hands-on experiences, and some learn visually.

As an African American principal, it is incumbent upon me to find out why a child is not learning. If there is a discipline problem, then I meet with the parents and the teachers. First we talk about the discipline problems and then discuss the child's academic progress. I believe that there is something in the classroom that is making a child misbehave and not achieve.

Generally, African Americans are left out of the textbooks. Therefore, we are left out of the teaching. All aspects of American and Florida history need to be understood. I think the real history is omitted to make history palatable. History has become a myth.

There are more African American students in Special Education because they are not being taught. Let me give you an analogy. Two children run 100 meters and they both run it in 10.1 seconds, everything being equal, the one who comes out of the block first will probably win. I take that same example and apply it to education. African American students are not getting out of the block because they are put in programs like Special Education. They are scratched before they even get in the race. Some African American students are not even allowed to get in the block.

Many African American children are labeled when they first walk into classrooms. Because a child is behaving inappropriately does not mean he or she cannot learn. When a teacher at Northboro wants to test a child for Special Education, before the child is tested teachers have to meet with the parents and demonstrate to me that they have made every attempt to work with the child in the classroom.

Gifted classes in public education seem to be for the children of the affluent. When African Americans are in a gifted program, some teachers do not think they should be there and turn them off. Before desegregation, we had gifted students. I have to ask myself if after desegregation, did God just take everything away from us and we could no longer be creative?

Frankly, I think everyone is gifted in some way. American education needs to get away from labeling children—Gifted, Special Education. Children tend to become what they are labeled. All children are gifted at something. Educators should be concerned with developing the potential of all children.

African American children come to school caring and wanting to learn. They want to explore. They want to achieve. The major key for African American children having a successful school experience is going to be the teachers. Teachers make the difference in how children will respond to school from the minute they first walk in the classroom. Teachers' acceptance of African American students makes the difference in the learning opportunities they will have. If they are provided with opportunities to learn then they will soar. When they start soaring the teacher has to keep providing opportunities so they can soar higher.

As an African American principal, what do you consider to be your personal contribution to African American students' school experiences?

At Northboro, we have some African American children who have not been in a formal learning setting until they enter kindergarten. The idea of school is new to them. They are given time to explore. They observe and become familiar with their surroundings. They want to know how many African Americans are there. They want to see someone of their ethnic group when they walk in. They believe that they will be treated fairly if there are people like them at the school. I work at providing an environment that is positive and caring, and that the setting is attractive. The environment has to be one where everyone in the class will work together as a team.

As a Montessori school, we have a lot of equipment. When the children first walk in a classroom and see all the equipment they think school is about playing games. However, they come to understand that those materials will be learning opportunities. The way in which the opportunities are provided goes back to the teachers.

When I came to Northboro nine years ago, the school population was between 96 and 98 percent African American. I needed to make some changes to get students prepared. I set high expectations for the teachers and the students. As a principal, I have to be an advocate for the children and the parents at the school.

Northboro is now a Montessori school and we have done some things differently. I originated the idea of implementing the Montessori program and the Reading Recovery Program. I made these changes because minority students need certain types of opportunities to achieve.

Through the programmatic changes, I have been able to turn children around and our discipline problems are down. Yes, we still have discipline problems. Yes, I do suspend students. However, I visit homes frequently in an effort to minimize discipline problems and reduce suspensions.

When I walk in a home, I want everyone to know who I am, and I am going to help. I let parents and students know that I am going to do what it takes to make sure the students learn. To fulfill this promise, I need teachers who are supportive of what I am trying to achieve. When I am hiring, I look for that first. I told someone the other day, if Michael Jordan decided to play basketball again would you have him on the bench. She said, "No." Therefore, when you find good educators or teachers they should not sit on the bench. They should be in the forefront. My job is to identify teachers who care about children, can teach all children, and are committed to them receiving an outstanding education.

Periodically, I go into classrooms to observe. Each day I stick my head in the classrooms. I want the teachers and students to know that I am concerned about them. People know if you care about them. They know if you are genuine.

We need to get the phonies out of education. The phonies are those who pretend to care about children and use children to become more powerful and wealthy. The phonies are those that allow students who cannot read to continue moving from first to second grade with no interventions.

Janice B. Henry

Janice Henry was born, grew up, and was educated in Fayetteville, North Carolina. She is an elementary school teacher. She received her baccalaureate and master's degrees in elementary education. Both degrees are from Fayetteville State University. Fayetteville State is a public historically black university.

Henry has twenty-eight years of teaching experience. She has taught in Florida, North Carolina, and Oklahoma, and has state teaching certificates in each state. She has two Florida Teacher Certificates, one for early childhood education and the other for kindergarten through sixth grade. She has taught kindergarten through third grades. Most of her teaching is in second grade. She is a second-grade teacher at Del Prado Elementary School in Palm Beach County School District.

In addition to participating in continued professional development courses and workshops, Henry has served on numerous county and state education committees in Florida. Her membership on Palm Beach County committees includes Instructional Action Council, Elementary Language Arts Curriculum Development Team, and District Instructional Reading Materials Committee. Her membership on State of Florida committees includes Science Framework for Pre-service Teachers, National Science Foundation Statewide Systematic Initiative in Science, and National Writing Project.

Janice Henry recently spoke with the author about American and African American public schooling. That conversation follows.

The doctrines of equality, equity, and quality are always attributed to American education. What do those doctrines mean to you?

It would mean that all children are taught equally and they receive an equal education. However, I have found through the years that this is not necessarily the case. For example, in the school in which I presently teach, 72 percent are white and 55 percent of the school population are classified as gifted. We have very few minority children in those classes. For the ones in the gifted class, the same matrix is not used to determine their eligibility. In fact, they drop the matrix. I do not think that is equal. The matrix is the rating scale that is used for tests. This scale might include IQ, academic skills, or social skills.

I think black children are capable if they are taught in a manner in which they can express themselves. I find that in the schools in which I have taught in Florida, that increasingly African American children are not getting the education that they should. They are being placed in Exceptional Student Education (ESE) classes other than gifted education. ESE, which includes gifted, also includes Specific Learning Disabilities (SLD), behavioral problems, and all of the other exceptionalities that occur. If they are not placed in ESE classes then they are classified as slow learners. They are being retained at a greater rate than the white children in the schools.

How has American education changed during your twenty-eight years of being a teacher?

Having taught twenty-eight years, I have seen it come full circle. When I first began teaching, I started teaching in Broward County in Florida. I was in a school of migrant children, primarily. I had twenty-eight third-graders. They were eager to learn. I did grouping in reading and math. I have seen it go from ability grouping to teaching whole language and back to ability grouping. A cycle keeps repeating itself. The concepts are the same, but the names change. When I examine it closely, it is something that I have done previously. We are back to about where we were when I started teaching twenty-eight years ago. In early childhood education, we have come full circle. We have been through the Piaget period and the Montessori period, and now we are back to phonics as the best way for children to learn to read. I do not see any drastic changes. I see a cyclical pattern.

How has the teaching profession changed?

Now that has changed. Teachers do not get the respect that is due from the public, parents, and children. We are expected to wear many different hats in the classroom. Not only are we educators, we are psy-

chologists, social workers, and doctors. We are expected to handle a multitude of problems. The problems were possibly there in previous years,
but it was not as evident as it is today. We have an increasing number of
children who come to school from problematic home environments.
Teachers have to try to manage the effects of these problems in the classroom. At times, very little instruction is done because we are dealing with
the home problems that manifest themselves in the classroom.

A classic example. We have more single-parent children in the
classroom. We have more children who have social problems that teachers have to deal with in the classroom. These problems can interfere
with the learning of the other children in the classroom.

The social problems I am talking about are children who do not
want to associate with other children because they may be from another
country. In the school that I am in, the children from Haiti, specifically,
are not accepted by the African American children, nor are they accepted
readily by the Caucasian children. We also have children who are abused.
Teachers have to deal with parents and the evidence of the abuse. Other
children who know about the abuse have a tendency to tease the children in the abusive situation. For example, last year I taught a child
whose father was abusing the wife. The father's name was in the newspaper. The child was suffering because he and his classmates knew that
the father's name was in the newspaper. His classmates teased him. Although teachers try to run interference, teachers cannot always get a
handle on every situation until it has gotten to be a big problem.

Have students changed in the past twenty-eight years?

They have changed. Children are still receptive, but they have so
many outside influences going on in their lives that they bring it into the
classroom. I think they have lost a certain amount of respect for
adults—all adults. They see so many adults who are acting like children.
The children, in turn, emulate the behavior that they see around them.

Some experts say that there are no children who suffer from drug
fetal syndrome. I believe that we do have children in our classrooms that
evidence this syndrome. For example, children who cannot sit still for
very long. I know that young children are not supposed to sit and be at-
tentive for a long period, but these children seem to be in constant motion. They are constantly fiddling at their desks. Their attention spans
are extremely short. Moreover, it is not just one child. In an average
classroom of twenty-five children, a teacher can have five or six children
who show the symptoms of short attention spans, and the inability to sit
still. They are yelling out, and generally have no self-control. This type of
behavior was not there before in such a large number. I can only attribute it to some type of outside influence. You can talk to teachers in the

average classroom and they are able to name immediately two or three children who cannot sit still, cannot follow written directions and very few oral directions, and have extremely short attention spans. Therefore, I would say you have to attribute it to something in our society that has not been there before.

We are supposed to have a six-hour day for instruction. When you break the day down into actually how many minutes are spent teaching, it is not six hours.

Let us talk about the schooling of African American children, specifically. I want to start with a question about your identity. Do you consider yourself an African American who is a teacher or a teacher who is African American?

I am an African American who is a teacher. That means that my heritage is very important to me. I carry it as a symbol and I would hope that the African American children that I have in my classroom see me as role model to them. Someone they might want to emulate. In addition, I have the reputation as an excellent teacher. There are Caucasian parents and children who respect me for the teacher I am. For example, a Caucasian girl drew a picture of the two of us. She colored both of our faces brown. I think she did it subconsciously. Although I am African American, I can be a role model for white children also.

How does the school curriculum reflect the culture of African Americans?

I think that the curriculum deals superficially with the culture of African Americans. We still have our one month a year, February, in which emphasis is placed on our culture, past and present. The curriculum is such that it does not go much beyond that, and we should be doing it all through the year. African Americans have contributed to many aspects of society. These facts should be built into the curriculum. I would say it should be embedded in the curriculum. It should be a natural part of the curriculum instead of being a superficial addition, which is what it is now.

At one time, black parents emphasized knowing about the African American experience and contributions. Today, even a lot of African American parents are not stressing the deeds of our ancestors. Therefore, our children come to school not aware of their history. It is not important to black children and I think it should be very important to them.

There are so few African American teachers. Many of us in the classroom are thinking about getting out. I wonder what is going to happen to African American children in the future and our culture being taught. A few Caucasian teachers try, but they do not have a real understanding of our culture. They do it based on what they have read in a book.

What are the instructional needs of African American students? Are they different from the instructional needs of other children? Are those needs met?

In some instances, African American children's instructional needs are different from other children. We have some African American children who come to school who are totally unprepared. Few of them are read to at home. They do not have the basic concepts with which many children come to school. These concepts include reading readiness, penmanship, and listening skills. I am basing this only from my experiences as a teacher. Some African American children have parents who are very involved in their development before entering school. There are African American students who have had a wealth of experiences, which prepares them to go to school. But the gulf is widening between African American children who come prepared and those who do not come prepared. I attribute this mostly to socioeconomic backgrounds. If parents have not had certain experiences, they cannot provide them for their children. Many African American parents are willing, but they do not have the experiences and money. There are African American children who have never been outside of the city in which they live except when they are bused to school. They have no idea of the world outside of their neighborhoods except for what they see on television.

Generally, the instructional needs for some African American children are different. This goes back to socioeconomic background. If you have children coming to you who have not been read to, who have not had a lot of opportunity for oral expression, then teachers have to provide those experiences for them. The earlier the teachers start, the more progress these children will make. African American children need to be read to. They need to be talked to and given the chance to express themselves. They need to hear the King's English. But if they do not hear it, how can they repeat what they have not heard? Definitely, our children have some needs that are not being met and the instructional approaches should be a little different.

Black children are visual learners, for the most part. When they are being taught there needs to be a multitude of manipulative and visual experiences for them. They seem to grasp the concepts faster if it is done visually.

Our children do not do as well on tests because a lot of it has to do with a certain type of logic or processing. Can we teach African Americans to think logically for these situations? I think that they can be taught some skills, and some strategies. They can be taught test-taking skills. If they are given the opportunity to have test-taking skills taught to them, they could probably do equally as well as other children.

How do testing, test taking, and assessment programs affect or influence the education of African American children?

First, too much emphasis is being put on testing, generally. This is across the board, especially when you are talking about young children. It puts pressure on all children, undue pressure.

I think testing has a negative influence for African American students. Test results are not interpreted the same way for African American students as they are for Caucasian children. Let me talk specifically about aptitude tests. I find that the person who interprets the matrix for the aptitude tests has a lot to do with how children are classified. Frequently the test scores are interpreted by people who do not know exactly what they are looking for or what they should be looking for when they interpret African American students' scores. Another interpreter might classify children differently.

For example, an African American child might be a slow learner. That means that the teacher will have to keep repeating things for this child. That does not mean the child has a learning disability and needs ESE services. Learning disabilities include dyslexia, visual perception problems, or processing problems. Very few African American children, from my observations, have learning disabilities.

In addition, children respond differently to people who are testing them. I think that there should be a certain rapport between children and the test administrators. Test administrators might be someone the children have seen once or twice on campus, but they do not really know these people. Children respond differently with someone they know and with whom they have had positive experiences. I have difficulty with the testing that is being done with our children. Black children are not given the benefit of the doubt or a chance in relation to testing and the interpretation of test scores.

Some of the items on the test are not familiar to black children. This has to do with the experiences they bring to school. If the child is not familiar with what is in the item, why would you ask them the question?

Teacher expectations, parental expectations, and society's expectations play an important part in how well African American children do on early achievement tests. Those are considered more important than what is actually taught.

There is a mutually reciprocal relation between teacher expectations and students' achievement. If African American children feel that there are high expectations of them, then they will try to meet those expectations. They will do anything to please their teachers if they feel the teachers care about them. If the children feel or sense that the teachers do not care about them, then their attitudes become, "Why try?" I am seeing more and more of the "why try" attitude. Too many of our children feel that their teachers do not care about them and do not expect them to do as well as other children.

If you walk into the average classroom today, look at the placement of African American children in those classrooms. Are they at the front of the classroom? Or are the majority of them at the back of the classroom? How many times are they being called on to answer questions? Where are they placed in a line?

All teachers need to take a step back and look at these things. I do not think that all teachers consciously do it. There is a possibility that it is done unconsciously. Nevertheless, it is happening to our children— African American children.

Black children are overlooked not only because of the behaviors of the teacher, but also because our children do not necessarily project themselves in ways that say, "Look at me," "Pay attention to me." Black children tend to have one of two responses to what happens to them in classrooms. Either they are very silent in the classroom because I think they have been ignored so much. Alternatively, they exhibit negative behavior that is not considered acceptable in the classroom, rather than behave in ways that are considered acceptable.

There is a great deal of research that concludes African American children are disproportionately suspended and expelled. What is your experience?

This research is accurate. In the school populations in which I have taught, and the one in which I am teaching, African American students are sent to principals' offices more frequently than other children are. They are accused more frequently of being disruptive. At the elementary level, we have very few children who are expelled. If anything, they are placed in in-school suspension. In-school suspension is the removal of a child from the classroom to some place in the school for a determined period of time. Nevertheless, African American students are placed in in-school suspension more than Caucasian students. This means that they are being removed from other students and regular instructional settings more.

I do not think that African American students are more disruptive than Caucasian students are. I think that they are not understood. Again, children come to school with a lot of baggage. For example, in the school in which I teach, a lot of the African American children are bused to school. Either before they get on the bus or while on the bus something unsettling might happen to them that morning. Maybe the other children were picking on them or they had a fight with a sibling. Something sets them off and in turn, they bring it into the school. It snowballs from there. They are frustrated about what happened to them before they even get to school.

Most of the African American students at my school begin their day being picked up at 7:00 in the morning and get home about 2:30 or 3:00 in the afternoon. Each day they are on the bus a total of thirty to forty minutes on Interstate 95. This is a long day for young children. African American children leave their parents and neighborhood, and are bused to another city.

Primarily, African American children are bused. When the concept of neighborhood schools was dismantled, our children lost a great deal. They lost the closeness that they had of the community being there to surround them and give them the pat on the shoulder or the swat on the rear, if they needed it. I think that busing has a lot to do with their perceived disruptive behavior.

What do you think it is like to be a six-, seven-, eight-, or nine-year-old African American child in a public school today?

I think that it is hard on them. If they are not in a neighborhood school or are not in a school that is predominantly black, they may be one of three or four African American children in a classroom, if they are lucky. They are surrounded by children who are not like them, and it is likely that the teacher is not African American. There are very few people in their schools with whom they can identify. I would think that being in school is scary.

Young children have fears of which they are not aware. They cannot always express their fears. Instead, they display their fears in other ways, such as stomachaches, acting up, or telling teachers that they want to go home.

African American children are moved completely away from familiar surroundings and put in an environment that is foreign to them. For a five-year-old African American child, I think being in school would be very scary and induce a lot of fear. By the time our children are older—eight or nine years old—they have probably developed defense mechanisms. They project an image of being tough, which is interpreted by some teachers as being hostile. However, inside they are still children and they have fears. Yet they cannot afford to let anyone know about them. Without their defense mechanisms, they are left defenseless.

How did school desegregation affect the education of African American students?

I began teaching just as schools were being desegregated. I never taught in a school that was officially classified as segregated. I would say that desegregation has impeded the progress of African American children.

I went to an all-black school. All of the children were expected to learn. When they graduated, the majority were able to read. We did not have the problems that black children have today. We were taught by African American teachers in our community. They worked twice as hard with less to make sure that we achieved. I think that the teachers were dedicated to making sure that black children learned and were educated. Black teachers had a sense of caring about the children they taught and pride about what black children accomplished. We were the generation that would follow them. School desegregation took that away.

At one time, the professional fields open to African Americans were limited. Generally the choices were in education, medicine, or law. A lot of us chose education. Today, we have more career options, and fewer African American college students are selecting education. There will not be the pool of minority teachers that are needed.

Studies show that very soon the schools will be made up mostly of minority children, and they will not have the minority teachers to teach them. There are a small percentage of white teachers who care about the education of African American children. There are a few, who are very caring, who really want to do what is best for our children. I think, in spite of their caring, these white teachers will have problems because they have not experienced what we have to live through and what is needed for African Americans to be fully functioning, productive, and accomplished people in America. Caucasian teachers do not have a true understanding of what it is to be an African American in America. It takes more than just caring about African American children. You can care and still not be able to teach the children the processes and concepts that they need.

Can this understanding be taught to a Caucasian teacher? I do not know. I know that attempts have to be made for Caucasian teachers to learn. There are an increasing number of courses on how to teach African American children. I am still wondering if the courses are effective. I would think that some things could be taught, but some things have to be a part of the teachers. With all the courses on how to teach African American children, we still have children who have a sense of alienation in school, and we still have an increasingly large number of African American students who are not making the grade. It seems to be becoming more evident everyday.

What do you see as some of the challenges still facing African American children in school?

How can they hold on to their heritage, and still be successful and accepted. Be accepted as an American and an African American who is capable of learning, producing, and being productive people in our society. Children will do as much or as little as is expected of them. If teachers do not expect them to do much, they are not going to do it. If teachers expect, and if needed demand, they produce, they will flourish.

What needs to occur for African American children to obtain schooling that is based on the doctrines of equality, equity, and quality?

What can I say? Maybe a flood. It has been talked about since the end of slavery and it still has not occurred. I do not know if it is possible for it to happen.

When we talk about the school system it is as though it is some distant, inanimate object. People are the system. I do not think that the day will ever come when the three doctrines are accomplished. I say this because of people and the mindsets that most Caucasians have of African Americans. Like I said, "a flood." Just wipe the whole thing out and start all over again. Maybe that time we can get it right.

Superficially, we might have accomplished equality in schooling. Black students get new books. We do not have to use the books that the white children used previously. Supposedly, resources are distributed equally. However, I know of cases right now in predominantly black schools or schools with a large minority population that do not have certain things that are in schools that are predominantly Caucasian. Although the school board says every school has the same resources.

Parent Teacher Associations (PTAs) are an example of unequal distribution of educational resources. PTAs in the more affluent schools have a large percentage of parents who are able to volunteer their time and give their money to the PTAs. However, in schools that are not in the affluent areas there is not the same level of parental involvement or availability of additional funds. Most African American parents do not have the money to give to the school to buy the extras that may be needed. They are not able to volunteer at school during the day because they are working.

In addition, there is the situation of the lack of equal access to knowledge, generally. For example, all of the schools in the district where I teach have computer laboratories. That is at school. Most African American students do not have access to computers at home. Whereas children in the more affluent areas have their own personal computers in their homes and in their bedrooms. Therefore, they are able to leave the computer laboratory at school, go to their computers at home and do research. Many African American children do not even have access to public libraries because they have no way of getting to the libraries and the libraries are not in their neighborhoods. Their parents cannot take them to the library because they are working or do not have a way to get them there. Yet, the child has research to do.

The busing factor makes it virtually impossible for African American children to participate in after-school programs. Most African American children are bused into neighborhoods where their parents do not have an automobile to get to the schools, and public transportation does not connect the home and school communities. Bused black children tend not to be able to take part in after-school activities. If they stay for after-school activities they will not have a way to get home. African American children not being able to participate in after-school activities isolates them more. Our children feel like they are not part of the school they attend.

Economics limits many black parents from being involved in their children's schools, as they may want to be. It also limits many African American children from developing a sense of belonging in the school. African American parents are as interested in their children learning and doing well as other parents are. In African American families usually both parents are working and cannot get off from work to volunteer. Most African Americans are not "middle class." They do not have jobs that have paid personal leave. If they take a day off from work, even to volunteer in schools, they lose a day of pay. For most African Americans it takes two incomes to support the family.

Any final comments?

Black children can be taught and they can learn. Black children are taken out of their communities and put into environments in which they are neither comfortable nor helped to be comfortable.

Do we care more for animals than we do black children? When the pandas were brought from China, they go through an entry period for adjustment. Every effort is made to make sure that their environments or their habitats are similar to what they had in China. They were brought to the United States in pairs. Therefore, the pandas have companionship and a sense of not being alone. That is why they are able to thrive and live as long as they do.

We are taking African American children out of their neighborhood, out of their environment, and putting them into unfamiliar environments. With all of this disruption in their lives, they are expected to respond and reciprocate. Many African American children are tossed into this nonsupportive school environment completely alone. This type of situation has to be scary for African American children.

As an African American teacher, sometimes it is arduous. When the school in which I am currently teaching first opened, I was the only African American teacher on the faculty. I felt I had to do more than the other teachers were doing because I was on display. I was the example for the race. It was constantly in my mind that if I failed then I failed my race. They were constantly looking at me, not necessarily for me to fail, but to see what I could do. Therefore, I exceeded their expectations of me. I had to prove myself, constantly, although I know I am an excellent teacher. I put in long hours after school. I was usually one of the last teachers to leave each day.

After twenty-eight years of teaching, I still feel I have to do more than the Caucasian teachers do. Presently, there are four black teachers where I teach and we all have the same feeling of needing to exceed the expectations. In addition, we are the last ones to leave each day.

SCHOOLING OPTIONS FOR AFRICAN AMERICAN STUDENTS

In response to the pessimistic reality for a large number of African American students in public schooling settings, some African American parents have chosen to provide their children with a different type of schooling experience. These parents take control of the education of their children and enroll them in schools that are compatible with their own personal and cultural values, goals, and expectations of education. Their responses can be seen as a proactive solution for nurturing, developing, and fostering the educational achievement and attainment of their children. These schools represent the type of institutional autonomy Carter G. Woodson spoke of in *The Mis-Education of the Negro* (1933). Most of the schooling options are private and a few are public. Whether private or public, all of these schooling options are regarded by African American parents as viable means to the ends of educational equality, equity, and quality.

As illustrated in Chapter 2, precollege schools specifically established by African Americans for African Americans are not a new phenomenon in the history of African American and American education. The resurgence of independent black schools began in the early 1970s. In 1990, the Institute for Independent Education reported that there were 284 African American independent schools that served approximately 53,000 African American students, or 8 percent of all African American school age students (Kifano 1996).

All independent, or private, black schools are not African-centered schools. African-centered schools have a specified focus. The Council of Independent Black Institutions (CIBI) defines "Afrikan-centered education as the means by which Afrikan culture—including the knowledge, attitudes, values, and skills needed to maintain and perpetuate it through the nation building process—is developed and advanced through practice" (CIBI website).

Independent black schools vary in their philosophies, goals, approaches, and practices. However, the reason they exist is singular. These schools are considered safe havens where African American children can flourish and thrive intellectually, emotionally, psychologically, and socially.

In large part, private schools' operating budgets are dependent on tuition. Over the past thirty years, some of these schools have had to close because of the lack of sufficient operating funds.

These schooling options establish educational standards that stress academic excellence. Generally, their curricula incorporate aspects of state education standards and objectives. What makes these schools unique is their focus on the sustainable development of African Americans through culturally relevant curricula and teaching styles. In these schools, the early development of African American children's understanding of the importance of and necessity for their social responsibility and service are integral parts of the academic curricula.

SCHOOLING OPTIONS RESOURCE INTERVIEWS

The author had an opportunity to talk with the headmaster of an independent black school, International Preparatory Institute (IPI). IPI is one of the oldest private African American schools still in operation in the nation.

Vivien Davenport

Vivien Davenport was born in Washington, Georgia, in Wilkes County. In 1945, she moved to Atlanta to attend Booker T. Washington High School. She has five degrees. Her bachelor's degree in elementary education is from Morris Brown College, a historically black institution in Atlanta. She has two master's degrees, one in elementary education and the other in library science. Her education specialist degree is in school administration. She received her Ph.D. degree in counseling from Atlanta University, which is historically black.

For eighteen years, she was employed by Atlanta public schools, primarily as an elementary school teacher and elementary school librarian. She also served as a high school librarian. In addition, she was an instructor in the adult education evening program. Upon receiving her doctoral degree, she was appointed vice president for student affairs at Morris Brown College. She has traveled extensively, served on several boards and has been honored with two presidential appointments.

She is the founder and headmaster of IPI, a private black school located in southwest Atlanta. This quadrant of the city is predominately black. While there is a high concentration of black professionals, people from a cross section of socioeconomic levels reside in the quadrant. IPI was founded in 1978 as the International Center for Child Development. This school was for children two to five years old. In 1980, IPI was incorporated and expanded to include kindergarten through third grade. In 1989, grades four and five were included. In its twenty-two years, 440 black children have graduated.

IPI is fully accredited by the Georgia Accrediting Commission. In addition, it is a member of the Georgia Association of Independent Schools as well as the Atlanta Area Association of Independent Schools.

People learn about IPI in a variety of ways. Although it is advertised in such magazines as *Atlanta Parent,* many people hear about it through word of mouth and parent recommendations. Many of the children at IPI are siblings and cousins of IPI graduates.

A typical day at IPI begins with Davenport greeting each child personally as he or she enters the school, and the entire school singing "Lift Every Voice and Sing," the black national anthem. Family and community presence is the rule rather than the exception at IPI.

Vivien Davenport recently spoke with the author about the history, purpose, philosophy, mission, curriculum, instructional and assessment methods, and instructional staff of IPI. The following is that conversation.

What is the history of the International Preparatory Institute?

Let me begin by saying that I was consulting in school districts when I opened the school. It first opened as a child care facility. That, however, is not what I had in mind. Yet that was the extent of it at that point. It was then the International Center for Child Development. I operated it under that name for about a year or a year and a half. Although I started with the child care center somewhat as an initial phase—a beginning—I had written a program for a school.

Upon completing a consulting job in South Carolina and driving back to Atlanta, I started to thinking, "That is not the name. I have not fulfilled my desires for this place and the name is not right. What name—what name Lord, can I name the school that will fit in with what I am trying to do?" It came to me as plain as day, International Preparatory Institute.

I knew that a child care facility was not enough for my people in this area. I wanted to give blacks an option for their children in southwest Atlanta. When I returned to Atlanta, I changed the name of this facility and began to implement the program that I desired.

I began with two-, three- and four-year-olds and a kindergarten in this one facility. One day, my uncle, Luther Frazier, asked me if I needed more space and if I knew that the house next door was available. The house was in foreclosure. I did not know that and thought it was a good idea to purchase it. I purchased that building and renovated it. Then I was able to add first, second, and third grades. The house had a double-car garage behind it that was not complete. I completed the garage. There were now three classrooms for first, second, and third grades. Nevertheless, IPI would not be complete until it had fourth and fifth grades, a media center, and a resource area. The house next door was purchased and renovated and an extension to the double-car garage was done. This made it possible to add the grades and the re-source area as well as the media center.

Why did you think you needed to add fourth and fifth grades?

I felt that if the children could do well through the fifth grade, they could move forward with successes in their school experiences. If they could grab hold to all of the skills through those grades, they could go to any middle schools and high schools, and be successful. But, they needed a good foundation at the elementary level.

When I was an administrator at Morris Brown, some students re-ceived federal money for skills programs for developmental reading and math. They should have known how to do it before they left elementary school. This suggested to me that I needed to do something. I needed to go back to my roots.

My roots were the elementary school level. My grandmother and mother were elementary school teachers. I was an elementary school teacher, but somehow, I moved away from that realm. Therefore, I came back to where I felt I needed to be and where my services were most beneficial.

What is the philosophy and mission of IPI?

IPI's philosophy is to provide prekindergarten through fifth-grade school children with the skills and experiences necessary to: (1) respond logically in a diverse world, (2) become innovative and creative, (3) develop critical thinking skills, (4) possess positive behavior and at-titudes about future goals, (5) understand and accept change, and (6) rise to high expectations. The philosophy is accomplished through the "I Can" attitude. This encourages students to be productive, committed, and focused. In this regard, IPI seeks to provide a high-quality education with an international perspective based on the five Rs: Reading, Writing, Arithmetic, Respect, and Responsibility.

IPI's mission is threefold: (1) to strengthen the basic essentials of education in the early and elementary school years, (2) to educate students two to twelve years of age in basic educational requirements, thereby providing the skills and tools essential to achieving the quality of education requisite to assure very high standards, (3) to fulfill its commitment to the task of developing fully functioning children in a global society.

What are the educational scope and focus of IPI?

I think black children need to be well rounded. They will have to deal with all kinds of people. You never know where you are going to end up in this world. IPI is a traditional, independent school that has a lot of flavor. We are training our children to be totally well rounded in many, many areas whereby they will be able to move throughout the world if they have to. Not immediately after they leave IPI, of course. IPI is the beginning. IPI's curriculum is somewhat competency based and multicultural. The children are expected to meet certain competencies. In addition, the children have to know about various cultures and understand them.

There are two schools at IPI: Early and elementary. We can house about 130 children in both schools. The Early school we characterize as the beginning period of the initial school program. At first it was thought of as a day care, a child care center. Then I started thinking, it is not a day care. It is an Early school. It is the first phase of a child's schooling. It is not a play school. It is part of our academic program. There are skills and essential, fundamental concepts children at this age need to acquire.

We use Core Knowledge for the children in the Early school. In the elementary school, we use Quality Core curriculum from the State of Georgia. However, we reinforce and enhance the state curriculum by using Core Knowledge as a supplement, to give it extra flavor.

IPI's children in the Early school learn the fundamental enriching skills that they need to move successfully to the elementary school. The Early school is our feeder school for the elementary school, for the most part.

At IPI there are twelve full-time teachers in addition to itinerant staff. Our itinerant staff includes a Spanish teacher to teach Spanish as a second language, and a Sign Language teacher who teaches the children to sign mainly for the purpose of communicating with those who sign only. Spanish and Sign Language are part of our core curriculum.

As part of the extracurricular activities for the after-school program, we offer piano lessons taught by an itinerant person. This young lady plays the organ music that you hear at the Atlanta Braves games. She also does the music program for IPI. Additionally, we have a professional dancer who teaches dance. Our itinerant staff members are professionals in their fields. We try to provide the best quality for our children that we possibly can.

IPI operates on three cycles. Cycles One and Two are the regular school year. Cycle Three is what we call Summer Shops. The Summer Shops are designed to bring a high quality program of a different nature to children during the summer. The focus of Summer Shops is to interrelate some academic skill reinforcement with enriching camp-oriented experiences.

The children have to be taught to read, to write, and to do arithmetic. Yet that is not enough. They have to know what this economy is about and how to manage their money. We take the children, ages two through fifth grade, to the bank where they open bank accounts. Each month they go to the bank window to make their own deposits.

They have to know how to make sound choices and decisions. They have to know how to communicate with others who are different from them. That is why I added Sign Language and Spanish as a second language. There are people who cannot speak or hear. Our children need to be able to communicate with them and not take it as something unusual. IPI children are learning to speak Spanish because of the increasing number of Spanish-speaking people in Atlanta.

We had an exchange program. I have taken children to Mexico, Ecuador, and Jamaica. We have had exchange students come to IPI to spend three weeks. We have tried to expose our children to experiences that will help them to have a good, full life—a whole life. We do not go out of the country any more because the liability is too great.

Presently, the school participates in the Culture Trek experience. This unique program creates global awareness for IPI children. Designed to allow children to visit other cultures without leaving the campus, the foreign ambassadors perform a variety of culture-related activities, which include dances, songs, games, storytelling, and crafts, on the site.

We have a touring choir. The children sing beautifully. They sang at Tuskegee University in Alabama and Fort McPherson in Georgia. Once a year they sing at Ebenezer Baptist Church. That was Martin Luther King's church.

IPI was started to expose black children to a lot of experiences that I wanted to do with children and could not do when I had somebody pulling my strings and telling me in which direction to go.

What are the credentials, attributes, and composition of your full-time teaching staff?

The teachers in the Early School have to have an associate degree in early childhood, and they have to complete at least twenty hours of professional development each year. Every year they take courses at

Clayton State College, or they attend workshops or seminars that are approved by the Georgia Department of Human Resources.

The elementary teachers must have a bachelor of science degree in elementary education or early childhood. In addition, they have to have a teaching certificate from the state, or work toward obtaining a state teaching certificate. They are required to obtain a minimum of ten hours of professional development each year. Frequently, they go beyond the minimum.

The average years of teaching experience of IPI elementary teachers is ten to twelve years. The teachers are experienced professionals. One or two of the teachers have been at IPI since its inception. The other teachers have been here fourteen or fifteen years. One teacher is completing her first year here.

We are eligible for Title I services. The Atlanta Public Schools provide one Title I teacher and a paraprofessional. The Atlanta Public School System has to provide these two employees based on the number of children at IPI who need reinforcement in reading and math. The need for Title I services is determined by test results on the Iowa Test of Basic Skills. Based on the guidelines of Title I, we qualify for two Title I staff people. The Title I teacher and paraprofessional report here. IPI is their teaching site. They are here every day, five days a week. They take small groups of the students who qualify for Title I services. They have a separate area. They work with four or five students who need some reinforcement in a particular skill in reading or math.

In addition to credentials, IPI teachers must possess other attributes. Many times people have the credentials, but the credentials mean nothing if they do not have some other things. I look for teachers who are cordial, professional, and speak well. Teachers must speak well. Teachers have to dress professionally; they are representatives of IPI. Teachers must be warm and loving to the children. They must be able to solve problems when they arise. They have to have self-control.

What are the teachers to gain for professional development?

The purpose of professional development is to have teachers stay abreast of the trends. I do not go along with all of the new trends. Some things I think are basic. Nevertheless, all of us can learn something. When they attend courses, workshops, and seminars, it is more for enrichment and enhancement than for them to change what they are doing. Professional development gives them ideas about how they can do what they are doing better. I do not believe in making changes when something is working. I just want to add some flavor, to enrich and enhance.

Many times in education when something is working with the

children someone decides to change things, and the new thing does not work as well as what was already being used. I believe in staying with what works, and enrich and enhance that.

What are the admission procedures?

We have what we call "Written Plan for Enrollment." The plan includes a face-to-face interview with the parents or legal guardians of the child, and the child. The interview is conducted before the child is admitted. The purpose of the interview is to discuss policies and procedures, and obtain necessary health, addresses, telephone numbers, and permission information.

How is IPI funded?

Funding is from tuition and fees from parents, primarily. We do not try to get other moneys to operate. We have a fundraiser at the beginning of the school year to buy computers, software, and whatever else we need. The money goes where it needs to go. We have been able to sustain ourselves.

The children wear uniforms.

Yes, they do. It shows belonging, basically. It lets people and the children know that they are members of the IPI family. It eliminates competition, also.

Earlier you said that you started IPI to meet the education needs of the southwest Atlanta area. What did you see as the needs?

The needs I saw were that a number of black youth who graduated from high school were not proficient in reading, writing, and doing arithmetic. I knew that I needed to do something about that.

When I was teaching in the public schools, there were certain things that I knew as a professional teacher that I could do better or that needed to be done, without anybody telling me what or how to do it. However, I could not always do those things. With my own school, I can do it the way I know it should be done and get results. That was the reason why I decided to start this school.

I do not tell teachers at IPI how to do things. I trust their professional judgment. I just want the children to learn. I do not tell teachers, "You should teach reading this way." I do not care how they teach reading. I just want to make sure the children can read and scores are where they should be. It does not matter to me how they teach it.

In the public school system, teachers are told how to teach as well as what to teach. In addition, there were constant changes. One year, teachers are using Curriculum A, and the next year somebody tells them they have to use Curriculum B. Before the teacher can become acclimated to one thing, it is changed to something else. I do not see the need to change the curriculum constantly. I see the need to teach what you have. If you teach what you have, and enrich it, I guarantee you black children are going to have some success.

At one time, we looked at the whole language program. We started using it for a short period. One of my daughters is the reading teacher here. She said, "Mom, let us take another look at this. This is not for us. We need to go back to what we were using—the Houghton Mifflin system. We have always used it and we have always done well with it."

The whole language program had a lot more included in it, but it did not correspond with the skills that were needed for our children to learn to read. In addition, by the time the teachers were trained to use it and to teach it, we would have lost a lot of learning time for the children. So we went back to what we had been using and just added a few things. We have been very successful with that. This is an example of what I mean when I say too many changes. I do not tell teachers what to teach and how to teach. They know what the children need because they know the children.

I remember a public school principal who had been a reading teacher. She was determined to have reading taught in one particular way. But, some children did not benefit from being taught that way. Sometimes you can go through the front door and sometimes you have to go in the back door. However, it has to be left to the teacher to figure out how to get to the children.

How do you assess the children's achievement at IPI? Is the Iowa Test your primary assessment measure?

The Iowa Test of Basic Skills is not our primary assessment measure. Our teachers' tests are our primary assessment measure. The teachers develop their test based on the skills that they teach. They teach, assess, and reteach if necessary.

We use the Iowa Test of Basic Skills when the students first come to IPI to ascertain where they are at that point. Then we use the Iowa Test at a midpoint to determine how much the children have accomplished from the beginning to the midpoint. At the end of the year, we use another level of the same test to determine if they are ready for the next grade.

When the children come back from the summer break, they are administered the same Iowa Test of Basic Skills that they were administered at the end of the school year. The purpose of this testing is to decide how much they have retained over the summer. We give the same test midpoint to determine how much they have accomplished, and then we move it up a level. So teacher-made tests and the Iowa Test of Basic Skills are the only two assessments that we administer.

We compare teacher-made test results with scores from the Iowa

Test of Basic Skills to see the difference in what the children are doing on both tests. We look at these things so we can judge where the child is falling short, where the child is progressing, and to determine how much further we can move the child. For instance, if the child scores high on all of the parts of math except computation, then we look at why this child is not scoring well in that area. It is possible that a child could do well on the teacher-made test and not on the Iowa Test of Basic Skills. We review this to determine what is happening to the child and to see what assistance the child needs. I consider the teachers' tests to have more value than the Iowa Test of Basic Skills.

I give a standardized test to make sure our children are knowledgeable about test-taking skills. Testing is all part of going into the outer world. The children will have standardized tests when they leave here so we test them. Eventually, they get accustomed to taking tests. They become test-wise. If it were not for that, I doubt I would give them a standardized test. They would take teacher-made tests, and that would be sufficient for me.

We also give them preparation activities for taking tests. In the classes, and sometimes in the after-school program, they are given certain exercises, such as filling in the circles on an answer sheet. Frequently, black children have problems with the instructions, or how to approach these tests. Many times it might not be because of their lack of knowledge about the content. It might be the instructions. Generally, directions for standardized tests can be read only once. A child might accidentally bubble in the wrong thing. Therefore, we give them exercises in taking these types of tests.

Do children have homework?

Yes they do, beginning in the Early school. Homework is assigned regularly with a specific academic purpose in mind. Homework accounts for one third of the child's grade. It is necessary that homework is completed as assigned and returned.

Assigned homework for each class must be completed before pupils can proceed to the next learning experience. This is necessary because each learning experience is built upon the former. To complete these experiences, the child needs the help, encouragement, and support of his or her parents. Therefore, each parent must share the responsibility with the school.

How do you link the family and the community into the life of IPI?

First, let me say that parents are always welcomed, and they are constantly here. IPI's parents are a major cornerstone in the foundation of the school and its successful operation. Being committed to a quality education, our parents are expected to work with their children and teachers within the classroom as well as on the varied committees whose focal point is to enhance the effectiveness of the school's total curriculum and the development of the total child. Willingly, our parents develop the kind of positiveness that tends to contribute to the school being a family-oriented and community-directed institution.

We have what we call a parent-pupil support concept. It is not the usual PTA. When I was working in the school system, we had the PTA. At the beginning of the year parent attendance would be high. Maybe it was because we opened a new school and everybody was excited, or their child was in a program. However, eventually it reached the point that the only people who attended the PTA meetings were the principal, teachers, and the parents who did not need to be there.

I decided that I wanted to do something different. We do not just conduct business, pay dues, and go home. We do not have dues. We have a parent group that is chaired by a parent. We have the parents' development activities to make them better parents and to help them be good parents. The parents develop their programs based on parents' suggestions on topics on which they need information. I provide some input, but these are really the parents' programs. We might have speakers to talk with parents about parenting or family financial concerns.

Next month, we are going to have an informal family night. We will sit and chat, maybe around the fireplace. We will eat food they have prepared and have a storyteller. Children, parents, and teachers will be there.

Parents are asked to volunteer in the school. We have a list of committees. Each parent is expected to serve on at least two committees.

One committee is "20 Men," which is composed of the fathers. The mission of "20 Men" is to serve as mentors to the children; expand the awareness of IPI by sponsoring school-, community-, and business-related activities; and assist in the continual improvement of IPI's operation, capability, and capacity. They take the children on field trips. One recent field trip was to Booker T. Washington High School, the oldest black high school in Atlanta, to look at the material in the archives.

As far as the community is concerned, I am chair of a community organization. Therefore, the community is always in IPI. Maybe not always as a part of the school as such, but they are here talking and working on things that are happening in the community to make it a better community. I chair the Neighborhood Planning Unit in this community. Therefore, I am constantly working in the community.

How do you handle discipline?

Good behavior is essential in maintaining a positive learning environment and in developing responsible citizens. Self-control is closely linked to academic success.

We have a disciplinary policy that is given to the parents at the beginning of the year. If the teacher cannot handle the problem in the classroom by talking to the child or taking away something he or she enjoys, then the child is sent to me. Usually, the teacher can handle the situation. If a child comes to me, then the parents are called in.

Sometimes parents cannot get the behavior corrected, and I can get it corrected before the parent. If the parent cannot get some kind of resolution to the problem, the child is sent home for a day or two. Suspension is our last resort, and is rarely used. I have expelled one or two children in the past twenty-two years. Expulsion occurs when a child's behavior is continually extremely disruptive.

Parents send their children here to learn and if teachers constantly have to focus on a disruptive child, they cannot teach the other children. I cannot have that. We have had very few children with whom the teachers are not able to work successfully. If a teacher cannot get a child's attention, a teacher cannot teach the child.

One of the ways we avoid extreme disciplinary actions is through the admissions process. We interview all of the parents and children before the children are admitted. If while I am interviewing a child is disruptive and the parent does not try to handle it, then I know that IPI is not the right place for that child. If a child is disruptive and the parent is putting forth an effort to try to handle it while I am interviewing, then we will give the child a chance here. Most of all, where discipline is concerned, we have to have the support of the parents.

After twenty-two years, you have graduates. What do you know about the success of your graduates?

We always hear that schools like to receive IPI graduates because they do well in school and are well-mannered. We have not systematically kept track of our graduates. The graduates or their parents call or stop by to tell us what they are doing, or we receive graduation invitations. The majority of our graduates do very well.

My granddaughter was one of the first students here. She is working towards her Ph.D. degree, and teaches third grade in the Atlanta public schools. She will probably be the next headmaster at IPI.

We have a young graduate who is attending the Interdenominational Theological Center (ITC). ITC is a historically black institution for advanced theological education. It is in Atlanta. He is a minister of his own church.

We have graduates who are enrolled or graduated from such colleges as Tennessee State University, Georgia Southern University, and Agnes Scott College. Several of our graduates continue their education in private, predominately white schools in the city, such as Westminster and Woodward. They continue to succeed.

Any final comments?

I know that education is global. As I have indicated earlier, we are trying to give black children those things that can get them on their way to participate in a global society. The world is big, not because they will go somewhere else, necessarily. It is big because the world is coming to Atlanta. All types of people are in Atlanta. There is a lot of competition in this city.

Integration never occurred. However, desegregation occurred somewhat. Before desegregation, blacks had their own neighborhoods. We had our own stores, our own barbershops, our own restaurants. We had everything. The economy in the black neighborhood was much better than it is now. Desegregation diluted much of what we once had. I want our children to know all about that. It is going to take more than reading, writing, and arithmetic to help them survive. In order for me to help the children to understand that, I need the parents to know also.

I try to teach the children the concept of trade-offs. I am trying to help the children know—and I tell the parents, too—they cannot spend their last penny and live from day-to-day or paycheck-to-paycheck. Finances—savings and investments—are their backups.

I talk with parents about being good parents. I talk with them, for example, about not teaching their children to lie. Sometimes parents unconsciously teach their children to lie. For example, the teacher tells a parent, "Johnny was not at his best today. He disrupted the class." A parent will say to the child, "Johnny, did you do that? You did not do that. I know that you did not do that. Did somebody make you do that?" The parent is teaching the child to lie. If you teach children to lie, you are going to teach them to steal and so on.

I am 66 years old. I guess I have a lot of my grandmother in me and she was an old-time schoolteacher. I believe in many new things, but then I believe in building on the old. I do not believe that you can do away with the old and just use the new. There are some basic precepts I want to instill in black children. They need to respect themselves, others, and their community. Their parents and teachers are their role models and they will take them forward. I cannot lose those precepts. I do not want our children to lose them.

Blacks have a rich heritage. Children at IPI take black history classes. They go on black history tours. I want them to know every time they pull up to a traffic light that somebody like them invented it. I want them to know that black people have made contributions. We have been responsible for giving something to society. We have done a lot.

Finally, I try to teach our children responsibility. Many days I have to say, "Mommy, please do not bring this second-grader's book bag in.

He or she can take his or her own book bag." Or, "He or she can be responsible for doing some things for him or herself." At a young age, you have to let children do for themselves. If you do not, you are breaking children's desire to do, thereby, giving them the "I do not have to" attitude which breeds irresponsibility.

Derrick L. Moité

Derrick L. Moité is the parent of a five-year-old student at the International Preparatory Institute (IPI). He is a graduate of Morehouse College, a historically black male college in Atlanta, and is employed with Delta Air Lines. Moité shares the reasons why he and his wife selected a private black school for their daughter.

When it was time for your daughter, Courtney, to enter prekindergarten, what were your concerns about her education?

I want to give a little background about my wife's and my early education first. We both attended Catholic schools that were black. As we reflected on our educational background, we decided that private schools offered a foundation that was stronger than what public schools would offer. We felt that it was very important to look into private schools at an early age. We intend to do the same with her younger brother, Kendall. We wanted to find an African American private school for many reasons. Our primary reason was that we think it is very important for young people to know their heritage and to learn it at a young age. This is especially true for African American children.

The difference in what Courtney is getting and what her parents got is that through the school curriculum we did not have a great deal of exposure to our heritage at a young age. We had to wait until much later in our education. African American culture and history only received attention during Black American History Month in school. We wanted to make sure that Courtney received an exposure to her African American heritage and received a strong base for academic learning.

With these two objectives in mind, we did not have to look far. Friends recommended the International Preparatory Institute (IPI) to us. But, more importantly, the headmaster was a student at Morris Brown College where Courtney's great-grandmother, Mrs. Mary S. Jackson, taught. My grandmother and her friends spoke highly of Dr. Davenport. Dr. Davenport is a success, personally and professionally. She introduces the concept of success to IPI children from the day they enroll.

It was important that our child-rearing patterns and beliefs coincided with the philosophy and teaching practices of the school Courtney attended. The size of the school was a consideration. We wanted a school setting where children would get individual attention as well as classroom attention. I recognized this as being very important in the development of the child and the basic skills that are needed. Courtney's mother's and my active participation in her education was important to us. We considered all of this in making our decision to enroll Courtney in IPI.

It is amazing to see how well Courtney has progressed. At only five years and four months, she reads very well. She is reading books that I was reading at seven years old. IPI is setting standards for this young lady. IPI's requirements and expectations are very high. I wonder if they may be too high for a child her age. She has homework consistently every night. She may have two or three lessons on which she has to focus. Although it is one page, I wonder whether it is too much. At the same time, I see that Courtney enjoys the homework. She is being challenged and she accepts the challenges. Challenges I feel that only IPI can provide for her and is providing very well.

We believe that Courtney's reading skills are crucial for her future school success. We believe that phonics is a good way to accomplish this. I noticed that in public schools, phonics is not used frequently, although there is talk about using it again. In my opinion, phonics will help children to enunciate well, spell well, and expand their vocabulary. Courtney is learning the basics in mathematics. The five-year-olds engage in mathematics activities to learn mathematics concepts that I was not exposed to until first grade.

What do you feel Courtney gets from a school like IPI, a black independent school, that she would not get in a public school environment?

She gets individual attention. The teachers care about her achieving. She is taught self-discipline from the first day. The self-discipline transfers from the classroom and her studies to the home. Through self-discipline, she is learning to do the right things, to follow through in assignments and homework, and the discipline needed to learn. We reinforce the self-discipline at home in what we expect of her.

Most importantly, Courtney's thirst for knowledge is being satisfied. Her hunger for learning is being fed, whether or not she knows it. When new concepts are introduced to her, she absorbs them like a sponge.

Learning is open-ended at IPI. There are no barriers to learning, as far as I can see. Teachers constantly challenge Courtney as well as all the students. I appreciate that.

How is parent involvement part of the educational process and development of the children?

Parent involvement at IPI is very important. We are like road signs for the headmaster and teachers to know if the school is going in the right direction. If a parent says, "I like what you are doing for my children," then this is a good sign. If a parent says, "I do not like what is happening with my child," Dr. Davenport listens and finds out what may be needed. Together, the headmaster, teachers, and parents work to make sure that the child is receiving what he or she needs.

The parents at IPI are not underachievers and they do not expect their children to be underachievers. They want their children to have the best education possible. Dr. Davenport expects the parents to be involved in their child's education and the school. Parents know that they can come to the school and be involved in the school. Not only involved, but also have input into the direction the school is taking. There is active participation and engagement on the part of parents. Dr. Davenport tells the parents that she expects them to be involved and how she expects them to be involved when she interviews each family before the child is enrolled.

IPI has a Grandparents' Day. This is another example of how IPI believes in the unity of the family as well as the importance of cultural education. Grandparents or the elders of the family are the family historians. They have a wealth of information about each individual in the family, past and present. They are a means of passing on the family culture and history to the young ones. IPI recognizes this, and believes that it is very important for every family member to honor the elders of their families. IPI takes responsibility beyond its gates. It takes responsibility for the family because IPI is more than just a school. It is another extension of the family.

Describe the admissions process.

When a family expresses an interest in IPI, Dr. Davenport meets with the family. She finds out the background of the family as well as the child. In the family interview, Dr. Davenport wanted to know why we chose IPI. She asked about our educational goals for Courtney and our expectations of the school. She told us what she expects of the parents and the importance of parents' involvement for the cognitive and affective development of Courtney. She emphasized that parent involvement creates a good relationship not just from an educational standpoint, but from a family standpoint also. She stressed that the involvement is very important to all—the child, the parents, and the school.

After she meets with the family, she meets with the child. This meeting is separate from the parents. I do not know what she discussed with Courtney. However, I anticipate that she was finding out what Courtney knows, her temperament, and her behavioral pattern to determine if Courtney is going to be a welcomed addition to IPI or a distraction to IPI.

What are some of the extracurricular and after-school activities and school programs in which Courtney has participated?

Courtney is a member of the mass choir. She enjoys singing and participating in school programs. As a member of the choir, she participated in the Christmas concert and the African American history program.

There are other activities available. For example, the Girl Scouts, and they have started a Boy Scout troop. IPI has a drill team. Courtney has not expressed an interest in these activities. However, we let her know that these activities are available. Next year, in first grade, we will see if she wants to participate in the activities at school more. She has interests outside of school, such as soccer.

Courtney is very outgoing, but she is more of a family child. She likes being with her family. Sometimes she has to be encouraged to join other organizations. I believe that in first grade, Girl Scouts will be one activity that we will introduce to her.

Any final comments?

I would say that when possible, an increasing number of African American parents are enrolling their children in private black schools, because they want more than a school. They want an environment that is an educational extension of the family. African American private schools are small. Some people equate the size with how well the school is doing. If that were the case twenty-two years ago, when IPI started with six to ten people in one school, IPI would never be where is it right now. Dr. Davenport not only sees what the African American family needs in a private school, but she is also looking at what the other top private schools are doing to keep IPI top-notch.

ADDITIONAL SCHOOLING OPTIONS

African American Immersion Schools

African American immersion schools are the result of a task force that was established in 1990 by the Milwaukee, Wisconsin, school board. The task force was to "document the current status of African-American males in the Milwaukee public schools" (Leake and Leake 1992, 783).

The findings of the task force were consistent with national studies concerning the education of African American male students in public schools. African American males were disproportionately suspended and, for the majority of the males, academic achievement was below average. Upon further study, the task force found similar statistics for African American females.

Based on the recommendations of the task force, the Milwaukee school board authorized coeducational immersion schools that are accessible citywide. The goal of these schools is to "eliminate the institutional and attitudinal influences that impede the academic success of African-American students" (Leake and Leake 1992, 784). These schools infuse the district's curriculum with an African-centered education model, incorporating African American culture, history, and experiences. The schools have corporate sponsors, and the University of Wisconsin–Milwaukee School of Education staff are affiliated with the schools.

The two African American immersion schools in Milwaukee are the Dr. Martin Luther King, Jr., African American Immersion Elementary School, which has prekindergarten through fifth grade, and Malcolm X Academy, a middle school, with grades six through eight.

Supplementary Programs

Supplementary programs are after-school and weekend activities that are offered by organizations. The activities can include mentoring, tutoring, and cultural events.

The W. E. B. DuBois Learning Center in Kansas City, Missouri, provides a supplementary program for over 400 students a year. The program is designed to meet the increasing academic and social needs of children in Kansas City. It is "an alternative for those economically disadvantaged parents who want a quality education for their children" (W. E. B. DuBois Learning Center website). The program is staffed by volunteers from a variety of professional fields. The volunteers serve as tutors and mentors, organize events, and identify resources. The objectives of the program are fostering self-confidence and self-esteem, exposure to role models and mentors, and improving and enhancing students' academic performance in reading, mathematics, science, and computer science.

REFERENCES

Asante, Molefi Kete. 1991. "The Afrocentric Idea in Education." *Journal of Negro Education* 60, no. 2: 170–180.

Barrington, John M. 1991. "The New Zealand Experience: Maoris." Pp. 309–327 in *Minority Status and Schooling: A Comparative Study of Immigrant and Involuntary Minorities.* Edited by Margaret A. Gibson and John U. Ogbu. New York: Garland Publishing.

Benson, Ciaran. 1995. "Ireland's 'Low' IQ: A Critique." Pp. 222–233 in *The Bell Curve Debate: History, Documents, Opinions*. Edited by Russell Jacoby and Naomi Glauberman. New York: Times Books.

Bond, Horace Mann. [1934] 1966. *The Education of the Negro in the American Social Order*. Reprinted with a preface and new chapter by the author. New York: Octagon Books, Inc.

Council of Independent Black Institutions. http://www.cibi.org.

Grant, Carl A. 1995. "Reflections on the Promise of *Brown* and Multicultural Education." *Teachers College Record* 96, no. 4: 707–721.

Kifano, Subira. 1996. "Afrocentric Education in Supplementary Schools: Paradigm and Practice at the Mary McLeod Bethune Institute." *Journal of Negro Education* 65, no. 2: 209–218.

Klich, L. Z. 1988. "Aboriginal Cognition and Psychological Science." Pp. 426–454 in *Human Abilities in Cultural Context*. Edited by S. H. Irvine and J. W. Berry. New York: Cambridge University Press.

Lane, Charles. 1995. "Tainted Sources." Pp. 125–139 in *The Bell Curve Debate: History, Documents, Opinions*. Edited by Russell Jacoby and Naomi Glauberman. New York: Times Books.

Leake, Donald, and Brenda Leake. 1992. "African-American Immersion Schools in Milwaukee: A View from the Inside." *Phi Delta Kappan* 73, no. 10: 783–785.

Lee, Yongsook. 1991. "Koreans in Japan and in the United States." Pp. 131–168 in *Minority Status and Schooling: A Comparative Study of Immigrant and Involuntary Minorities*. Edited by Margaret A. Gibson and John U. Ogbu. New York: Garland Publishing.

W. E. B. DuBois Learning Center. 2000. http://www.duboislc.org.

Woodson, Carter G. [1933] 1991. *The Mis-Education of the Negro*. Reprinted. Philadelphia: Hamik's Publications.

Chapter Four

❧ Historically Black Colleges and Universities

Over the last decade of the twentieth century, a phenomenon the press called "white anger" emerged. The rhetoric around this undefined set of issues usually involved an assertion that special programs or special opportunities for people of color had gone too far, and that people of color already had accomplished their goal of equal opportunity.

This misguided argument usually centers on the premise that the opening of admissions to blacks at historically white institutions has achieved equal access and the historical necessity of HBCUs is no longer relevant. That is not so. By 1991, HBCUs had produced 70 percent of all African Americans holding baccalaureate degrees. By 1995, 60 percent of blacks with doctorates received their baccalaureate degree from an HBCU. HBCUs only have one-fifth of the African American university enrollment but graduate over one-third of all African Americans attaining a degree. The mission has just begun. HBCUs nurture young, aspiring African American men and women in a supportive, affirming environment—an environment free of racial tension, which eases cultural shock—and introduces a large number of African Americans into the nation's mainstream.

HBCUs are the Garden of Eden of equal opportunity. The possibility of a more just society grows from the education model provided by HBCUs. Unlike historically white institutions, HBCUs have always been institutions of inclusion and not exclusion. HBCUs have never by law or tradition excluded individuals because of race, color, creed, or national origin.

HBCUs also serve as custodians of the archives for African Americans and as centers for the study of African American culture and history. The history is stored there, waiting to be rewritten to accurately report the role of African Americans in the United States (Jackson 1996).

This chapter provides an overview of HBCUs. Included are brief discussions on the history, definitions, accomplishments, and challenges of these institutions as well as their relation to higher education desegregation. Eighty-six regionally accredited four-year, professional, and graduate-level HBCUs are listed. Interviews with a president emeritus of an HBCU and a current HBCU faculty member are provided. Two programs specifically designed to assist HBCUs in addressing their needs are presented. Four organizations established specifically to promote HBCUs are described. Finally, HBCUs that have repositories of African American culture and history are noted.

HBCUs: AN OVERVIEW

Approximately 75 percent of the HBCUs currently operating were established between 1865 and 1899. Over 90 percent of those founded during that period were located in the South.

"Organized originally for liberal arts purposes, the [black] college slowly instituted industrial education as one of its basic functions" (Bullock 1967, 159). The shift from liberal arts aspirations to industrial adequacy was a direct outgrowth of the need for economic development of the newly freed African Americans. Due to racial confinement, the agricultural industry continued to dominate as one of the sure avenues to employment. As such, many private HBCUs' early beginnings were as industrial institutes. The Tuskegee Institute, Hampton Institute, and Benedict Institute are examples. State-supported African American institutions, many of them land-grant institutions and some private institutions, identified their areas of focus with the letters "A" (agricultural); "I" (industrial); "M" (mechanical); "N" (normal, for a teacher training school); and "T" (technical) in their names. While many public HBCUs continue to have these designations in their names, today their academic offerings are not limited to those areas.

As some HBCUs were moving in the direction of industrial education, private seminaries were also being established. These include Walden Seminary, which became Philander Smith College; Atlanta Baptist Seminary, which became Morehouse College; Atlanta Baptist Female Seminary, which became Spelman College; and Bennett Seminary, which became Bennett College. Bennett began as a coeducational institution and in 1929 was established as a women's college.

The continuation of racial division after emancipation in the South specifically and in the United States generally fostered the need for HBCUs to move closer to their original focus—liberal arts education. "The many daily needs of the segregated Negro community justified giving young Negroes higher professional training" (Bullock 1967, 164). Leadership was needed in all professional fields of endeavor. Liberal arts education was seen as the means to provide the leadership training. "Based on current trends, it is estimated that over 300,000 blacks will graduate from [historically black colleges and universities] in the next twenty-five years" (Roebuck and Murty 1993, 4). There is no reason to conclude that the trend will change.

In 1996, the National Center for Education Statistics reported that in 1994 approximately 280,000 students attended HBCUs. Between 1976 and 1994 enrollment at HBCUs increased 26 percent, with the greatest increase occurring between 1986 and 1994. The status and condition of African American education as described in Chapter 1 and Chapter 3 is indicative of the continued need for HBCUs. The remainder of this chapter expounds on the necessity and demonstrates the role of HBCUs in American higher education.

HBCUs DEFINED

The basic definition of an HBCU is a postsecondary institution specifically established to educate African Americans. One hundred and nine postsecondary institutions meet this definition. Twenty are two-year degree institutions, and the remaining eighty-nine offer four-year degrees and higher.

The National Association for Equal Opportunity in Higher Education (NAFEO) expanded this definition. The Federal government modified this basic definition. Both of their definitions include private and public two-year, four-year, graduate, and professional degree institutions. NAFEO includes postsecondary institutions that are predominantly black. Using its definition, there are 118 NAFEO member institutions (1999).

The Higher Education Act of 1965 defines historically black colleges and universities as " . . . any historically black college or university that was established prior to 1964, whose principal mission was, and is, the education of black Americans, and that is accredited by a nationally recognized accrediting agency or association determined by the Secretary [of Education] to be a reliable authority as to the quality of training offered or is, according to such an agency or association, making reasonable progress toward accreditation."

There are eighty-nine HBCUs that offer four-year degrees or higher. For the purpose of this book, two criteria were used to define historically black colleges and universities. First, they are four-year colleges and higher that were founded specifically to educate African Americans. Second, they are regionally accredited as reported by their respective regional accrediting agencies as of January 2000. Eighty-six HBCUs meet these two criteria. This means that of the eighty-nine HBCUs that offer four-year degrees and higher, 97 percent are regionally accredited.

The eighty-six institutions that meet this book's definitional criteria for HBCUs are located in nineteen states, one territory, and the District of Columbia. Forty-six are private. Six were founded before the Civil War. Thirty-two HBCUs, or 37 percent, were founded within the first ten years after the Civil War. Seventeen HBCUs, or 20 percent, were founded during the twentieth century. African Americans from across all socioeconomic strata, and with varying levels of academic readiness for college when they first enroll, graduate from HBCUs.

Following are the eighty-six HBCUs that meet the definitional criteria for this book. The highest degree indicated is based on what is reported by the institutions' regional accrediting agencies.

Alabama

Alabama A&M University
Founded: 1875
Control: Public
Highest Degree: Three or fewer doctorates
City: Normal
Telephone: (256) 851–5000
Website: http://www.aamu.edu/

Alabama State University
Founded: 1874
Control: Public
Highest Degree: Four or more doctorates
City: Montgomery
Telephone: (334) 229–4100
Website: http://www.alasu.edu/

Concordia College
Founded: 1922
Control: Private
Highest Degree: Bachelor's
City: Selma
Telephone: (334) 874–5700
Website: http://higher-ed.lcms.org.selma.htm

Miles College
Founded: 1905
Control: Private
Highest Degree: Bachelor's
City: Birmingham
Telephone: (205) 929–1000
Website: http://www.miles.edu

Oakwood College
Founded: 1896
Control: Private
Highest Degree: Bachelor's
City: Huntsville
Telephone: (256) 726–7000
Website: http://www.oakwood.edu/

Stillman College
Founded: 1876
Control: Private
Highest Degree: Bachelor's
City: Tuscaloosa
Telephone: (800) 841–5722 or (205) 349–4240
Website: http://www.stillman.edu

Talladega College
Founded: 1867
Control: Private
Highest Degree: Bachelor's
City: Talladega
Telephone: (205) 761–0206
Website: http://www.talladega.edu

Tuskegee University
Founded: 1881
Control: Private
Highest Degree: Three or fewer doctorates
City: Tuskegee
Telephone: (800) 622–6531 or (334) 727–8496
Website: http://www.tusk.edu/

Arkansas

Arkansas Baptist College
Founded: 1901
Control: Private
Highest Degree: Bachelor's
City: Little Rock
Telephone: (501) 374–7856
Website: Not available

Philander Smith College
Founded: 1877
Control: Private
Highest Degree: Bachelor's
City: Little Rock
Telephone: (501) 370–5215
Website: http://www.philander.edu

University of Arkansas, Pine Bluff
(Formerly Arkansas AM&N College)
Founded: 1873
Control: Public
Highest Degree: Master's
City: Pine Bluff
Telephone: (870) 543–8000
Website: http://www.uapb.edu/

Delaware

Delaware State University
Founded: 1891
Control: Public
Highest Degree: Master's
City: Dover
Telephone: (302) 739–4917
Website: http://www.dsc/edu/

District of Columbia

Howard University
Founded: 1867
Control: Private

Highest Degree: Four or more doctorates
City: Washington, DC
Telephone: (202)806–6100
Website: http://howard.edu/

University of the District of Columbia
Founded: 1867
Control: Public
Highest Degree: Master's
City: Washington, D.C.
Telephone: (202) 274–5000
Website: http://udc2.org/index-b.htm

Florida

Bethune-Cookman College
Founded: 1904
Control: Private
Highest Degree: Bachelor's
City: Daytona Beach
Telephone: (904) 255–1401
Website: http://www.bethune.cookman.edu/

Edward Waters College
Founded: 1866
Control: Private
Highest Degree: Bachelor's
City: Jacksonville
Telephone: (904) 355–3030
Website: http://www.ewc.edu/

Florida A&M University
Founded: 1877
Control: Public
Highest Degree: Three or fewer doctorates
City: Tallahassee
Telephone: (850) 599–3000
Website: http://www.famu2.edu/

Florida Memorial College
Founded: 1879
Control: Private

Highest Degree: Bachelor's
City: Miami
Telephone: (800) 822–1362 or (305) 626–3600
Website: http://www.fmc.edu/

Georgia

Albany State University
Founded: 1903
Control: Public
Highest Degree: Master's and education specialist
City: Albany
Telephone: (912) 430–4600
Website: http://argus.asurams.edu/asu/default.asp

Clark Atlanta University
Founded: 1989 (Merged)
Clark College (Founded 1869); Atlanta University (Founded 1867)
Control: Private
Highest Degree: Four or more doctorates
City: Atlanta
Telephone: (404) 880–8000
Website: http://www.cau.edu/

Fort Valley State College
Founded: 1869
Control: Public
Highest Degree: Master's and education specialist
City: Fort Valley
Telephone: (912) 825–6211
Website: http://www.fvsc.peachnet.edu

Interdenominational Theological Center
Founded: 1958
Control: Private
Highest Degree: Three or fewer doctorates
City: Atlanta
Telephone: (404) 527–7700
Website: http://www.itc.edu

Morehouse College
(Male only)

Founded: 1867
Control: Private
Highest Degree: Bachelor's
City: Atlanta
Telephone: (404) 215–2632
Website: http://www.morehouse.acu.edu/

Morehouse School of Medicine
Founded: 1975 (As part of Morehouse College)
Control: Private
Highest Degree: Three or fewer doctorates
City: Atlanta
Telephone: (404) 752–4500
Website: http://www.msm.edu/

Morris Brown College
Founded: 1881
Control: Private
Highest Degree: Bachelor's
City: Atlanta
Telephone: (404) 220–0270
Website: http://www.morrisbrown.edu

Paine College
Founded: 1882
Control: Private
Highest Degree: Bachelor's
City: Augusta
Telephone: (706) 821–8200
Website: http://www.paine.edu/homeus4.htm/

Savannah State University
Founded: 1890
Control: Public
Highest Degree: Master's
City: Savannah
Telephone: (800) 788–0478
Website: http://www.savstate.edu

Spelman College
(Female only)
Founded: 1881

Control: Private
Highest Degree: Bachelor's
City: Atlanta
Telephone: (800) 982–2411
Website: http://www.spelman.edu

Kentucky

Kentucky State University
Founded: 1866
Control: Public
Highest Degree: Master's
City: Frankfort
Telephone: (502) 227–6000
Website: http://www.state.ky.us/ksu

Louisiana

Dillard University
Founded: 1864
Control: Private
Highest Degree: Bachelor's
City: New Orleans
Telephone: (504) 283–8822
Website: http://www.dillard.edu/

Grambling State University
Founded: 1901
Control: Public
Highest Degree: Three or fewer doctorates
City: Grambling
Telephone: (318) 274–3395
Website: http://www.gram.edu

Southern University and A&M College
Founded: 1880
Control: Public
Highest Degree: Three or fewer doctorates
City: Baton Rouge
Telephone: (225) 771–4500
Website: http://www.subr.edu/

Southern University at New Orleans
Founded: 1959
Control: Public
Highest Degree: Master's
City: New Orleans
Telephone: (504) 286–5000
Website: http://suno.edu

Xavier University of Louisiana
Founded: 1917
Control: Private
Highest Degree: Three or fewer doctorates
City: New Orleans
Telephone: (504) 486–7411
Website: http://www.xula.edu

Maryland

Bowie State University
Founded: 1865
Control: Public
Highest Degree: Master's
City: Bowie
Telephone: (301) 464–3000
Website: http://bsu.umd.edu/

Coppin State College
Founded: 1900
Control: Public
Highest Degree: Master's
City: Baltimore
Telephone: (410) 383–5400
Website: http://www.coppin.umd.edu/

Morgan State University
Founded: 1867
Control: Public
Highest Degree: Master's
City: Baltimore
Telephone: (443) 885–3333
Website: http://www.morgan.edu

University of Maryland–Eastern Shore
Founded: 1886
Control: Public
Highest Degree: Master's
City: Princess Anne
Telephone: (410) 651–2200
Website: http://www.umes.umd.edu

Mississippi

Alcorn State University
Founded: 1871
Control: Public
Highest Degree: Master's
City: Lorman
Telephone: (601) 877–6100
Website: http://www.alcorn.edu/

Jackson State University
Founded: 1877
Control: Public
Highest Degree: Master's and education specialist
City: Jackson
Telephone: (800) 848–6817
Website: http://www.jsums.edu/

Mississippi Valley State University
Founded: 1946
Control: Public
Highest Degree: Master's
City: Itta Bena
Telephone: (601) 254–3344
Website: http://mvsu.edu/

Rust College
Founded: 1866
Control: Private
Highest Degree: Bachelor's
City: Holly Spring
Telephone: (601) 252–8000
Website: http://www.rustcollege.edu

Tougaloo College
Founded: 1869
Control: Private
Highest Degree: Bachelor's
City: Tougaloo
Telephone: (888) 424–2566 or (601) 977–7700
Website: http://www.tougallo.edu/

Missouri

Harris-Stowe State College
Founded: 1857
Control: Public
Highest Degree: Bachelor's
City: St. Louis
Telephone: (314) 340–3366
Website: http://www.hssc.edu

Lincoln University
Founded: 1866
Control: Public
Highest Degree: Master's
City: Jefferson City
Telephone: (573) 681–5000
Website: http://www.lincolnu.edu/

North Carolina

Barber-Scotia College
Founded: 1867
Control: Private
Highest Degree: Bachelor's
City: Concord
Telephone: (704) 789–2900
Website: http://www.barber-scotia.edu

Bennett College
(Female only)
Founded: 1873
Control: Private
Highest Degree: Bachelor's

City: Greensboro
Telephone: (910) 370–8624
Website: http://www.bennett.edu/

Elizabeth City State University
Founded: 1891
Control: Public
Highest Degree: Bachelor's
City: Elizabeth City
Telephone: (252) 335–3400
Website: http://www.ecsu.edu/

Fayetteville State University
Founded: 1867
Control: Public
Highest Degree: Three or fewer doctorates
City: Fayetteville
Telephone: (910) 486–1371
Website: http://www.fsufay.edu/

Johnson C. Smith University
Founded: 1867
Control: Private
Highest Degree: Bachelor's
City: Charlotte
Telephone: (704) 378–1010
Website: http://www.jcsu.edu/

Livingstone College
Founded: 1879
Control: Private
Highest Degree: Master's
City: Salisbury
Telephone: (704) 797–1000
Website: http://livingstone.edu

North Carolina A&T State University
Founded: 1891
Control: Public
Highest Degree: Three or fewer doctorates
City: Greensboro
Telephone: (910) 334–7500
Website: http://www.ncat.edu/

North Carolina Central University
Founded: 1910
Control: Public
Highest Degree: Three or fewer doctorates
City: Durham
Telephone: (919) 560–6100
Website: http://www.nccu.edu

Saint Augustine's College
Founded: 1867
Control: Private
Highest Degree: Bachelor's
City: Raleigh
Telephone: (919) 516–4000
Website: http://www.st-aug.edu

Shaw University
Founded: 1865
Control: Private
Highest Degree: Master's
City: Raleigh
Telephone: (919) 546–8200
Website: http://www.shawuniversity.edu

Winston-Salem State University
Founded: 1892
Control: Public
Highest Degree: Master's
City: Winston-Salem
Telephone: (800) 257–4052
Website: http://www.wssu.edu

Ohio

Central State University
Founded: 1887
Control: Public
Highest Degree: Master's
City: Wilberforce
Telephone: (937) 376–6348
Website: http://www.centralstate.edu/

Wilberforce University
Founded: 1856
Control: Private
Highest Degree: Bachelor's
City: Wilberforce
Telephone: (937) 376–2911
Website: http://www.wilberforce.edu

Oklahoma

Langston University
Founded: 1897
Control: Public
Highest Degree: Master's
City: Langston
Telephone: (405) 466–4000
Website: http://www.lunet.edu/

Pennsylvania

Cheyney State University
Founded: 1837
Control: Public
Highest Degree: Master's
City: Cheyney
Telephone: (610) 399–2000
Website: http://www.cheyney.edu

Lincoln University
Founded: 1854
Control: Public
Highest Degree: Master's
City: Lincoln
Telephone: (610) 932–8300
Website: http://www.lincoln.edu

South Carolina

Allen University
Founded: 1870
Control: Private

Highest Degree: Bachelor's
City: Columbia
Telephone: (803) 376–5735
Website: http://www.scicu.org/allen/auhome.htm

Benedict College
Founded: 1870
Control: Private
Highest Degree: Bachelor's
City: Columbia
Telephone: (803) 256–4220
Website: http://bchome.benedict.edu

Claflin College
Founded: 1869
Control: Private
Highest Degree: Bachelor's
City: Orangeburg
Telephone: (803) 535–5349
Website: http://www.claflin.edu

Morris College
Founded: 1891
Control: Private
Highest Degree: Bachelor's
City: Sumter
Telephone: (803) 934–3200
Website: http://www.scicu.org/morris/mchome.htm

South Carolina State University
Founded: 1896
Control: Public
Highest Degree: Three or fewer doctorates
City: Orangeburg
Telephone: (803) 536–7000
Website: http://www.scsu.edu/

Voorhees College
Founded: 1897
Control: Private
Highest Degree: Bachelor's
City: Denmark

Telephone: (804) 524–5000
Website: http://www.voorhees.edu

Tennessee

Fisk University
Founded: 1867
Control: Private
Highest Degree: Master's
City: Nashville
Telephone: (615) 329–8500
Website: http://www.fisk.edu/

Lane College
Founded: 1882
Control: Private
Highest Degree: Bachelor's
City: Jackson
Telephone: (901) 426–7500
Website: http://www.lanecollege.edu

LeMoyne-Owen College
Founded: 1862
Control: Private
Highest Degree: Master's
City: Memphis
Telephone Number: (901) 774–9090
Website: http://mecca.org/LOC/page/LOC.html

Meharry Medical College
Founded: 1876
Control: Private
Highest Degree: Three or fewer doctorates
City: Nashville
Telephone: (615) 372–6000
Website: http://www.mmc.edu/

Tennessee State University
Founded: 1912
Control: Public
Highest Degree: Three or fewer doctorates
City: Nashville

Telephone: (615) 963–5000
Website: http://tnstate.edu/

Texas

Huston-Tillotson College
Founded: 1876
Control: Private
Highest Degree: Bachelor's
City: Austin
Telephone: (512) 505–3027
Website: http://www.htc.edu

Jarvis Christian College
Founded: 1912
Control: Private
Highest Degree: Bachelor's
City: Hawkins
Telephone: (903) 769–5700
Website: http://168.44.172.2

Paul Quinn College
Founded: 1872
Control: Private
Highest Degree: Bachelor's
City: Dallas
Telephone: (214) 302–3250
Website: http://www.pqc.edu

Prairie View A&M University
Founded: 1876
Control: Public
Highest Degree: Master's
City: Prairie View
Telephone: (409) 857–2626
Website: http://www.pvamu.edu/index.html

Texas Southern University
Founded: 1947
Control: Public
Highest Degree: Three or fewer doctorates

City: Houston
Telephone: (713) 313–7011
Website: http://www.tsu.edu/

Wiley College
Founded: 1873
Control: Private
Highest Degree: Bachelor's
City: Marshall
Telephone: (800) 658–6889
Website: http://199.171.201.14/college

Virgin Islands

University of the Virgin Islands
Founded: 1962
Control: Public (Territory)
Highest Degree: Master's
City: St. Thomas
Telephone: (340) 776–9200
Website: http://www.uvi.edu/

Virginia

Hampton University
Founded: 1868
Control: Private
Highest Degree: Three or fewer doctorates
City: Hampton
Telephone: (757) 727–5000
Website: http://www.hamptonu.edu/

Norfolk State University
Founded: 1935
Control: Public
Highest Degree: Three or fewer doctorates
City: Norfolk
Telephone: (757) 683–8600
Website: http://www.nsu.edu/

Saint Paul's College
Founded: 1888
Control: Private
Highest Degree: Bachelor's
City: Lawrenceville
Telephone: (804) 848–3111
Website: http://www.utoledo.edu/~wfraker.stpaul.html

Virginia State University
Founded: 1882
Control: Public
Highest Degree: Master's
City: Petersburg
Telephone: (804) 524–5000
Website: http://vsu.edu/

Virginia Union University
Founded: 1865
Control: Private
Highest Degree: Three or fewer doctorates
City: Richmond
Telephone: (800) 368–3227
Website: http://www.vuu.edu

West Virginia

Bluefield State College
Founded: 1895
Control: Public
Highest Degree: Bachelor's
City: Bluefield
Telephone: (304) 327–4000
Website: http://www.bluefield.wvnet.edu/

West Virginia State College
Founded: 1891
Control: Public
Highest Degree: Bachelor's
City: Institute
Telephone: (304) 766–3000
Website: http://www.wvsc.edu

ACCOMPLISHMENTS AND CHALLENGES OF HBCUs

There are those who argue that except for a handful of HBCUs, they are at best junior colleges and should be designated as such. Primarily non–African Americans generate these arguments. A few African Americans agree with this assertion.

The pivotal role these postsecondary institutions have played and continue to play in African American education and American education is evidenced by their tangible accomplishments and outcomes. A selected list of accomplishments follows. All organizations have challenges to address. A selected list of challenges are listed as well.

Accomplishments

The U.S Department of Education, Office of Civil Rights, reports that during their existence HBCUs have:

1. Produced more than 80 percent of all degrees conferred to African Americans in medicine and dentistry. The two institutions that conferred these degrees were Howard University and Meharry Medical College. At the end of the twentieth century, 19.7 percent of the medical and dentistry degrees awarded to African Americans were from these two institutions.
2. Provided undergraduate training for three-fourths of all blacks holding a doctorate degree, three-fourths of all black officers in the armed forces, and four-fifths of all black federal judges.
3. Led in institutions awarding baccalaureate degrees to black students in the life sciences, physical sciences, mathematics, and engineering.
4. Continued to rank high in terms of the proportion of graduates who pursue and complete graduate and professional training.
5. Accounted for 50 percent of black faculty in traditionally white research universities (1991 and 1999).

The White House Initiative on HBCUs reports that "in 1995, these institutions matriculated 26 percent of all African American students enrolled in four-year colleges, awarded master's degrees and first-professional degrees to about one in six African American men and women, and awarded 27 percent of all baccalaureate degrees earned by African Americans nationwide" (Website 1999).

The U.S. Congress reports in the findings section (Item 9, F) of the Individuals with Disabilities Education Act (IDEA) Amendments of 1997, "as recently as 1991, historically black colleges and universities enrolled 44 percent of the African-American teacher trainees in the Nation. However, in 1993, historically black colleges and universities received only 4 percent of the discretionary funds for special education and related services personnel training under this Act." This finding is significant when one considers the percentage of African American children who are identified and placed in special education programs, as noted in Chapter 1 of this book.

HBCUs have a higher retention rate of African American college students than historically white institutions (Constantine 1994). The high retention rate generally is attributed to two factors: (1) a supportive environment, and (2) the readiness of HBCUs to provide remediation for students who need it.

Of the top fifteen baccalaureate institutions of black Ph.D. degree recipients, twelve are HBCUs (*Black Issues in Higher Education* 1999). Three out of four African American females who earned a doctoral degree in the sciences between 1975 and 1992 received their baccalaureate degrees from an HBCU (Leggon and Pearson 1997). HBCUs have an international influence on the African diaspora. A number of influential African leaders came to the United States to be educated at HBCUs, returning to their countries to apply the training (*Academe* 1995). HBCUs are tangible examples of staff and faculty diversity in higher education. In 1993, 24 percent of the total staff at HBCUs were non-black, and 34 percent of the total faculty at HBCUs were non-black (Griffith 1996). No historically white colleges and universities can report similar percentages for staff or faculty diversity.

Finally, Jill M. Constantine conducted a study on the long-term wage level of African Americans who received their baccalaureate degrees during the 1970s. The researcher found "that students who attended HBCUs in the 1970s apparently later enjoyed substantially higher value added to wages than black students who attended historically white or racially mixed four-year institutions" (1995, 541). The finding was attributed to the higher post-baccalaureate degree attainment of blacks who graduate from HBCUs as compared to those who graduate from historically white institutions.

Challenges

Generally, four challenges face HBCUs singularly or in some combination. These challenges are financial resources, president turnover, historical identification preservation, and Internet access.

The issue of financial resources is two-pronged: one issue is student expenditure and the other is faculty salary. The National Center for Education Statistics (1996) reports that "during the 1993–1994 academic year per student expenditures at public HBCUs are lower than those at other public institutions." In addition, due to the slow rate of growth, private HBCUs spent about 14 percent less per student than all private postsecondary institutions. "Increases in faculty salaries at HBCUs generally kept pace with those at other colleges, though salaries at HBCUs remained somewhat lower. In 1993–94, female faculty at HBCUs earned 86 percent of the average for all female faculty compared to male HBCU faculty who earned 79 percent of the average for all male faculty. Within HBCUs, men's salaries averaged 12 percent higher than women's salaries, compared to a 24 percent difference for all institutions" (National Center for Education Statistics 1996, vii).

HBCUs, especially public HBCUs, are experiencing a rapid exodus of presidents. In the public institutions, the turnover is attributed primarily to a hostile political environment. Some have suggested that overall, the high turnover rate is due to incompatibility of expectations between the presidents and the boards of trustees (Maggett 1996).

The full consequences of the *United States v. Fordice* decision, discussed in Chapter 5, are yet to be realized. The *Fordice* decision is concerned with the desegregation of higher education systems in Mississippi. The United States Supreme Court requires the establishment of racially neutral institutions. Some blacks see it as a possible blessing in disguise, while most blacks think it is a frontal attack on public HBCUs. What remains to be seen is if "racially neutral" means predominately white. What is known is that the fear of the *Fordice* decision having a negative impact on public HBCUs may be well founded. Before the *Fordice* decision, three public HBCUs had student enrollments that were predominately white. These schools were West Virginia State College, Bluefield State College in West Virginia, and Lincoln University in Missouri. Bluefield State is probably the most alarming example of what can happen to a public HBCU when one considers the *Fordice* decision. Although Bluefield is identified as an HBCU, little remains that supports that identification. Currently, 8 percent of the student population is black. Of the 82 faculty members, three are black. Bluefield State began desegregating in 1954, the year of the *Brown v. Board of Education* decision. In 1968, a state referendum passed that closed the dormitories. This is also the same year that Bluefield State had its first white president. The referendum occurred during an era when college students across the country were protesting the Vietnam War and demanding input in university policies and the academic curriculum. With the dormitories closed, and remaining closed today, Bluefield State is a commuter school. The black population in West Virginia has not exceeded 5 percent. Bluefield State, like West Virginia State, relied on attracting out-of-state black students to enroll. With the dormitories closed, out-of-state recruitment efforts were useless. Champions of HBCUs are concerned about the impact of *Fordice* because the decision could accelerate demographic shifts similar to those at Bluefield State at other public HBCUs, thereby eroding the black cultural identity of these institutions.

From October 1994 through January 1995, the ERIC Clearinghouse on Urban Education surveyed forty-nine HBCUs about their Internet capability. Thirty-five institutions reported having some level of Internet access for students, faculty, or administrators, or some combination of the three. Fourteen were building an infrastructure for access. Some of those fourteen are subsumed in the thirty-five mentioned earlier. Ten had no Internet access nor any plans in the near future for access (website).

Internet access, specifically, and technology, generally, are critical for HBCUs to remain competitive. While several HBCUs have the capacity, there remain many that, because of financial constraints, have not been able to focus their full attention on this educational resource and administrative tool. This is particularly true of many small, private HBCUs.

HBCUs AND DESEGREGATION

The information on HBCUs and the effect of desegregation on them is from personal correspondence with Raymond C. Pierce, the deputy assistant secretary for civil rights at the U.S. Department of Education (21 August 2000).

The collection of cases concerning higher education desegregation is known as the *Adams* cases. These cases, based on legal suits that began in 1970, were brought by individuals and by the National Association for the Advancement of Colored People (NAACP). In these cases, the U.S. Department of Education Office of Civil Rights (OCR) is accused of not meeting its responsibility to enforce Title VI of the Civil Rights Act of 1964. The 1977 district court decision in *Adams v. Califano* motivated OCR to "aggressively seek compliance with Title VI." *Adams v. Califano* revealed that OCR was not doing what was needed to facilitate higher education desegregation in states where there had been segregated higher education systems. The district court ordered OCR to require statewide desegregation plans for these states' higher education systems. Nineteen states that operated "colleges that had been created solely for the education of African Americans under state sponsored segregation" were affected by this district court decision. These states were: Alabama, Arkansas, Delaware, Florida, Georgia, Kentucky, Louisiana, Maryland, Mississippi, Missouri, North Carolina, Ohio, Oklahoma, Pennsylvania, South Carolina, Tennessee, Texas, Virginia, and West Virginia.

Pierce, in his correspondence to the author, wrote:

> Of these 19, Tennessee was involved in a private litigation in which the Department of Justice ultimately intervened resulting in a court ordered remedial plan. North Carolina was also involved in private litigation that resulted in a consent decree monitored by OCR. Thirteen states submitted desegregation plans that were accepted by OCR. Three states, Louisiana, Alabama, and Mississippi submitted plans that were unacceptable and OCR referred those states to the Department of Justice for enforcement through litigation. One state, Ohio, refused to submit a plan and it too was referred to the Department of Justice for litigation.

The desegregation plans addressed two concerns. First, academic programs that were likely to attract a cross-section of the total student population, based on race, were placed in HBCUs. For example, Savannah State University in Georgia offers programs in marine biology and computer science technology. Second, avenues of access to the white institutions were developed. This was done primarily through intense recruitment and race-specific financial aid. Minority students would be recruited and provided with financial assistance at the University of Georgia.

In the 1980s, states that met the two parts of the desegregation plans, which had become a "contractual approach" to review compliance, had their cases closed. These states were Arkansas, Delaware, Georgia, Missouri, North Carolina, Oklahoma, South Carolina, and West Virginia. Pierce states:

> The [Supreme] Court, guided by principles enunciated in earlier cases in the elementary and secondary school setting, such as *Brown v. Board of Education,* established guidelines for ascertaining whether a *de jure* system has, in fact, been dismantled. . . . Based on this Supreme Court ruling, OCR developed an updated federal policy on higher education desegregation that did not rely on a checklist analysis but one that utilizes a "vestiges" analysis. Since 1994, a vestiges analysis has been at the

core of federal policy on Title VI compliance in higher education desegregation cases. In [*Fordice*], the Supreme Court identified several areas
that should be examined to determine if there are any remaining vestiges of the past system of segregation. Pursuant to the [*Fordice*] decision OCR examines several areas for possible vestiges including the following: mission statement, funding, and physical facilities of HBCUs,
and the unnecessary duplication of programs between HBCUs and
TWIs [traditionally white institutions].

Pierce also provided the status of the remaining cases on OCR's
docket, which included Ohio, Florida, Pennsylvania, and Kentucky. The
Ohio case that had been referred to the Department of Justice was returned to OCR and in January of 1998 OCR accepted a compliance plan
from the state. The plan is designed to bring the state of Ohio into compliance with Title VI through specific state commitments addressing three
areas affecting Central State University: funding, facilities, and programs.

In February of 1998, OCR accepted a compliance plan from Florida designed to address issues identified by OCR as possible remaining vestiges [of *de jure* segregation]. That agreement requires the state to further strengthen programs and improve facilities at Florida A&M,
strengthen student retention programs that assist minority students attending the state's TWIs [traditionally white institutions], and address
issues of recruitment and student preparation for high-stakes tests.

In March of 1999, OCR accepted a compliance plan submitted by the
Commonwealth of Pennsylvania. Pursuant to that agreement the state
is required to provide for specific funding for Cheyney State University
for facilities renovations and program expansion in addition to addressing issues impacting minority student participation at Penn State
University.

In January of 2000, OCR accepted a compliance plan submitted by
the state of Kentucky designed to address the remaining vestiges identified through our investigation. The agreement requires the state to
develop a new education plan for Kentucky State University, provide
specific funding for program expansion, renovate several campus
buildings, and address certain faculty-related issues. OCR began review
of Texas in late 1998. The Virginia review was also begun in late 1998.
With the initiation of the Maryland review in late 1999 OCR had fully
activated and/or reached resolution agreement in all of the open
Adams cases on our higher education desegregation docket.

ORGANIZATIONS ESTABLISHED TO ASSIST HBCUs

Four organizations and one office were established specifically to complement and empower HBCUs and their administration, faculty, and students. Three are nonprofit, one is governmental, and one is a professional organization. The histories and missions of these organizations follow.

National Association for Equal Opportunity in Higher Education

NAFEO was founded in 1969. National attention had been focused on inequality in precollege education by the *Brown* decision. However, this type of attention had not occurred for African American higher education. It appeared that there were no avenues for redress. NAFEO keeps the interests, concerns, and needs of HBCUs on the agendas of the executive, legislative, regulatory, and judicial branches of federal and state governments. It promotes the formulation and implementation of policies, programs, and practices to protect and amplify HBCUs. It accomplishes this through education and training, management consulting, evaluation and research studies, institutional development, and project management. An annual conference is held in Washington, D.C.

National HBCU Faculty Development Network

Founded in 1996, the National HBCU Faculty Development Network is a professional organization designed to promote effective teaching and student learning through collaborative faculty endeavors across HBCUs. Its activities strengthen the network and its leadership role as a catalyst and coordinator for collaboration. It convenes an annual symposium to enhance the collective experiences of HBCUs' faculty.

Office for the Advancement of Public Black Colleges

The Office for the Advancement of Public Black Colleges is part of the National Association of State Universities and Land-Grant Colleges (NASULGC). NASULGC was established in 1887 for the purpose of supporting and promoting postsecondary public education through constituency awareness, partnerships with member institutions and the federal government, and strengthening the work of HBCU land-grant institutions and urban universities. Membership is voluntary.

The Office for the Advancement of Public Black Colleges facilitates NASULGC's work with the 17 HBCU members. The HBCUs are collectively known as the 1890 Institutions because that is the year of the Second Morrill Act, which established black land-grant institutions.

United Negro College Fund

UNCF was incorporated in 1944. It is the oldest organization in the United States that supports HBCUs. Member institutions of UNCF are regionally accredited, private four-year HBCUs. Currently, there are thirty-nine member institutions.

Frederick D. Patterson, president of Tuskegee Institute, now Tuskegee University, initiated the idea of private HBCUs "[pooling] their small monies and [making] a united appeal to the national conscience." This idea gave birth to UNCF.

UNCF realizes its mission with a variety of programs that provide financial assistance to their students, raise operating funds, and supply technical assistance. Some UNCF programs are: Infrastructure Development Assistance Program; Financial Aid for Graduate Study; Precollege Program; Study Abroad Programs; Curriculum Development and Teaching Program; Faculty Development Programs and Fellowships; and scholarships based on geography, academic majors, merit, and need.

White House Initiative on HBCUs

In 1980, President Jimmy Carter signed Executive Order 12232. This executive order established the White House Initiative on HBCUs. The order authorizes a federal program in support of HBCUs. Subsequent presidents signed similar executive orders.

In Executive Order 12677, President George Bush established the President's Advisory Board on Historically Black Colleges and Universities. The board advises the president and the secretary of education on these institutions. In addition, the board "issues an annual report to the President on HBCU participation in federal programs; advises the Secretary of Education on increasing the federal role in strengthening HBCUs; and reports to the President on how to increase the private sector role in strengthening these institutions."

In 1993, President William J. Clinton's Executive Order 12876 characterized the mission of the White House Initiative on HBCUs as a means " . . . to advance the development of human potential, to strengthen the capacity of historically black colleges and universities to provide quality education, and to increase opportunities to participate in and benefit from Federal programs."

To increase the participation of HBCUs in federally funded programs, thirty U.S. departments participate through grants, contracts, and other agreements. Annually, each department is required to present a federal plan and report on how it assisted HBCUs. In addition to the U.S. Department of Education, the other federal agencies are Agriculture, Agency for International Development, Appalachian Regional Commission, Commerce, Central Intelligence Agency, Corporation for National Service, Defense, Energy, Environmental Protection Agency, Equal Employment Opportunity Commission, Health and Human Services, Housing and Urban Development, Interior, Justice, Labor, National Aeronautics and Space Administration, National Credit Union Administration, National Endowment for the Arts, National Endowment for the Humanities, National Science Foundation, Nuclear Regulatory Commission, State, Transportation, and Treasury.

HBCU RESOURCE INTERVIEWS

The author had the opportunity to talk with a president emeritus of an HBCU and an HBCU faculty member. Following are their experiences and insights on HBCUs and these institutions' roles in African American education and higher education in America.

Arthur E. Thomas

Arthur Thomas, a native of Philadelphia, Pennsylvania, received his baccalaureate degree in history with a minor in geography from Central State University, a public HBCU in Wilberforce, Ohio. He received his master of science degree in educational administration from Miami University in Ohio. His doctorate, from the University of Massachusetts at Amherst, is in educational administration with a specialization in the rights of children. He is president emeritus of Central State University, and was the first alumni to serve as president. In addition, he holds the title of Distinguished Professor of Education. Before his ten years of leadership at Central State, he served as the vice president for academic affairs for eight years.

Thomas's other professional experiences include director of the Bolinga Black Cultural Resources Center, assistant dean of the medical school in continuing education, and assistant dean of continuing and community education. All of these positions were at Wright State University. He directed the Center for the Study of Student Citizenship Rights and Responsibilities, a legal services program designed to protect the rights of children. He was the director of the Model Cities Education Program in Dayton, Ohio. He has served as an assistant principal and as an elementary and secondary school teacher. He coached football and track at the high school level. Thomas also has many years of teaching experience at Central State University.

While at Central State and Wright State, he was known and respected for his work with international programs. The international program grants and contracts included funding from the U.S. Agency for International Development (USAID) and agencies in Senegal, Mali, Ghana, and Egypt. During Thomas's tenure, 123 students from 23 African countries attended Central State University.

President William Jefferson Clinton appointed Thomas as part of the official U.S. delegation headed by Rev. Jesse Jackson to monitor the elections in South Africa. In 1988, Thomas became a member of the President's Board of Advisors on Historically Black Colleges and Universities. Presidents George Bush and William Clinton appointed him to this position.

Following is the author's conversation with Arthur Thomas. He shares his experiences and views about HBCUs, their role in American higher education, their strengths and challenges, and the political environment in which they exist.

What is the mission and role of HBCUs today in America's higher education system?

There are different missions for different people. There are different missions for different institutions. The mission that most black leaders hold for Historically Black Colleges and Universities is to maintain access to a better life through education for African Americans and the other poor and oppressed people. For white people, the mission of HBCUs changes as their attitudes change.

Let me explain how this thing called "access" works. Right after World War II, Michigan State University was an ordinary school. The president was John P. Hanna. John P. Hanna's concern was access. He believed that if you let enough people in school, though not all of them will graduate enough of them would graduate to positively impact society. He accepted academically unprepared white people who did not have social skills, social graces, or professional goals. He took these white people and provided them access to an education and a future. He gave them all an opportunity. Some of them graduated, and some of them did not. Some of them went on to become truly great men and women. They then supported Michigan State in the legislature, the Congress, and through corporations. The graduates provided support to the extent that it is now one of the premier universities in the world. Access was the issue.

When Dwight Eisenhower made his great landing during World War II, he knew that he would lose x number of men. It was calculated. His strategy was that "as I take this beach, x number of my men will die, but this beach is important enough for me to take to win this war." He engaged in battle and took the beach, knowing some would die. As blacks try to attack the beach of access for our people, we will have casualties.

My point is access has always been an issue in this nation. Access was the issue when poor, ignorant immigrants from Europe got off the boats and went to school. Public schools were developed because access was the issue for white people. Access was always the issue for white people.

My grandfather was a sharecropper. During the summer, my mother would send my brother and me to South Carolina. We would watch my grandfather being called "boy" by a boy. We watched my grandfather work all day and half the night on this white man's farm making sure the white man became rich. I watched my grandfather as a sharecropper and I have seen what has happened in my family over a period of generations. My mother went only to the tenth grade and then had to go to work. Later, after I graduated from college, she returned to school to complete her high school education and graduate from college. I received my college degree. My son received his college degree. My grandchildren will receive their college degrees. My cousins are lawyers and working on their Ph.D.s in engineering and other fields. Education has very positively affected my family. There is no question about the fact that education is the real source to survival. Not only survival, but to improving one's condition.

Now all of a sudden when black people demonstrate in great numbers that we are progressing, that we are moving forward, access is becoming an issue that white people see the need to change. Now all of a sudden, black people should go to junior colleges and technical schools. Now all of a sudden, black people should have to pass certain standards before they are permitted to go to college. Now all of a sudden, according to white people, through affirmative action black people are being given advantages.

White people do not have the right to decide what our priorities should be and black people should not listen to them. The white man should be the last man in the world to decide that affirmative action has had its day. How can he decide that affirmative action has had its day when he and his ancestors enslaved us, degraded us, and dehumanized us for 400 years? How can he decide that affirmative action has had its day when he and ancestors treated us like dogs, horses, cows, and chickens for 400 years? He gave up a little progress, a little freedom when we demanded it. Now all of a sudden, he decides that we have had enough freedom, that we have had enough affirmative action. We need to say that now is the time to go back to the 1960s on this racist white system to ensure that our young people still have access.

HBCUs were initially built not only to provide access to black youngsters; they were built to provide access to black youngsters through the minds of black people. In the minds of white people, they were built to contain and segregate black people.

When you trace the history of historically black colleges, they are usually on some back road. For example, Central State is on a road that was a glacial esker. When the ice age receded, the boulders created a trail. When engineers decided to build the road that leads to Central State, they followed that trail. On the other hand, US 675 was carefully planned and built so that Wright State University could have access to all the people that it wanted. Therefore, you have a university that is flourishing at thirteen thousand to fourteen thousand, while whites deliberately, premeditatedly, and maliciously planned the stunting of the growth of Central State.

There are some blacks who assist whites in the destruction of some of our institutions. They say, "We should adhere to the standards. We should develop all of our schools as 'elitist institutions.'" They completely forget the fact that if we can provide enough youth with access, then we will build our race to a much more productive, positive level. These recently developed new versions of House Negroes would not have survived in the schools they now want poor children to attend.

My position as an educator has always been to provide access. My position has also always been that you cannot be an educator without being a civil rights activist. You have to do both. The same attitudes prevailed in the white community during slavery where they said if you teach a slave how to read or write, we will hang you; if we catch blacks learning to read and write, we will hang them, because we do not want blacks to be literate. That same condition still exists today. It is modified. It is incognito. It is done in a "dignified way," but many white people do not want large numbers of black people educated. They do not want black people to compete with their children for jobs, wealth, and power. White people still want us to shine their shoes and clean their toilet bowls because this makes them feel superior, powerful, and in control.

The sad issue is that growing numbers of "successful" Anglo-Saxon Negroes feel the same way.

What challenges are facing HBCUs today?

White schools now see the value in black athletes filling their stadiums although they do not graduate. White schools now see the value in bringing youngsters to white campuses so they can get the financial aid packages, although they do not graduate. White schools now see there are black students who are superior academically to their students. If they have to have some of us, then they want our best. Therefore, the challenge now is to keep the doors of historically black colleges and universities open. The challenge now is to not let our people become victimized by the stereotypes that black people cannot do anything right.

There are 134 synonyms in the dictionary for the word "black"; 75 percent of them have negative connotations. Seventy-five synonyms in the dictionary for the word "white"; 75 percent of them have positive connotations. "Black" is lazy, shiftless, and no good. You are blackballed, blackmailed, and blacklisted. The angel food cake is white and the devil food cake is black. Therefore, we still have the stereotypical attitude that if it is a black school, it is inferior and there is something wrong with it. If it is a white school, it has to be all right simply because it is white. Many white schools are not regionally accredited whereas 98 percent of all black schools are regionally accredited. Black schools will survive just as our people have survived. Black schools will survive because committed black people will see to it. Black schools will survive because white racists will continue to demonstrate by their racist actions the need for black schools to continue to exist. If black schools do not survive, then black people, black culture, and black heritage will not survive.

The Clinton-Gore administration has done an outstanding job of providing potential resources for poor and oppressed people. They have initiated legislation and worked with the Black Caucus and others that support us to implement that legislation. They placed outstanding blacks and other minority group members in many critical positions.

The problem is the white schools and their organizations still have more power and control. They exert that power and control to maintain their dominance over resources and decisions.

There are also many white people in career program positions in the federal government who simply slow down the process and wait for the next administration. They do not know about black schools. They do not want to know about them. They believe that our schools are inferior. They view their responsibility as being to block access to federal resources for black schools. Federal resources are important because many states interpret "states' rights" as being separate and unequal, and want to turn back the clock.

Sadly, we have a growing number of Negro Anglo-Saxons who believe their attainment is because of their own abilities. Gaining the acceptance of white people is more important to them than the progress of our people and our institutions. Their behaviors and actions have the same impact on our people and institutions as the white people described in the preceding statement.

Another way to look at the challenges is to examine the percentages of total expenditures of the federal budget for postsecondary institutions received by black institutions. Realize that the remaining percentages went to historically white institutions. In 1999, historically black colleges and universities received from the Agency for International Development, which sponsors programs overseas, 7 percent; Department of Agriculture, 9 percent; Department of Defense, 3 percent; Department of Education, 7 percent; Department of Energy, 3 percent; Department of Health and Human Services, 2 percent; Department of Housing and Urban Development, 18 percent; U.S. Information Agency, 3 percent; Justice Department, 3 percent; Department of the Interior, 20 percent; Labor Department, 47 percent; National Aeronautics and Space Administration, 6 percent; National Credit Union Administration, 19 percent; National Endowment for the Arts, 1 percent; National Endowment for the Humanities, 1 percent; National Science Foundation, 1 percent; U.S. Nuclear Regulatory Commission, 6 percent; U.S. Small Business Administration, 4 percent; Social Security Administration, 32 percent; U.S. Department of State, 4 percent; U.S. Department of Veterans Affairs, 2 percent; Department of Commerce, 1 percent; Department of Transportation, 8 percent; Department of the Treasury, 20 percent. The total awards of federal money to white schools were $32,406,669,831. Black schools received $1,344,697,091, or 4 percent of the total awards of federal money to postsecondary institutions.

If you take that information and then look at how the states fund HBCUs in relation to how they fund white schools, then you get a good idea of what the issue will be for the continued existence of HBCUs. Let me use Ohio as an example. We have many racist legislators in the state of Ohio; one thought it more important to fund programs for hogs at The Ohio State University than black people at Central State University. In the 1960s, 1970s, and 1980s, we had smart, militant, and courageous black legislators like C. J. McLin, Jr., William Bowen, and Bill Mallory who fought for black people and black institutions. They maintained a Democratic balance that kept the conservatives in check. After forty years of checks and balances, the Republicans gained control of the governor's office, the senate, and the house. The Republicans retaliated by attempting to dismantle and destroy programs and institutions that had been designed to protect and create access for black, poor, and oppressed people. One legislator stated that his attempt to destroy Central State University was his way of getting revenge on a now-deceased powerful black man.

The state of Ohio refused to respond to the fact that the federal government told it that it was guilty of discrimination against Central State University in 1981. The state had still not responded as late as 1997. During the Reagan and Bush administrations the federal government pulled back. The Clinton administration came back and reiterated the discrimination charge. Governor Vonovich still refused to address the issue. Central State is in the same predicament it was in nineteen years ago. The state of Ohio is still not putting enough money into Central State. The university has been denied at least $110 million since 1981.

Black people are another challenge for HBCUs. Black people have to stop letting whites decide that our youngsters do not have the ability or should not go to college any longer. We have to start identifying our youngsters at the kindergarten, first-, second-, third-grade levels, and start preparing them for college. We need to start, right now! We have to start developing their skills and refuse to let, blindly, our youth go to junior colleges where many are not going to graduate either. We have to say that we want these youngsters to go to four-year historically black colleges and universities where we know that they will get the love, trust, respect, and education that they need. Not only do we need to say it; we have to do what is necessary to make it happen.

HBCUs are successful with graduating black college students. What is it that HBCUs provide black students?

First, black college students at HBCUs see a black woman president or a black man president. They see blacks in leadership.

On a daily basis, the youngsters are told that we expect them to succeed. On a daily basis, the youngsters who may not have all of their financial aid papers in order get the help they need until those papers are in order. On a daily basis, if somebody is shot at home or somebody dies from an overdose at home, they get the understanding and the sensitivity to those issues that they need. We work with them through the rough times. On a daily basis, if a young lady gets pregnant, there is somebody to whom she can talk, and who works with her until she can continue her education. In continuing, she can provide a better life for herself and her child. On a daily basis, students get the same type of care and support they get from their families as well as the expertise and skills they need to continue to develop at any level after they leave that historically black college.

There is no question about it in my mind. The toughest schooling I ever had was at Central State University. There are a number of HBCU graduates from a cross-section of backgrounds who say the same thing about their HBCU experiences. The most demands that were ever put on me were at Central State University. The most caring people in an educational institution that I met in my life, people who cared about my success and me, were at Central State University.

What do you see as the impact on HBCUs of the anti–affirmative action movement in higher education?

It is a negative impact. Any time you take black people out of the loop, it is a negative impact on black people, period. The HBCUs do not want to survive just because they are HBCUs. HBCUs want to survive so they can continue to contribute to the progress of black people.

Not all black youngsters are going to attend HBCUs. We do not want black people to be denied access to anywhere they need and want to go. A black youngster in California who is knocking the top off exams in physics may need to go to a school out there where he or she can get in school and commute home on a regular basis. We do not want white people deciding where our opportunities should be. We have to have access to any place our youngsters want to go. We do not want to go backward. If we keep going the way we are going we will be back at Jim Crow, The Black Codes, and being denied the right to vote.

I wonder if somebody calculated how many hangings there were in 1899 compared to how many police assassinations there have been in the year 2000. I wonder if we would come out just about the same with hangings as we do now with blacks getting their heads dragged off in Texas or their brains blown out in New York City. In many respects, we are going backwards.

I am thankful to have had the opportunity to work with Louis Stokes, William Blakey, and Adib Shakir to develop a multi-million-dollar program that is operating in several HBCUs now dealing with the issue of "The Survival of the Black Male."

I am proud of my work with 23 African countries and 123 African students and disappointed that many blacks have some of the same attitudes as many whites toward Africa. Some of them say they want nothing to do with Africa. Malcolm X once said, "Some Negroes left their minds in Africa."

Some of our people are moving forward, but many of our people are moving backwards. Many of our people are moving backwards because of the diseases that confront us, because of the unemployment that confronts us, because of the lack of opportunities that confront us, and because of the real racist attitudes of white people. I do not see any real difference in the legislature in the state of Ohio and other states, and in what the white police are doing in New York. They are all denying black people opportunity. They are cutting short our potential. They are all saying, "Black people, you are not as good as white people, and you do not deserve the resources that white people have."

What is the most important thing African Americans need to understand about HBCUs?

HBCUs belong to us. They were created for us and if we are going to continue to progress, they must be used by us. We must advance them. We must improve them. We must use them for the cause of our people. We have to move HBCUs forward. They must become vital to the age of technology, to distance learning, and everything else. As far as public HBCUs are concerned, we put enough money into state taxes to provide the resources for those historically black colleges and universities. Private HBCUs put enough investments into the nation that they deserve resources put into them.

If black schools were not around do you think white schools would be competing for black youngsters? If black schools were not around, do you think we would have developed leadership like Kweisi Mfume, Jesse Jackson, Hazel O'Leary, Jocelyn Elders, Louis Sullivan, Marion Wright Edelman Young, Vernon Jordan, Alexis Herman, Thurgood Marshall, David Satcher, and Frederick Humphries, to name a few? If black schools were not around, do you think we would have some of the progressive attitudes that we have towards the economy and other issues that were really nurtured in historically black colleges and universities?

Many white people see us as their servants, not their equals. We have to understand that. They do not like black people who stand up to them. They do not like black people who confront them. They do not like black people who tell them that they are wrong. They do not like black people who tell them that they are racist. They do not like people who will not allow them or permit them to step on them. HBCUs are successful at developing these types of blacks. HBCUs develop blacks who can compete, who stand up, who refuse to be denied while simultaneously trying to keep the door open for other black people as they move along.

"None of us is free until all of us are free." My job is not done until every sister in the projects has at least a bachelor's degree; until every little brother and little sister in the projects has access to the job that he or she wants; until every grandmother and every great-grandmother in the projects has what they want and believes that they have developed to the maximum of their potential. That was my goal the first day I started teaching. That is my goal today.

What do non–African Americans need to understand about HBCUs?

That we will fight for survival just as hard as they fought to steal America from the Native Americans, and Africa from the Africans. That black people are wise to racist white media propaganda about our institutions and our people. That we do not have time to waste explaining, apologizing, and making excuses to them to get their support. That we feel the same way about our institutions that they feel about their institutions.

What are your thoughts on regional accreditation and HBCUs?

Anything in which we do not participate in the formulation of—anything in which we do not participate in from the ground floor—is something that is going to be used against us negatively in America. That is the way it has been and that is the way it will always be until we do something about it.

If the doctrines of equality, equity, and quality of postsecondary education were exercised, and if African Americans had full access to white institutions, would we still need HBCUs?

When Thurgood Marshall and those brilliant lawyers were preparing for the Supreme Court decision in 1954, the main issue as I recall was not about sitting down next to white people. The main issue was that all the resources needed to make black students the absolute best were in the white schools. Therefore, if black children were going to have access to the best chemistry labs, to the best physics labs, to the best biology programs, to the best English programs, the best language programs, then they would have to go to white schools to get them. The issue was having access to the best possible educational programs.

Malcolm X said it best when he said, "Sitting down next to white people on the toilet is not a revolution." We need access. We need the very best in our schools. Where there are too many white people in the institutions, then the institutions become white. You have to think white. You have to act white. You have to do white. White schools have failed at developing black Ph.D.s in physics, chemistry, math, and computer science. They have failed because they do not want to succeed. Black schools must succeed because white schools have failed.

The new frontier for our people will not only be economics, civil rights, and the Internet. It will also be genetics, urban space planning, human transplantation, environmental issues, germ warfare, to name a few. We cannot rely on placing our future in the hands of those that have systematically oppressed, dehumanized, and denied us.

The mission of HBCUs is to educate and to transmit the cultural heritage. There are about 3,000 white institutions in the nation. They all transmit their cultural heritage. They will talk about George Washington,

Abraham Lincoln, and Thomas Jefferson. They all talk about Woodrow Wilson, even though he segregated the public toilets in Washington, D.C. They all talk about Franklin D. Roosevelt, even though he told jokes about blacks in the White House. They transmit their cultural heritage. Well, we need to transmit our cultural heritage too, and we do that through HBCUs. Transmitting the cultural heritage is the responsibility of HBCUs. The issue is bigger than equality, equity, and quality. It is transmitting the cultural heritage; it is economic, political, and cultural survival.

When people talk about equality, equity, and quality, I do not know about whom they are talking. I assume they are talking about white people. They are false doctrines because they were not meant to include us in the first place. That is what throws blacks off all of the time. We start thinking white people are talking about us with these doctrines. They are not talking about us. They are talking about white people. Once we get that clear in our minds, then we can focus on educating our people. When they say "all men are created equal," they were not and still are not talking about us. If they were talking about us, why would they spend so much more money per child in the white suburbs than they spend in the black inner city? Why would police protection be so much better in the white suburbs than it is in the inner city? Why would blacks be dying at sixty-five while whites die at seventy-five? Why do we have a higher rate of AIDS, a higher rate of tuberculosis, and a higher rate of hypertension? Why are so many of us in jail? The average black man dies at sixty-five. On the average, we do not live long enough to get social security. White women live the longest.

Any final comments?

Based on my experiences and first-hand knowledge, there are outstanding models of black academic excellence. Anybody interested in advancing the cause of historically black colleges and universities needs to go to these campuses and talk to these presidents. They need to look at the progress these HBCU presidents have made and the directions they are taking Historically Black Colleges and Universities. These presidents are doing by demonstration and action. They are not just talking.

Some examples are Frederick Humphries at Florida A&M University, William Harvey at Hampton University, Delores Spikes at Maryland Eastern Shore, Ernest Holloway at Langston University, Earl Richardson at Morgan State University, John Henderson at Wilberforce University, and Norman Francis at Xavier University. There are of course many others. All HBCUs are doing an outstanding job in some capacity for our children and for our people. They all confront racism, oppression, and conspiracies every day of their existence. All black schools move our people forward individually and collectively every day of their existence. They have not brought us this far to leave us.

Linette P. Fox

Linette Fox is originally from Anson County, North Carolina. At the age of eleven, she moved to Charlotte. She received her bachelor's degree from Bennett College in business education with a concentration in accounting. Bennett is a historically black women's institution in Greensboro, North Carolina. Her MBA degree, with a concentration in management, is from the University of North Carolina at Greensboro. Her doctorate in management and organization development with an emphasis in entrepreneurship is from The Union Institute in Cincinnati.

She is a tenured assistant professor of business administration at Johnson C. Smith University. Johnson C. Smith is a private HBCU. Her primary teaching focus is in management; however, on occasion she teaches economics and some interdisciplinary courses. In addition to her teaching and mentoring responsibilities, she is the director of the Urban Research Group.

Her other professional experiences at Johnson C. Smith were as director of the Banking and Finance Center and chair of the Department of Business and Economics. She has been at Johnson C. Smith for sixteen years.

Fox began her college teaching career at North Carolina Central University, a public HBCU in Durham. She taught in the public administration program. Her academic expertise, particularly in accounting, afforded her the opportunity to provide technical assistance to governmental agencies, public organizations such as the Employment Security Commission, and community-based organizations. Upon leaving North Carolina Central, she taught at Barber-Scotia College, a private HBCU in Concord, North Carolina, in the Department of Business and Economics.

The following is the conversation the author had with Linette Fox about her experiences as an HBCU faculty member, the students, and her work with them.

Frequently, you have characterized yourself as "a child of the community." What do you mean by that?

Until I was eleven years old, my grandmother reared my sister, brother, and me. During the great migration north, most of her sons and daughters migrated to the North for improved employment. My grandmother insisted that my mother, in particular, and some of her other children, not take the grandchildren with them.

My grandmother was unsure of how we would be reared and what the possibilities were. Moreover, some people in the South negatively stereotyped the North in terms of raising children. So my grandmother did not want that to happen. That was one of the reasons why we did not go. The other reason was my grandmother was a widow and she needed the majority of the grandchildren to help maintain the farm because we were sharecroppers. So she needed that kind of assistance. She took care of eight of her grandchildren. It was not until much later in life that I understood that whole transaction. I always thought, "Now what happened that I ended up here."

When my grandmother passed away, I ended up in Charlotte with my mother's sister and her husband. There were some personal issues. My mother was not considered stable in terms of her borderline alcoholism. I thought that she was probably capable. But her brothers, sisters, and mother felt she was not, and they did not think that it was good for children to be brought up in a household where alcohol was consumed on a regular basis. I do not think it was an official vote. But my aunts and uncles decided that my mother's children should go in different directions just to avoid what they believed to be a household that was not conducive to what they believed would be a sound family structure for the children. I ended up in Charlotte with my mother's sister and her younger two children. I came to the house as the oldest child, which meant that I served as my aunt's assistant and helped with the other children. I must admit that I missed my older sister. Fortunately, she graduated from high school and moved to Charlotte to begin her career by the time I started junior high school. Although she did not live with us, she played a major role in my emotional and economic well being.

We were very active in the church in our community. Along with the family, a lot of my upbringing, background, and values came from the church. I discovered later that most people did not know to whom I belonged because my last name was different from my aunt's last name. My last name was Pratt, and there was nobody in the church whose last name was Pratt.

My aunt and uncle frequented the church but not as much as I did. Since the church was down the street, we could walk there. My aunt and uncle were rather strict, and we really could not go anywhere else except church. At church, everybody just reached out to me—our minister, my Sunday school teachers, and women in the church.

We were poor. When I needed anything, my older sister and the community helped. If I was not going to participate in a school activity because I did not have proper clothing, which would happen on occasion, somebody in the church would make sure I had what I needed. There was somebody up the street, there was somebody in the back of us, somebody on the other street. All of these people were looking out for me, encouraging me as well as providing assistance with homework whenever I needed it.

My aunt and uncle both worked outside of the home. My aunt and uncle's goal for us was to get a high school diploma. They did not want anything to happen until we got that diploma. However, they were not really focused on going to college. The other voices in the community and at the church felt I should go to college. They were telling me, "You want to do that" or "You want to do this." They would do whatever they needed to help me. They identified resources such as people in other communities who were familiar with colleges and universities. They made sure that I saw the guidance counselors and talked with them about college. There was always that kind of support at church and in the community. All of these influences had an impact on me. That is why I say I was a child of the community.

What do you consider the role of HBCUs in American higher education?

Considering that this is the third HBCU in which I have taught and I received my undergraduate degree from an HBCU, I think that the role of the HBCU primarily is to continue to increase the number of African American young people who get their bachelor's degrees. I know there are HBCUs that also provide master's degrees and a handful that offer doctorates. I think that the HBCU environment is more conducive to learning and enhancing the self-image and confidence of undergraduate black students in particular. This is especially true when compared to majority universities. Majority universities may be more appropriate for some black students. However, I do not believe that they can provide or are even willing to provide the support that many black college students need to improve the potential quality of their lives.

The HBCU role is to be that instrument for continuously increasing the numbers of African American males and females to get that bachelor's degree, and move out into the world of work into positions that they probably would not have been able to get had they not been able to go to college. In addition, the role of HBCUs is to increase the number of African Americans who complete graduate school, at both the master's and doctoral levels.

At HBCUs, the small classes are more conducive to the black students who are not as competitive as other students are, as well as black students who are very competitive. I have experiences with a few students in business administration who have gone to majority institutions but somehow or another they just did not make it. One student in particular graduated from here two years ago and is currently working on her master's degree at the University of South Carolina. She left Wake Forest and came to Johnson C. Smith University because "it wasn't happening" for her there. She graduated from Johnson C. Smith University with honors and was offered top jobs. Had she not had a Johnson C. Smith University to come to, she may have dropped out of college and just been out there. Therefore, I think the HBCU plays a major role in increasing the numbers of college graduates within the black community.

At Johnson C. Smith, we are beginning to look into recruiting more Hispanics and other minorities. We believe that some of those young people have similar educational challenges as African Americans.

What is the purpose of the interdisciplinary courses?

At Johnson C. Smith, we have made our liberal studies program more interdisciplinary. This program is used to focus freshmen and sophomores, and introduce them to the departments in which they will major. This gives students an opportunity to interact with the faculty in a variety of departments from the beginning of their college careers. In addition, this increases their potential of completing the requirements for the program that they choose.

Our goal is to have freshmen declare their major at the end of the second semester. Students do not receive an academic advisor until there is official documentation that they declared their majors. Prior to major declaration, students receive advising from mentors. This way they can begin getting advisement from their department major faculty as soon as possible. We want them to have declared their majors by the first semester of their sophomore year. We have not been able to get 100 percent of declared majors by that time.

Each March, we sponsor "March to Your Major." It is like a departmental fair. Freshmen are required to attend. They spend time with faculty in majors in which they are interested. At the end of the event, they completed a form declaring their major. About 25 percent are undecided after this event. I think that is probably going to happen no matter what.

What are the challenges of teaching at an HBCU?

The first challenge is limited resources. This includes human, material, and financial resources. Johnson C. Smith University is a private institution. The funds are not supplemented by the state of North Carolina. We operate primarily on tuition and grants. Therefore, we do have limited financial resources. We also have limited human resources. For example, I am currently director of the Urban Research Group and I have very little administrative assistance. In fact, I have someone who comes in on Monday, Wednesday, and Friday from 2:00 to 5:00. It seems to be the popular time for this young lady to have to take care of some personal matters. So unfortunately, sometimes she is not here. Material resources, we are doing a little better in that area because our student population has increased. Consequently, we have a few more opportunities to buy supplies. That has been very helpful. Because of the Urban Research Group grant, I have been able to secure some of the things that are needed for this particular project. The grant helps to supplement the department and the department supplements the project. This includes access to the computer, the copier, and the fax, to name a few.

Another challenge is what I call "the be twice as good strategy." This strategy requires a lot more time in terms of the classroom teaching, mentoring, coaching, and motivating students. To be twice as good means I have to do twice as much. Sometimes this gets in the way of doing some of the things that are valued at universities—for example, research. I do not have that much opportunity to play that game of doing research and getting it published. I did have a chance to publish a case study in *African American Enterprise Casebook, Volume I* and *African American Enterprises Casebook Teaching Notes, Volume I.* The book was edited by Chi Anyansi-Archibong. The textbook was written with HBCU faculty members at North Carolina Central, North Carolina A&T, Howard University, and a few other universities. I am proud of this accomplishment. I use the book in my small business management class. The book contains case studies that represent successful black entrepreneurs.

I would like to do more research and publishing. However, it requires a different kind of time. Time that is taken from the teaching, mentoring, and coaching. Personally, the teaching, coaching, mentoring, motivating, and encouraging of students is more important. As an HBCU faculty member, I guess it is a question of my values versus someone else's. I do believe strongly that the proof is in the pudding. The more we can do for the students to help them to be ready when they go into the world of work or to graduate school, the better it is going to be for all parties (students, faculty, university, community).

The third challenge is the need to wear more than one hat. Some people say, "Just say no." Nevertheless, there is a need to wear many hats. Many committees work to achieve the goals and objectives of the university. There have to be people who will serve as chair on these committees. I have served as chair of several committees. Some of the committees are much more demanding than others. Some of the demanding committees I chaired are the Judiciary Board, the Educational Policies Committee, and Liberal Studies 235. I do it because of my interest in the university and the students. Interacting with my colleagues at other

HBCUs and some of the conversations that we have indicate that we have similar issues and we have similar rewards and similar challenges.

How would you characterize the students at JCSU?

The majority of the students at JSCU, of course, are black. About 99.5 percent of our students are black. The white students and sometimes Asian and other minority students are here because of the exchange program. Occasionally, we do have a white student who is enrolled as a full-time student of the university.

A large percentage of the students are first-generation college students. Many of them are on financial aid. In fact, there are probably a much larger percentage of them on financial aid than would be at some of the public HBCUs. Much of the aid that they receive at private HBCUs is in the form of loans. A large portion of the students, particularly in my department, which is business administration, work. Surprisingly, many of them work thirty to forty hours a week. They indicate that they need to work in order to pay for college. You can imagine what a challenge that creates for them.

I see some of their material goods. Depending on how well I know the students, I tell them to look at the brand name things they are wearing. I talk to them about reducing credit card balances and how they could work fewer hours if they limited their wardrobe a little bit. By the same token, I do understand that many of us think of ourselves in terms of the way we would hope that others would think of us. Sometimes what we look like paints that picture, at least in our minds. I understand that self-concept/self-image for some is fragile. Students feel the need to have things and those things might make them feel like they are valuable. I try to explain to them that it is better to be than to have. Most of them do not listen to me. Even my own children do not want to her me say that.

At Johnson C. Smith University, we have students who come from various levels of achievement, from the very high achiever to the minimal achievers. One of our roles is to be there for students who probably would not have the opportunity to get their college degrees if it were not for the HBCUs. We have students who did not look good in terms of the SAT scores, in terms of class standing and transcripts. They have also been some of our better students. I do not have a problem with taking the spectrum of achievement. I think it is a good thing. Many of the students at Johnson C. Smith University major in three areas: business administration, computer science, and communications, although all other areas have been increasing in terms of majors over the past three years.

Recently, we have had an increase in the student population. That means we have an increase in applications. Whenever that happens, of course, the university can be a lot more selective. Overall, the students at Johnson C. Smith University are like students at state funded HBCUs. The state HBCUs may have a little more in terms of resources and the availability of scholarships.

You have initiated and received funding for several programs. What are some of them?

I want to talk about three programs. First, there is the Students and Free Enterprise Program. This was my internship when I was working on my doctorate at The Union Institute. This program brings in a few funds through competitions. I do receive a small fellowship at the end of the year each time I take students to competitions, whether they win or not. Fortunately, they do win. They place generally at the first runner-up level. They have won some special competitions. These competitions result in cash awards and these cash awards provide the income that is needed for other things.

The second grant is the Urban Research Group Grant. The purpose of this grant is to provide service to community-based organizations by providing faculty research expertise for community-based organizations. We assist by doing three things: (1) identify community needs by surveying the members of the community, (2) enable communities to document those needs for funding sources, governmental agencies, or whomever they may want to share their needs and concerns with, and (3) we assist communities in expressing their concerns and quantifying those concerns through the research we provide. We have a research group project. It is made of a group of faculty members from various disciplines who have joined to write a grant to the Council of Independent Colleges.

An important element of the Urban Research Group Grant is for each community-based project to have students involved. In fact, this is a strategy we use to increase the potential for students to develop their research skills and to provide an opportunity for them to provide community service at the same time. Generally, the community-based organizations do not pay for the research. When a community organization does have funds, they are more than willing to share the cost of the research.

We are pleased with the Urban Research project. It has strengthened the university's image in the community. It has helped the community to understand a little more about what we do at the university. The feedback that we have received from community leaders is that we are doing a wonderful job and they do not want this project to stop at the end of the current funding. We are all working together so the project can continue. The community leaders would like for us to extend our services to include some technical assistance, such as training in grant writing, management, supervision, and team building. This type of training will help community organizations address the problem they have in terms of securing funds and getting their points across about community situations they have and the needs they have.

The third grant, which is part of the Urban Research Group Grant, is one that I wrote in response to a request based on the reputation of the group. The Alcohol Beverage Control (ABC) Board approached me to determine if we could provide assistance for them with their grants program. Through this ABC Board program, funds are established to provide grants for community organizations that want to provide substance abuse prevention education. We applied for this grant and it was approved. The source of funding for this project is the ABC Board.

We assist the community organizations in creating their grant proposals primarily in the area of what we call SMART objectives. SMART is an acronym for objectives that are Specific, Measurable, Achievable, Realistic, and Time based. We work with them through these objectives. We established a structure for them so that they provide formative and summative evaluations. They provide qualitative and quantitative information to us. We take that data, analyze it, and produce an evaluation report for the ABC Board. The report provides the Board with indicators of how effectively the funds are being spent.

Before this project began, the board believed that they were not receiving enough acceptable grant proposals from community groups. The community groups were having trouble measuring results and addressing accountability issues for the recipients of the grants. The goal of the ABC Board for this project is to increase the quality of the proposals that they receive from the community-based organizations. It is our responsibility to work with the community-based organizations to achieve the goal. I have received feedback from the ABC staff that this year's proposals were much improved. Last week I received a call from the board asking us to continue the project.

Johnson C. Smith University students are involved in many ways in the ABC Board project. They code data, input data, administer surveys, and assist in designing some of the instruments that we use, such as feedback and evaluation instruments. This happens both in class and outside of class. Students are also tapped for internship opportunities at some of the community-based organizations. They are available for any workshops or training sessions that we do or that the community leaders do. Through their involvement, students are developing communication skills, leadership skills, management and planning skills, and they are representing the university well. This is always a plus for the image of the university. The feedback we get from students who participate in the project indicates that they benefit tremendously. We believe that student involvement is important for two reasons. One reason is it helps develop their research skills. The other reason is it is an opportunity for them to provide community service.

Johnson C. Smith University is a member institution of the United Negro College Fund (UNCF). While you were working on your doctorate, you received a grant from UNCF. What was the purpose of the funding and how did you use it?

I received the UNCF IBM Doctoral Fellowship. The fellowship is for faculty from HBCUs who are pursuing their doctorates in the area of management or business administration. I received the doctoral fellowship for two years. Having the fellowship afforded me the opportunity to study full-time for my doctorate. Before my nomination for the fellowship, I do not think UNCF had any experience with non-traditional doctoral programs.

The fellowship was very helpful. It gave me a chance to be out of work for two years, and my tuition and fees were covered. It did not provide for everything for my household. Therefore, in that regard, I am grateful to my husband who paid all of our bills.

Any final comments?

I received information about The Union Institute's doctoral program from the Johnson C. Smith University Office of Academic Affairs. The president of our university at that time, Dr. Robert Albright, and the people in the office of academic affairs were very aware of my work at the university, and were pleased with the leadership roles that I had taken. In addition, they were pleased with my impact on students, my student evaluations, and my performance appraisal. They wanted to do what they could to help me get a doctorate. They understood my family obligation, with two children who were teenagers. I could not get away and study for a doctorate. I could not leave my children here in the care of others.

There were not any doctoral programs nearby that provided the doctorate in management. In addition, three traditional programs, to which I applied, had extremely limited enrollment. The traditional programs generally accepted two or three people a year. Unfortunately, I did not have the political connections that would make me one of the two or three. I did make it as far as the interview for two of the institutions to which I applied. About eight people were interviewed. Need I say more? The family issues and the availability and accessibility of traditional doctoral programs are a challenge for many HBCU faculty members.

The Union program became a viable option for me. I had a conference with Robert Albright and we talked about my plans. He was more than willing to nominate me for the UNCF fellowship for studying at The Union Institute.

He complimented me for my willingness to go on and try to get the doctorate and to do it in a nontraditional way. I did not realize it, but apparently he thought it would be difficult because of the need to work independently and the tremendous amount of discipline that it would require. I knew this would be required.

The Union program was one of the best education experiences I have had. It was tough. In fact, my two doctoral committee adjuncts commented on how much I had to do to complete the requirements of my degree. Professor Lyons at Tennessee State University was an adjunct on my doctoral committee. She told me that if I ever decided to get another doctorate, it would be a lot easier to go the traditional way. Perhaps that is true, but I would not trade my Union experience for anything in the world.

I very much appreciate the way the program is structured. The emphasis is interdisciplinary, with a focus on social relevance and the importance of work on self, while working on the academic side of everything. All of that came together very well for me. Of course, it was challenging to assume the role of chair of my doctoral committee. However, having you, Dr. Jackson, as my first core faculty advisor (teacher, researcher, mentor, coach, editor) made it manageable and exciting. What a tremendous opportunity for personal and professional growth. I cannot thank you enough.

Based on my background and my experiences, the Union was made for me and I really thank God for that. I tell others about the Union and its HBCU Initiative. I cannot emphasize enough what an outstanding experience it was for me.

TWO PROGRAMS DESIGNED TO ASSIST HBCUs

Increasingly, efforts are emerging from a variety of sectors to assist in strengthening and enhancing Historically Black Colleges and Universities. Two such efforts are described below. The first describes a partnership between a state and a private entity. The other describes an educational access program established by a university. A central theme of both programs is collaboration and cooperation among African Americans for the greater good.

Both programs are in white organizations. Because of this, two mandatory factors contributed to the success of both. One factor is an African American whose position in the organization reflects a sufficient level of authority to make the program a reality. The other factor is the necessity of the unchanging support for the programs by the presidents of the organizations.

The Historically Minority Universities Bioscience and Biotechnology Program Initiative

Eleanor Nunn is a native of Raleigh, North Carolina. She received her bachelor's degree from Shaw University, a private historically black institution in Raleigh. She majored in biology. Her two master's degrees are in science education and public administration, from Duke University and the University of North Carolina at Chapel Hill, respectively. She is a Ph.D. candidate at The Union Institute. Her field of study is technology and public policy.

Currently, she is the director of the Historically Minority Universities Bioscience and Biotechnology Program Initiative at the North Carolina Biotechnology Center. The program is commonly known as the HMU Program Initiative. The center is a private nonprofit research organization.

She brings to this position an eclectic professional background. She was the director of a Head Start program in Rochester, New York. She was employed by Louis Harris and Associates to conduct surveys on the economic status of people in rural North Carolina. She was the director of recruitment and a budget analyst for the state of North Carolina. Nunn has conducted consultative services for several universities to address affirmative action issues concerning minority students at majority universities. She was a high school science teacher in Rochester, New York, and in New York City. As a member of the Peace Corps, she was science department chairperson and teacher at an agricultural college in Northern Nigeria.

Nunn has served on several state, national, and international committees and commissions focused on people of the African Diaspora and science. In March 2000, she returned to Nigeria to participate in "Biodiversity, Biotechnology, and Law" training to create an expert knowledge base and network in West Africa to address issues related to biodiversity, biotechnology industry, and activities in Africa.

The author had the opportunity to talk with Eleanor Nunn about the HMU Program Initiative's impetus, mission, goals, successes, and challenges, as well as HBCUs, generally. That conversation follows.

When, how, and why was the HMU Program Initiative established?

Officially, the HMU Initiative Program was established in 1993. It was established through special legislation passed by the North Carolina General Assembly. The background on the special legislation is interesting and unique. Speaker of the House of Representatives for the state of North Carolina Dan Blue spearheaded and sanctioned the program. Speaker Blue was the first African American to hold the position—at least, the first since Reconstruction. Speaker Blue provided the leadership for the collaboration of several black legislators; private citizens in key positions in nonprofit organizations; the president of the North Carolina Biotechnology Center, Charles Hamner, as well as Arch Nakaboo, who was vice president for finance at the center; and Andrea Harris, who was president of the Institute of Minority Economic Development. Their collaborative efforts planted the seed for the need to have a program that would help to jump-start the five public historically black universities and the one public Native American university toward improving their bioscience and biotechnology capacities. The five public Historically Black Colleges and Universities are Fayetteville State University, North Carolina Central University in Durham, Winston-Salem State University, North Carolina A&T University in Greensboro, and Elizabeth City State University. The public Native American postsecondary institution is University of North Carolina at Pembroke. For purposes of this interview, I will only focus on the five public HBCUs.

The early collaboration made it relatively easy for North Carolina legislators to be supportive of such an initiative. This is especially true in light of the fact that North Carolina was rapidly becoming one of the leading states in the South in biotechnology. While this big surge was taking place the three white universities were getting the attention and the money. These three institutions are Duke University, North Carolina State University, and the University of North Carolina at Chapel Hill. The Historically Black Colleges and Universities had not been totally involved in the process. As industries and manufacturing companies came into the state, they needed a pool or a source of potential talent. It suddenly dawned on people: what better place to look than at the HBCUs, who historically and traditionally had never been part of the research concept of biotechnology?

Technology involves research. Usually, educational institutions are the leaders in the development of new concepts and new ideas. Most often, these are nonminority institutions. The HMU Program Initiative is the state's acknowledgment of the potential at minority institutions to generate a level of talent that is very, very important to the whole technological portrait.

The pattern of marginalizing HBCUs in biotechnology occurred out of the history of historically separating the schools on a racial basis. The white schools, especially the larger white schools, always had the lion's share of resources and academic opportunities, while the minority institutions were shortchanged. As North Carolina moves towards more high technology in everything, and the country becomes more of a technological society, it is very clear that there are certain resources that are required to be competitive.

Historically, minority institutions have not been competitive because resources have been distributed unequally, unfairly, and of lesser quality. The reality is that although HBCUs and white institutions taught chemistry, biology, physics, and at one HBCU engineering, the HBCUs did not have access to the quality of equipment and the equity of resource distribution. This stymied the abilities of HBCU faculty to do the same kinds of things that some of the well-funded white institutions were able to do.

North Carolina is one of the leading states in the South where the emphasis in biotechnology is expanding. Companies all over the world continuously look at North Carolina as a possible site for either a corporate office or a manufacturing plant. These employers were willing to hire anyone who had the capacity to do what they needed to be done. It was necessary then to have a better and larger pool of potential talent available. The question became, can we relocate all of the needed talent to North Carolina to occupy these facilities, or do we develop our human capital to be sources of potential workers in the state? One of the potential sources within the state was the pool from HBCUs. Therefore, the state's economic development necessitated the program.

Historically, the source of potential workers has not been from the five public and six private Historically Black Colleges and Universities in North Carolina. There have always been HBCU students graduating with degrees in the sciences. Many have not considered the changing opportunities out there and the availability of those opportunities simply by adding a few courses or revising a few of the traditional courses that would make them competitive. HBCUs do not always have to revise their traditional curricula totally. Sometimes it is a matter of adding topics or courses to bridge the old with the new.

Through the program we have collaborated with these companies and placed youngsters in internships. This exposure lets them see that with the proper equipment and the proper course work, there is very little difference between a well-equipped undergraduate laboratory and a highly sophisticated laboratory. The techniques are the same.

What is the mission of the HMU Program Initiative?

As I mentioned earlier, biotechnology is a growing industry in North Carolina. Through the program, money is used to enhance the public HBCUs in the area of bioscience and biotechnology to enable them to attract students to these fields. Generally, curricula revisions and acquisition of academic resources is what has occurred through the program. In turn, HBCU graduates can fill some of the many, many positions that are available and are becoming available in biotechnology. The mission, therefore, is to enhance the capacity of North Carolina's five public HBCUs in the areas of bioscience and biotechnology, thereby creating a larger pool of African Americans in these fields.

What are the goals of the HMU Program Initiative?

The HMU Program Initiative is an economic-based program, although it is educationally undergirded. To have adequate minority human potential in these fields you have to be proactive. There has to be a plan that indicates at every level how you are trying to increase the number of minorities who are competitive in the sciences. You cannot just talk about it. Strategic planning and resources have to be available to assure a greater possibility of increasing the numbers.

One goal is to develop a competitive pool of African American students who can move from the undergraduate classroom into one of three places: (1) enter graduate programs in the sciences, (2) enter the technological workplace immediately after receiving the baccalaureate degree, or (3) enter graduate programs in the health-related professions.

Another goal is that the program is directed by the people who are most affected. These people are the universities' faculty, administrators, and students. Each school had to recognize its status and condition. This is not something that could be determined by the North Carolina General Assembly, the North Carolina Biotechnology Center, or anyone in a biotechnology firm. Typically, when institutions apply for grants they have to develop plans based on preconceived, established standards. Institutions are required to fit their needs to accommodate the granting organizations' standards. We did the reverse.

It was decided that each university would develop a plan. The plan would identify where they are, where they want to be, and what are their strengths and weaknesses. A review of the plans showed clearly that the schools were not homogeneous. Each of the five public HBCUs had varying degrees of strengths and weaknesses. The idea was that in order to move to the next level, each school needed support, and each school could identify what degree of support they wanted.

The HBCUs have science departments already. When you talk about developing curricula, what are you talking about?

Most HBCUs have biology. Very few of them have microbiology. Most HBCUs have chemistry. Very few have biochemistry. Most of the undergraduate programs did not have microbiology, genetics, or any types of programs that looked at and had the capacity to focus on bioinformatics or genetic engineering. This was true for three reasons:

(1) They did not have the equipment. (2) The faculty was not trained in these areas. (3) The curricula did not include these areas. Although biology was a component of every science department, now they needed to include bioethics, bioinformatics, microbiology, or some combination of the three. These are some of the pieces that are instrumental in making students competitive once they graduate and enter the technological or the biotechnological work environment, or graduate school.

Based on their needs assessments, we found that they all had one need in common. The science curricula had to be revised because the sciences are changing. To stay competitive, they had to recognize the need for change and do what was necessary.

The institutions whose involvement you have talked about are the public historically black universities. There are six private Historically Black Colleges and Universities in the state of North Carolina. Do these HBCUs have an opportunity to come under the umbrella of the program?

Absolutely. The funding was for the public HBCUs. The only reason the funding was done for the public institutions was that it was easier to operate within the public domain for a certain sense of continuity, strategically and politically. However, from the beginning the six private HBCUs in North Carolina have all been part of the process. They are represented on committees. I have worked with them individually to make them aware of the additional resources that the center can offer.

Separate and apart from the program, there are other opportunities through the center. Consequently, the private HBCUs as well as the public HBCUs have received grants awarded by the North Carolina Biotechnology Center. These awards would in all likelihood not occur if they had not been involved in the HMU Program Initiative process. The involvement of private HBCUs in the program enabled them to be part of the environment with which they were not familiar or in which they were not comfortable before the program.

What is the range of the awards outside of the program that are granted, and what are the types of needs addressed?

The center, as a private nonprofit entity, has a budget. The resources come from a variety of places—the government as well as other sources. There are different departments in the center, such as an educational unit and a business unit. There are opportunities for North Carolina–based universities to compete for various awards. The HBCUs have been very pleased to know that the North Carolina Biotechnology Center exists. In addition, they know that there are specific programs in which they may be interested. They apply for grants and if they are successful in receiving awards it ranges from a couple of thousand dollars to more than a hundred thousand dollars.

For example, recently the center awarded North Carolina Central University a fairly large award to help them get their biomedical/biotechnology research institute developed and established. Most of the money has been used to help expand curricula and to equip laboratories with supplies and equipment. Some of the smaller grants have been used to have guest scientists speak or conduct demonstrations for faculty and staff, and to have training programs for faculty enhancement.

The North Carolina Biotechnology Center is a private research entity, yet your program is a state-funded program. How did that collaboration or partnership occur and why?

Why was the program placed in a non-profit entity? First, because the president of the North Carolina Biotechnology Center was amenable to receiving this challenge. Second, because of the real lack of trust that many people had in terms of whether or not a university system would be interested in such an endeavor and could overcome the historic stigma of unfairly doling out resources. If extra funds were given, there was doubt that the universities that really needed these resources would receive them. To ensure that HBCUs would receive the resources, it was decided that a neutral noneducational entity with a strong passion for education and fairness would be given the opportunity to receive these funds. This made it possible to develop a program designed to enhance the capacity of the HBCUs in the area of biotechnology.

The HMU Program Initiative is in the Office of the President of the Center. What do you see as the advantages of that placement?

My first step in developing the program was to meet with the center's president about the kinds of things that one would expect in putting together a program from the ground up, generally. New programs, and especially new programs that will embrace moving people into what is considered nontraditional areas for them have to have the highest point of leadership supporting it. Dr. Hamner, the president of the center, was extremely committed to the program the first day, and his support continues. He has been very involved in making certain that the black universities accepted this program. Not because the state and someone external felt that this was important, but because the HBCUs recognized the program as a means to enhance their institutions.

The program is voluntary. The program has to meet each individual institution's needs. The HBCUs are not in any way to feel as though one institution had to be competitive with another. They do not have to duplicate efforts. The HBCUs have to create their individual program plans. Over time, the participants are expected to become collaborative and share information across institutions. It is important for the HBCUs to recognize that there can be strength in numbers.

What are the successes and the challenges of the HMU Program Initiative?

We are in the process of program evaluation. Future data will more accurately determine just what components have been more strategically significant in helping the program to recognize its successes.

However, there are indicators of success as viewed by the individual institutions and the global plan that was set forth for this initiative. A success is seeing a fully equipped, high-tech facility evolve where once it was an empty room. A success is once having a few students sitting in a classroom with just textbooks and a blackboard, and they are now in a high-tech, state-of-the-art-equipped facility where fifteen to twenty budding future scientists are engaged in research projects. A success is having collaborative relationships with scientists and health professionals in countries around the world. This was unheard of for young black college students at HBCUs. These are just a few examples.

I think the challenges are self-imposed. There are opportunities. There are ways to accomplish anything with a little creativity, commitment, and compassion. There will always be the challenges for faculty, for students, and even for the colleges and universities to do things as rapidly and as completely as they would like to have things done. I encourage people that challenges to which they are committed are just opportunities that will take a little more time to achieve than was initially thought.

In the Fordice *decision of the United States Supreme Court, Mississippi was ordered to determine if racially identifiable universities are a vestige of the historically segregated public higher education system. In several states, HBCUs are starting to lose their historical racial identification, mission, and focus. Either certain programs are being placed in public HBCUs as a means of altering the demographics, or HBCUs are designated as regional institutions. For example, Arkansas AM&N is now the University of Arkansas at Pine Bluff. In light of the mission and goals of the HMU Program Initiative, it seems that in North Carolina public Historically Black Colleges and Universities are maintaining their racial identity. First, is this observation correct? Second, what does that say about North Carolina and its HBCUs?*

Many people view North Carolina as a progressive educational state. The jury is still out. North Carolina acknowledges that it has eleven HBCUs, five of which are public HBCUs. The history of these schools has not been researched. Yet they provide strong basic education at the collegiate level. We do not want to see these eleven institutions necessarily become little havens of modest research competency. We still hold dear that there needs to be strong undergraduate scientific education. It is the choice of the HBCU graduates to go beyond the undergraduate level and to attend the major research institutions in the state. HBCUs are the pipelines for this to occur.

We want HBCUs to generate a strong cadre of black youngsters who have been exposed to a quality undergraduate education with all of the resources and facilities of any other undergraduate program. We would like to see these five public HBCUs be so strong that any young-ster worldwide would want to matriculate for a strong undergraduate foundation in technology and bioscience. That will only happen when an environment of quality, equality, and equity is created.

At the same time, the state does not want to erode the history of the public HBCUs. Their history is not just in education but in their grounding. HBCUs are ready to broaden their academic prospective while continuing their strong, capable, competent education.

HBCUs are a given in North Carolina. I do not see any institution being forced out of business. I do not think the state is going to take on try-ing to force institutions to close down or to consolidate or to disintegrate. I do not see public HBCUs losing their cultural identity in North Carolina.

As director of the HMU Program Initiative, you have opportunities to be involved with HBCUs across the country. What do you see as the challenges affecting the current and future status of Historically Black Colleges and Universities nationally?

The challenge is HBCU leadership recognizing the changes that are occurring and being ever mindful of the impact of those changes. The presidents or the leadership of black colleges and universities must be globally involved with events and recognize how events influence their individual institutions. They need to determine the impact they want these external events to have on their institutions. They cannot just go to the federal or state governments or other sources, wanting re-sources. They have to think and plan, thoroughly and clearly, the direc-tions they want their campuses, their universities, and their colleges to take, and the areas around their institutions to grow. Once they have identified the directions in which they want to see these things happen, then and only then are they going to have real control of what happens at their institutions.

I think HBCU leadership is going to have to be revitalized. Lead-ership is going to have to think outside of their campus. What happens on the campus occurs because of a number of external stimuli. It is be-coming increasingly important that education is viewed holistically and that blacks become more flexible in how we command situations and make demands. In short, changes can be very positive for any institu-tion if the leadership has given thought to where they want to see these changes move their institutions.

Any final comments?

The idea of trying to look at a tiny, atypical event that will affect just one life is important. The program will never be able to influence the masses. However, if one person is committed and wanting to be converted, then there are opportunities that can help a few. Even the few like African Americans in the sciences. Our numbers may be dwindling, but there are those students in science who want to be part of this changing or shifting paradigm. It is up to us to provide every opportunity possible. For me this is what the HMU Program Initiative is doing in its small way. My personal bias is that the time for this program has come.

The Union Institute HBCU Initiative

The author was the architect of The Union Institute HBCU Initiative. Following she describes her experience with the first four years of the initiative.

The Union Institute

Regionally accredited by the Commission on Institutions of Higher Education of the North Central Association of Colleges and Schools, The Union Institute (TUI), headquartered in Cincinnati, Ohio, is a national university offering baccalaureate degrees and the doctor of philosophy (Ph.D.) degree to adult learners. Without interrupting one's professional and personal life, the doctoral program offers education with the following distinctions: individualized, interdisciplinary, self-directed tutorial and independent study with nationally respected faculty; demonstrated field proficiency; a doctoral internship; completed dissertation-level projects; and attendance at an in-residence colloquium and three doctoral seminars.

Union was begun in 1964 by a consortium of presidents of higher education institutions who were interested in providing educational access to adult learners. In 1971, TUI became an independent degree-granting institution.

The Impetus of the HBCU Initiative

The HBCU Initiative was not Union's first affiliation with HBCUs. Two HBCUs were members of the founding consortium of the university; and HBCU administrators, faculty, and graduates have obtained Union Institute Ph.D.s since the 1970s. In the past five years, over 150 African

American professionals received their Ph.D. degrees from The Union Institute. In the July 1998 *U.S. News and World Report,* TUI was listed as one of the top five institutions in the country graduating African Americans with doctorates.

Embedded in TUI's mission is the social responsibility of the academy as a force for social change. As such, the HBCU Initiative is in response to Union's mission statement: "Facilitate and support education ventures addressed to serve previously excluded persons." The late Robert T. Conley, TUI president, and members of the graduate college faculty conceived the idea of addressing the historical imbalance of access for African Americans to terminal degrees. Dr. Conley placed his unwavering support as well as full institutional commitment behind this initiative. This was most evident in that, as the program coordinator, I reported directly to him, and he provided adequate institutional and financial support for program start up.

Two concerns are at the core of the HBCU Initiative. First, increasingly, historically black institutions are requiring terminal degrees for faculty to obtain tenure and for the institutions to meet regional accrediting agencies' standards. New faculty members at these institutions tend to have their doctorates when they are hired. Many faculty with long-term employment at the institutions have not been able to pursue or complete doctoral programs. The HBCU Initiative provides a means for the latter group of faculty, in particular, to earn their doctorates.

Second, in conversations with hundreds of HBCU administrators, faculty, and graduates, it was reported to me that traditional doctoral programs were not accessible to them for one of two reasons, or a combination of the two. (1) The need to relocate (short- or long-term) to attend an institution that offers a doctorate in the faculty member's field of study. Relocation can disrupt the HBCU, a career, and family life, as well as requiring additional expense. (2) The lack of faculty at historically white institutions who are willing to serve as mentors and commit themselves to black doctoral students. Many of the faculty members at historically white institutions have decided that black doctoral students, generally, are not qualified to pursue a doctorate. Some are not interested in black students' research focus on African Americans. In most of these institutions, there are few if any African American faculty members who have university status to work with doctoral students. Interview respondents believed that African American faculty would be more inclined to work with them. Repeatedly, African Americans are admitted to doctoral programs and allowed to complete the courses. Yet they are unable to secure a faculty adviser so they can take their written and oral examinations for doctoral candidacy. Being unable to secure a faculty adviser makes it impossible to proceed with the doctoral program.

These two concerns and TUI's mission statement translated into four cornerstones for the HBCU Initiative: (1) The assignment of faculty mentors during the application process or an assurance that each HBCU Initiative doctoral learner will secure a faculty adviser early in their doctoral process. (2) An Entry Colloquium and a seminar specifically designed to strengthen the faculty development network of HBCU faculty, administrator, and graduates. (3) Meetings with prominent African Americans committed to the initiative. (4) A commitment to maintain the integrity of The Union Institute admissions and doctoral program processes.

The Start of the HBCU Initiative

The initiative began in July 1995. The first entry colloquium was convened at Morris College in Sumter, South Carolina. This first group was composed of sixteen new doctoral students. Nine of them were faculty members or administrators from HBCUs in South Carolina and Georgia. Fourteen of them had received their baccalaureate degrees from an HBCU.

There are three reasons why HBCU graduates are involved in a program that focuses on faculty development. First, often HBCU graduates return to HBCUs to serve as faculty members, administrators, or in other professional capacities as a second career. Their involvement at this level reinforces the faculty development focus of the initiative.

Second, as the initiative participants complete their doctoral programs they will expand the network of scholars committed to conducting research on, as well as monitoring the conditions of, the African American community in general and the concerns of HBCUs in particular. In addition, several of the HBCU graduates who participate in the initiative are able to assist HBCUs by informing HBCU faculty and administrators of resources in their respective professional arenas that could be available to HBCUs.

The Goal of the Initiative

The HBCU Initiative affords an avenue of access for blacks with an HBCU affiliation to obtain their doctorates in the arts and sciences. Through the initiative a cadre of black scholars and scholar practitioners would develop. When taken together, the individual inquiry focus of each HBCU Initiative participant would generate accumulated understandings and explanations about the sociological, educational, economic, political, psychological, health, and environmental issues affecting African Americans. The initiative would: (1) provide an opportunity for HBCU faculty, administrators, and graduates to collaboratively dialogue, develop and implement new pedagogy, enhance curriculum, and further social change through their doctoral programs; (2) provide a meeting ground for carefully planned educational research and experimentation within and among HBCUs and their advocates.

The Design of the Initiative

Initiative design is an outgrowth of the program goal. The design had four elements: organizational infrastructure, admissions and mentoring, doctoral residency requirements, and weekend retreats.

There were three aspects of the initiative infrastructure. First, the administrative direction for the initiative was the responsibility of the graduate college dean for underserved populations. The responsibilities included daily administration and determination of the development of the program, public relations, and coordination of program components.

Second, the potential magnitude of the initiative required more than the verbal support of the faculty. The initiative necessitated the active involvement of the faculty. A ten-member graduate college faculty advisory committee was established to work closely with the dean. The committee made recommendations on the direction of the academic components of the initiative, served as liaison for the initiative and the general graduate college faculty members, represented TUI and gave professional presentations at conferences, and assisted with information meetings.

Third, the HBCU Initiative was a focused enterprise to assist systematically with the academic and credential concerns of HBCU faculty, administrators, and graduates. Recognizing this, it was essential to have a link between appropriate HBCU constituencies and The Union Institute. The HBCU National Advisory Council was formed. The eighteen-member council was composed of respected African American scholars, activists, and professionals representing a variety of fields and a cross-section of views about issues concerning African Americans. The commonality of the council members was their commitment to HBCUs and to fortifying their roles in American higher education. The council was a multifaceted consultative body to the dean, which provided informed advice and direction by sharing information to and from HBCUs.

Data informed us that a large number of African Americans who began doctoral programs at historically white institutions were deliberately discouraged, forcing them to exit programs without a degree. This occurred primarily because of their inability to obtain a faculty member who was willing to serve as a mentor and commit to black doctoral students. We wanted to address this concern early in the prospective doctoral student's experience with Union. A cadre of thirty-two graduate college faculty members volunteered to serve as mentors during the admissions process and until the students identified a permanent core adviser. Each HBCU Initiative applicant was assigned to one of the thirty-two faculty members. As mentors to prospective learners, the faculty members provided clarification of admission essays requirements and expectations, answered questions applicants had about Union and its initiative, and addressed any other concerns they might have. Finally, the faculty mentor wrote a letter to the faculty admissions committee describing their impressions of the applicant's abilities to complete the Union doctoral process.

Union's doctoral residency requirements consisted of a ten-day Entry Colloquium, three five-day seminars, and ten Peer Days. The Entry Colloquium and one of the three required seminars were specifically tailored for the initiative. HBCU Initiative learners attended an Entry Colloquium designated for them. This was done to facilitate collaboration and dialogue across HBCU campuses and to encourage graduates of HBCUs to advance the development and implementation of the network, new pedagogy, curriculum, and social change through their doctoral programs. The HBCU seminar was designed to provide an opportunity and a safe space for HBCU Initiative learners to engage issues unique to HBCUs and the larger African American community.

Finally, beginning in 1996, weekend retreats were held. These annual events provided an opportunity for HBCU Initiative learners to interact with members of the National Advisory Council, invited guests, and the public on issues related to the political, economic, and educational conditions of the African American community. The topics of the four retreats were: (1) "The Role of African-Americans in the Transformation of Society," held in 1996; (2) "Internet in the 'Hood: Cyberspace Access for Black Communities," held in 1997; (3) "Science and Technology in the Black Community: Past, Present, and Future," held in 1998, at which the keynote speaker was Charles S. Finch, III, M.D.; and (4) "Challenges of Black Leadership: Towards a New Conversation on Race," held in 1999, at which the keynote speaker was Manning Marable.

Accomplishments and Challenges of the Initiative

The HBCU Initiative has had a number of accomplishments. Most noted is that as of October 1999 eight initiative learners had graduated and over 50 learners were enrolled. Approximately 50 percent of them represented eleven HBCUs as faculty or administrators. The retention rate was approximately 96 percent.

Over 25 fields of study are represented in the HBCU Initiative. The broad range of fields includes social work, philanthropy and leadership, psychology (general, child, social, and educational), community organization, labor and personal relations, criminal justice, education and leadership, environmental studies, and medical sociology.

When interviews with HBCU Initiative graduates and learners are coupled with anecdotal notes, one repeated theme emerges in the responses. At least half of them had attempted doctoral programs at other historically white institutions and the other half were aware anecdotally of the defeating experiences at those institutions. For the first six to nine months in their doctoral program at Union they were "suspicious" that they were being "set up" for another frustrating experience that would ultimately lead to "failure again." All of them reported that camaraderie and peer support among HBCU Initiative participants were vital to sustaining their commitment and overcoming their fear and uncertainty. Furthermore, they reported that the assistance, accessibility, and openness of the faculty and administrators made them feel accepted as equal members of the Union community.

There is one primary challenge for the initiative. There remain a number of HBCU presidents and upper level administrators who have minimal or no knowledge of The Union Institute, its HBCU Initiative, or both. Union is increasing its efforts to remedy this.

A program designated for a certain population must be accommodating to the time period in which the population can participate. HBCU administrators and faculty were surveyed to determine the best time of the year to convene The Union Insitute's HBCU Initiative Entry Colloquium and the HBCU seminar. Since Union operates a twelve-month academic program, it was possible to accommodate the schedules of the HBCUs. The results of the survey indicated that the third week in July was the most appropriate time. Generally, this was the week after summer school ended and approximately ten days to two weeks before the new academic year began.

It was crucial that the HBCU Initiative learners did not feel isolated or marginalized from the general graduate college learner population. Every effort was made to ensure this did not occur. This was done strategically in four ways: (1) HBCU learners were never identified as part of the initiative except for administrative purposes for program evaluation. (2) All HBCU Initiative applicants had to complete and meet the standard admissions requirements and academic requirements of The Union Institute. (3) Generally, the graduate college concurrently convenes two consecutive seminars with the Entry Colloquium. For the initiative, the same practice occurred. During the HBCU Entry Colloquium, the HBCU seminar was convened. The second seminar was a general seminar opened to all graduate college learners. (4) HBCU Initiative learners completed their remaining two residency seminars through the general seminar program. The ten required Peer Days were completed in the same manner as all graduate college learners.

HBCUs AS CULTURAL AND HISTORICAL REPOSITORIES

All HBCUs represent repositories of African American culture and history. A few HBCUs, both public and private, have indicated on their websites that they have collections of art and rare books, archives, museums, and cultural centers that serve as places for the safekeeping and sharing of African American culture and history. These artifacts, heirlooms, and facilities are accessible to the public. These HBCUs are Alabama A&M University, Central State University, Fisk University, Florida Memorial College, Grambling State University, Hampton University, Howard University, Kentucky State University, Langston University, North Carolina A&T University, Tuskegee University, Virginia Union University, and Winston-Salem State University. Information on these repositories can be obtained through the institutions' websites, listed earlier in this chapter, or by contacting them.

REFERENCES

Academe. 1995. "The Historically Black Colleges and Universities: A Future in the Balance." *Academe* 81, no. 1: 51.

Black Issues in Higher Education. 1997. "Justice Department Asks Fifth Circuit to Reconsider Fordice." *Black Issues in Higher Education* 14, no. 10: 7–8.

———. 1999. "Top 15 Baccalaureate Institutions of Minority Ph.D.s." *Black Issues in Higher Education* 16, no. 19: 41.

Bullock, Henry Allen. 1967. *A History of Negro Education in the South: From 1619 to the Present.* Cambridge, MA: Harvard University Press.

Constantine, Jill M. 1994. "The 'Added Value' of Historically Black Colleges." *Academe* 80, no. 3: 12.

———. 1995. "The Effect of Attending Historically Black Colleges and Universities on Future Wages of Black Students." *Industrial and Labor Relations Review* 48, no. 3: 531–546.

ERIC Clearinghouse on Urban Education. 1996. "Historically Black Colleges and Universities: Internet Access Survey Results." http://eric-web.tc.columbia.edu/hbcu/survey.htm.

Jackson, Cynthia L. 1996. "Introduction." *The Role of African-Americans in the Transformation of Society: The Union Institute's Initiative with Historically Black Colleges and Universities* (First Weekend Retreat Proceedings). Cincinnati: The Union Institute.

Leggon, Cheryl B., and Willie Pearson, Jr. 1997. "The Baccalaureate Origins of African American Female Ph.D. Scientists." *Journal of Women and Minorities in Science and Engineering* 3, no. 4: 213–224.

Maggett, Linda L. 1996. "The HBCU Presidential Pressure Cooker." *Black Issues in Higher Education* 13: 26–28.

National Association for Equal Opportunity in Higher Education. 1999. *Institutional and Presidential Profiles of the Nation's Historically and Predominantly Black Colleges and Universities: Bridging the New Millennium, 1999–2000.* Silver Springs, MD: National Association for Equal Opportunity in Higher Education.

———. Internet site. http://www.nafeo.org/.

National Center for Education Statistics. 1996. *Historically Black Colleges and Universities: 1976–1994.* Washington, DC: National Center for Education Statistics. Also http://nces.ed. gov/pubs/96902.htm.

Roebuck, Julian B., and Komanduri S. Murty. 1993. *Historically Black Colleges and Universities: Their Place in American Higher Education.* Westport, CT: Praeger.

United Negro College Fund Internet site. http://www.uncf.org/.

United States Department of Education. Office of Civil Rights. 1991. *Historically Black Colleges and Universities and Higher Education Desegregation.* Washington, DC: U.S. Department of Education. Also http://www.ed. gov/offices/OCR/hq9511.htm. Last updated October 4, 1999.

White House Initiative on HBCUs Internet site. Last updated September 20, 1999. http://www.ed.gov/offices/OPE/hbcu/.

Chapter Five

✏️ Legal Influences on African American Education

There are three branches to the national government in the United States—executive, legislative, and judicial. The president of the United States heads the executive branch. Within the president's broad functions is the power to issue executive orders. Executive orders are rules, regulations, and instructions with which federal agencies are required to comply. The president also selects judges who serve in the federal court system, or the judicial branch. The judicial branch, made up of the U.S. Supreme Court and other federal courts, is responsible for interpreting the meaning of laws in the settling of disputes. The Supreme Court is the highest court, or the court of last appeal. The interpretation of laws or decisions by the Supreme Court, and to some extent the other courts, establishes public policy. Supreme Court decisions are to a great extent influenced by the social order of the times. The legislative branch, consisting of citizen-elected representatives, is bicameral, meaning it has two houses—the House of Representatives and the Senate—which are the lawmaking bodies. Along with enacting bills and acts, the legislative branch has constitutional authority to ratify amendments to the U.S. Constitution. Although each branch's function and span of control are distinct, the interplay between and among the three branches has shaped the environment of African American education, as it does all aspects of American society.

In this chapter, selected U.S. presidential executive orders, constitutional amendments, legislative acts, and U.S. Supreme Court decisions are presented. The first half of the chapter is an overview of executive and legislative actions that influenced African American education. The second half of the chapter is a general discussion of the ramifications of selected Supreme Court cases that configured the education of African Americans. In addition, overviews of the events surrounding the cases, as described in the court's opinions, are provided. The full court opinions can be accessed through the Legal Information Institute of Cornell University Law School, http://www.law.cornell.edu.

PRESIDENTIAL EXECUTIVE ORDERS

The concept of affirmative action was first put forth in President Franklin D. Roosevelt's Executive Order 8802. In the 1941 executive order President Roosevelt made it illegal for defense contractors receiving federal funds not to hire blacks because of race. The phrase "affirmative action" was first used in President Lyndon B. Johnson's Executive Order 11246, which was written in 1965 and titled "Equal Employment Opportunity."

The aim of Johnson's executive order was to redress discriminatory employment practices of organizations that received federal funding by directly allying the acquisition of federal contracts with contractors' employment practices. In the order he states, "The contractors will take affirmative action to ensure that applicants are employed, and that employees are treated during employment, without regard to their race, color, religion, sex or national origin." The contractors, or those who receive federal funding, are required by the order to develop practices and procedures that ensure equal access to consideration for employment with the full benefits and rights of other employees. Affirmative action was extended to postsecondary enrollment when these institutions accepted federal money for student financial aid and research grants, for example.

U.S. CONSTITUTIONAL AMENDMENTS

With the passage of the Thirteenth Amendment in 1865, slavery was made illegal in the United States and its territories. Yet the amendment stopped short of granting citizenship and its accompanying civil rights to blacks. John Hope Franklin and Alfred A. Moss, Jr., point out, "Most Southern whites, although willing to concede the end of slavery even to the point of voting for adoption of the Thirteenth Amendment, were convinced that laws should be speedily enacted to curb blacks and to ensure their role as a laboring force in the South" (1994, 225). Black Codes, laws enacted to reverse the effects of the Thirteenth and Fourteenth Amendments, were established as a means to this end. With the approval of President Andrew Johnson, Southern whites were given free range to control blacks as they deemed appropriate.

In 1866, after a battle between President Johnson and Congress, the Fourteenth Amendment was ratified. This amendment guaranteed citizenship rights and "the equal protection of the laws" to blacks and any individual born or naturalized a citizen and living within the jurisdiction of the United States. In the South, the response to the Fourteenth Amendment was to establish a *de jure* segregated society that was maintained through Jim Crow laws. Northern states, for the most part, maintained a *de facto* segregated society. De jure segregation is sanctioned by laws. De facto segregation is sanctioned through practices and traditions without the support of laws.

Many Southern states and a few Northern states did not consider the Fourteenth Amendment to include the right to vote. In 1870, the Fifteenth Amendment was ratified. It granted blacks the right to vote and stated that those rights could not be denied because of "race, color, or previous condition of servitude." Being able to vote gave blacks the opportunity to have input in the political system that governed their lives, including their education.

Although blacks had the right to vote, being able to vote was another matter. Southern states launched a frontal attack on the rights granted in the Fifteenth Amendment, passing laws that required blacks to pass literacy tests, to pay poll taxes, and to be removed from voting rolls if they were convicted of criminal actions. It became a practice to arrest and convict blacks for the sole purpose of removing them from the voting rolls.

A handful of Western states used literacy tests, and there were some Northern states that were subtler in barring blacks from voting. The Voting Rights Acts of 1964 and 1965 were enacted to strengthen the Fifteenth Amendment and banned the use of "qualification or prerequisite to voting" for any citizen of the United States.

LEGISLATIVE ACTS

The Civil Rights Act of 1964, the Elementary and Secondary Schools Act of 1965, and the Higher Education Act of 1965 gave the federal government authority to interface with states and their public education institutions. As stated in Chapter 1, education is the jurisdiction of the states. These three acts are considered to be part of the broader meaning of providing "for the general welfare" in the U.S. Constitution.

Title IV of the Civil Rights Act of 1964 addressed precollege and postsecondary public education desegregation. Authorization was given to the commissioner of education (now the secretary of education) to conduct a survey on the status of "the lack of availability of equal educational opportunities for individuals" in public schools. The survey, conducted in the United States and its territories, assessed the availability of opportunities based on race, color, religion, and national origin. The results of the survey were reported to the president and Congress.

States and their designated educational agencies could request assistance from the commissioner to formulate and implement desegregation plans. Grants were made available to school boards to provide in-service training for school personnel and to hire consultants. In addition, postsecondary institutions could apply for grants to assist school district personnel in effectively addressing "special educational problems occasioned by desegregation" (Title IV of the Civil Rights Act of 1964).

While Title IV outlined the principles in favor of desegregating schools, Title VI of the 1964 Civil Rights Act provided monetary sanctions. Title VI required that federal agencies and departments that awarded federal money to programs and other activities must do so in a nondiscriminatory manner. Departments and agencies were to issue rules, regulations, and orders that were consistent and complied with the objective of the act. Educational institutions that were not in compliance could be refused funding or not be re-funded. Title VI gave the U.S. Office of Education (which became the United States Department of Education in the 1980s) the authority to request desegregation plans from the states that systematically operated segregated education systems.

Title I of the Elementary and Secondary Schools Act of 1965 and a subsequent amendment, titled "Improving America's Schools Act of 1994," focused on the education of economically disadvantaged children. The purpose of the acts is to make it possible for school districts to provide opportunities for disadvantaged children to meet the states' education requirements. This is done primarily through remedial classes in reading and math.

Through this act, quality of life is inextricably linked to quality of education. In the 1994 amendment to the act, Congress states that it will provide the necessary funding each fiscal year so that by 2004 all children who are eligible for the Title I program are served. In addition, Title I provides federal assistance to school districts for programs designed to intervene when students are at risk of dropping out of school.

The Higher Education Act of 1965, and the amended 1998 act, broadened the degree of federal government intervention in postsecondary education. Quality in and access to higher education are the purposes of the act. Through the act, funds are appropriated for institutions that are accredited by agencies recognized by the secretary of education. These agencies include, but are not limited to, the regional accrediting agencies discussed in Chapters 1 and 6. Funding includes programs and activities to enhance teacher quality and institutional aid and to provide student financial assistance.

In the act, Congress acknowledges the significant contribution that HBCUs have made in the postsecondary education of African

Americans. Congress recognizes the unequal manner in which funds have been dispersed to white institutions and to HBCUs by the states and the federal government and admits the role the state and federal governments, because of these discriminatory actions toward HBCUs, played in creating the current precarious state of a large number of HBCUs. In Title III of the Higher Education Act, three sections focus on remedying the discriminatory practices. These sections are "Strengthening HBCUs," "HBCU Capital Financing," and "Minority Science and Engineering Improvement Program."

OPINIONS OF THE U.S. SUPREME COURT

Often, Supreme Court cases that set the direction of the education of African Americans are presented as quoted sections of the court's opinions. Readers must rely on an author's contextual interpretation of the significance and implications of the quotation. This author believes that readers should know the sequence of events that led up to and shaped the Supreme Court's opinions. The pretrial events are as important as the outcomes. These events provide insight into the legal, political, and social strife of African Americans in pursuit of educational equality, equity, and quality. The following discussion provides that information.

Plessy v. Ferguson (163 U.S. 537 [1896]) is the case that for African Americans determined racial identification. It also gave legal credence to the separate but equal doctrine. The circumstances leading to the case originated when the Louisiana General Assembly passed laws in 1890 establishing a segregated society. One of the laws instituted segregated train cars for blacks ("colored races") and whites. It was required that individuals occupy the car that was designated for their race. Persons who did not occupy the designated car could be fined $25 or placed in jail for not more than twenty days. In addition, if a conductor allowed a person to occupy a car that was not designated for that person's race the conductor could be liable for the same fine or jail term. Conductors could refuse to board passengers who would not occupy their racially identified car, and neither the conductor nor the railway company would "be liable for damages in any of the courts of the State."

Plessy bought a first class train ticket at a train station in Louisiana. He attempted to board the white car and was told by the conductor to board the black car. Despite the conductor's directive, Plessy occupied a seat in the white car. He was forcibly removed from the car by the conductor and a policeman and imprisoned. Plessy was criminally charged with violating the act. Ferguson was the criminal district court trial judge in New Orleans who found Plessy guilty.

On the bases of the Thirteenth and Fourteenth Amendments, Plessy took his suit all the way to the U.S. Supreme Court. He claimed that the 1890 act violated the two federal constitutional amendments. Plessy maintained that because he was seven-eighths white and one-eighth black he was entitled to "every right, privilege, and immunity secured to citizens of the United States of the white race." The U.S. Supreme Court upheld the decision against Plessy of the Louisiana Supreme Court. In the opinion of the U.S. Supreme Court: 1) The issue of racial identification was the jurisdiction of each state. 2) The Thirteenth Amendment was not in question because Plessy had not been placed in involuntary servitude—he was arrested. 3) The Fourteenth Amendment was not in question because as a citizen of the United States and Louisiana he was not denied "equal protection of the laws." It was on this point that the court established the doctrine of "separate but equal." In establishing this doctrine the justices used segregated education as an example of the reasonableness of separate but equal. "The most common instance of this is connected with the establishment of separate schools for white and colored children, which has been held to be a valid exercise in the legislative power even by courts of States where the political rights of the colored race have been longest and most earnestly enforced."

The *Plessy* case does not deal directly with education. However, the opinion has far reaching implications for the education of those identified as African American. Two key outcomes of this court opinion are the legal definition of who is identified as African American and the separate but equal doctrine. Status and treatment in the United States are based on racial identification. One outcome of the opinion that is frequently overlooked, except by many blacks, is the fact that in the *Plessy* case, the court determined that any person with black blood, no matter how microscopic an amount, is black. Once identified as black, one can expect the consequent circumstances and treatment. Although some may argue no such legal basis continues for the racial identification of blacks, clearly there are societal assumptions that continue to operate.

The separate but equal doctrine legalized in *Plessy v. Ferguson* required the establishment of equal facilities for both races. The responsibility for providing equitable separate facilities to meet this requirement was placed squarely on the shoulders of whites. The Supreme Court's interpretation of "equal protection of the laws" upheld states' rights to establish segregated societies. It will be seen in subsequent cases that separate never equated to equal, and there was no good faith intention on the part of states and/or education institution officials for this to occur.

McLaurin v. Oklahoma State Regents **(339 U.S. 637 [1950])** was the first case concerning equal educational opportunities for blacks in higher education. McLaurin, who had a master's degree from Langston (an HBCU), applied to the University of Oklahoma's doctoral program in education. Because Langston is a public institution, which at the time only offered undergraduate degrees, blacks seeking postbaccalaureate degrees in the state had to attend the University of Oklahoma. He was denied admission because he was black. In Oklahoma, it was a misdemeanor for blacks and whites to attend desegregated higher education settings, including classrooms, the library, and the cafeteria.

McLaurin filed suit based on the Fourteenth Amendment, citing that the decision of the school authorities and the Oklahoma law were unconstitutional and denied him equal protection of the laws. The Oklahoma District Court held that Oklahoma had a Constitutional duty to provide him the education he sought, and that the state law denying him admission because he was black was unconstitutional. The District Court trusted the state to fully comply with its decision and remedy the situation based on the constitutional edicts. The court did not grant an injunction, but maintained jurisdiction of the case.

The Oklahoma legislature amended the law. The amendment permitted blacks to attend historically white higher education institutions only if the same courses were not offered at the black higher education institutions. The change in the law could be viewed as the state conceding that in some situations desegregation had to occur, or it could be seen as an attempt to forestall McLaurin from taking his case to the U.S. Supreme Court.

McLaurin was admitted to the University of Oklahoma Graduate School. The president of the university was empowered to determine the conditions that afforded him "equal educational opportunities." He was to sit at an assigned desk in a room next to the classroom. He was to use an assigned desk on the library mezzanine, and was not to use any desks anywhere else in the library. He was to eat at an assigned table in the cafeteria. He could not use the cafeteria when other students were there.

McLaurin filed a motion in the District Court to have these impediments removed, again based on the Fourteenth Amendment. This time the court ruled that his equal protection of the laws was not being violated, and he appealed to the U.S. Supreme Court. Before the Supreme Court heard his case, a modification was made in his treatment. He was allowed to sit in the classroom. However, that section of the room was railed off with a sign that read, "Reserved for Colored." By the time the Supreme Court heard his case he was seated in a row that was designated for black students, without a sign. He was given a designated table on the main floor of the library. He could eat in the cafeteria when other students were there, but at a separate table.

The Supreme Court reversed the decision of the District Court, finding that McLaurin was being deprived of an education and equal protection of the laws. It concluded, "The result is that appellant [McLaurin] is handicapped in his pursuit of effective graduate instruction. Such restrictions impair and inhibit his ability to study, engage in discussions and exchange views with other students, and, in general, to learn his profession."

***Sweatt v. Painter* (339 U.S. 629 [1950])** is also a case concerned with equal educational opportunities for blacks in higher education. This case focuses on tangible equality in education facilities. Sweatt applied to the University of Texas Law School for the February 1946 term. He was denied admission because he was black. He sued in a Texas court against Painter, a university official, under the equal protection of the laws clause. At the time, Texas did not have a law school that admitted blacks.

The state court would not order the Law School to admit Sweatt. Instead it suspended the case for six months to give the state time "to supply substantially equal facilities" for African Americans. In December 1946, the state trial court denied Sweatt's case because in the six-month period of the trial university officials had arranged to open a law school for blacks. The school was scheduled to open in February 1947. When the black law school was opened, Sweatt would not enroll because the educational facilities were not equal to those offered at the University of Texas Law School.

Sweatt appealed to the Texas Court of Civil Appeals. This court remanded the case to the previous trial court "for further proceedings without prejudice to the rights of any party to this suit." The trial court and subsequently the Court of Civil Appeals found that the black law school had substantially equal facilities to those at the University of Texas. The Texas Supreme Court refused to hear the case.

What both Texas courts considered substantially equal facilities were these: The black law school did not have its own faculty. Four faculty members from the University of Texas Law School taught at both institutions but maintained their offices at the University of Texas. Of the 10,000 books ordered for the library less than a third had been delivered. There was not a full-time librarian. In addition, the black school was not accredited.

The white school, on the other hand, had sixteen full-time and three part-time faculty members. There were 65,000 books in the library with full-time librarians. Students at the University of Texas Law School had available to them moot court facilities, a law review, and scholarships. The school was accredited.

By the time the U.S. Supreme Court heard this case, Texas had made a few adjustments to the status of the facilities at the black law school. The black school had five full-time faculty members and twenty-three students enrolled. It had a library with 16,500 books, a full-time librarian, a practice court, and a legal aid association, and one graduate who became a member of the Texas Bar. The black law school had applied for accreditation.

The Supreme Court's decision that the petitioner was denied equal protection of the laws rested on three points. (1) Law schools are to provide the knowledge and practices of the legal profession. Individuals cannot be expected to be skilled in the profession if they are isolated from the people and institutions involved with the law. (2) The exchange of views and ideas about the law is fundamental to learning the profession; anything less is "an academic vacuum." (3) Compelling Sweatt to enroll in the black law school excluded him from 85 percent of the state's population. As a member of the Texas Bar he was bound to have to come in contact with that portion of the population in the form of other lawyers, witnesses, jurors, and judges, to name a few.

***Brown v. Board of Education* (347 U.S. 483 [1954])** is the landmark on which all subsequent education desegregation cases are based. The case was argued in 1952, and reargued in 1953. The *Brown* case is a consolidation by the U.S. Supreme Court of cases from Kansas, South Carolina, Virginia, and Delaware. Although the facts and localities of the four cases differed, the legal issue was the same.

The lawyers for the plaintiffs, Brown et al., wanted the black students to be able to attend public schools in their respective districts on a nonracial basis. Each state had laws that sanctioned education segregated by race. The plaintiffs based their cases on being denied equal protection of the laws. In Kansas, South Carolina, and Virginia, federal district courts ruled that the plaintiffs were not being denied equal protection of the laws. They based the ruling on the *Plessy* decision of "separate but equal." The Delaware Supreme Court held to the principle of separate but equal, but conceded that white schools were superior to the black schools, and the Delaware plaintiffs were able to enroll in the white schools.

In the argument to the U.S. Supreme Court in 1952, the plaintiffs disputed the separate but equal doctrine in education. They contended that "segregated public schools are not 'equal' and cannot be made 'equal.'" Therefore, the plaintiffs said, they were being denied equal protection of the laws. The court introduced its own questions about the issues of the case and the case was to be reargued in 1953.

Reargument was primarily focused on historical and contemporary thought on the Fourteenth Amendment. The court examined the original intent of the proponents and opponents of the amendment, particularly in light of the existing segregated society of the times. The justices determined that the proponents intended the amendment "to remove all legal distinctions" based on race, and the opponents intended a limited interpretation of the amendment. The justices then turned to the status of public education at the time the amendment was ratified. In the South, the majority of the whites were receiving private education and education for blacks was mostly nonexistent, due in large part to laws that continued to limit or prohibit the education of blacks. Public education in the South was not a consideration at that time. In the North, public education did exist. Yet the debate concerning this amendment was centered on the South and not the North. Public education in the North, at the time the amendment was written, did not approach the public education system in the 1950s. The justices decided that this information did not directly assist them in making a decision on the *Brown* case.

The justices decided that they had to look beyond the circumstances of the *Sweatt* case because the *Brown* case was about more than facilities and education resources being equitably proportioned. They posed the question, "Does segregation of children in public schools solely on the basis of race, even though the physical facilities and other 'tangible' factors may be equal, deprive the children of the minority group of equal educational opportunities?" They unanimously responded, "Yes." They concluded that "in the field of education, the doctrine of 'separate but equal' has no place."

The justices reached their decision by considering the contemporary elements of public education. These were: (1) Compulsory attendance laws and the large expenditures by state and local governments demonstrated the importance of education to citizens of the United States, (2) Good citizenship and the performance of fundamental capabilities as a citizen required an education. The justices noted the need for a high school education to serve in the armed forces. (3) Success in life is dependent on the accessibility of educational opportunities. (4) Based on testimony by psychologist Dr. Kenneth Clark, the justices found that segregation was detrimental to the psychological development of black children, creating a sense of inferiority. Therefore, given the contemporary society and what was known about psychology, "any language in *Plessy v. Ferguson* contrary to this finding is rejected." Taking their findings as a whole, they decided that segregation in public education denied blacks the equal protection of the laws.

How to remedy that condition was the next concern of the justices. The case was returned to the docket to argue two broad questions they posed. The questions were: (1) Should black students be immediately admitted to schools of their choice? Or should the court allow an incremental desegregation of the school districts? (2) Should the court develop specific mandates in the four cases comprising Brown, et al., and if it does what issues should be addressed? Or should the court appoint a "special master" who upon hearing evidence will recommend the specifics of the mandates? Or, should the court send the cases to the respective lower courts to develop mandates? If the court opts to operate on the last question, what directives should the Supreme Court give the lower courts, and what guidelines should the lower court be required to follow?

***Brown v. Board of Education* (349 U.S. 294 [1955]),** also known as *Brown II,* consisted of the arguments on the two broad questions that the justices had posed in 1954 on the manner of remedying *de jure* school segregation. The court noted the complexities associated with dismantling long-standing segregation in public schools. The U.S. Attorney General and the attorneys general from Florida, North Carolina, Arkansas, Oklahoma, Maryland, and Texas attended the hearing. A few other states sent *amici curiae* (friend of the court briefs) to illustrate what they had done to redress school segregation. The court acknowledged that there were some school districts in Kansas and Delaware that were moving in the direction of desegregating their public schools. Virginia and South Carolina had chosen to wait for a court order.

The court decided that there was no panacea to ending segregated public education. Community circumstances and problems would vary, and only those in close proximity to the community were able to assess and appropriately solve the problems. The primary responsibilities of school desegregation would rest on the shoulders of school officials. However, during the transition period, the lower courts in which the cases originated would have supervisory jurisdiction. The courts were to determine if school officials were making "good faith implementation of the governing constitutional principles."

The courts were to require the school district officials to begin the process of complying with the *Brown I* decision. School district officials were to submit a desegregation plan. The courts were to consider if the time frame of the plan would produce prompt and reasonable compliance. School district officials were to include in consideration of the plan impasses concerning administration, facilities, transportation, personnel, attendance areas, and amendments to laws and regulations. The courts were to consider if the school district responses to the impasses were adequate. The cases in Kansas, Virginia, and South Carolina were remanded to the District Courts. The Delaware case was remanded to the Delaware Supreme Court.

Green v. County School Board of New Kent County (391 U.S. 430 [1968]) was a case concerned with using a "freedom of choice" plan to achieve desegregation in public school education. Through "freedom of choice," students would be allowed to select the schools they attended.

New Kent County is a rural county in eastern Virginia. Approximately half of the county's population at the time was black. Housing patterns were essentially desegregated. There were two schools in the county. New Kent School, for whites, was located on the east side of the county and included grades one through twelve. George W. Watkins Schools, for blacks, was located on the west side of the county and was organized in the same manner. Because there were no attendance areas, the two schools were considered to be serving the entire community.

The total student population in New Kent County consisted of 740 blacks and 550 whites. Twenty-one school buses transported all of the students to and from the two schools. There was an overlapping travel pattern, meaning that buses taking black students to school were passing schools that whites attended before arriving at the black schools and buses taking white students to school were passing schools that blacks attended before arriving at white schools. Eleven of the buses traveled to Watkins School. Virginia's constitution and laws had stipulated that public education was to be racially segregated. Although these stipulations violated the *Brown I* decision, the school board continued to maintain a dual system. They continued the dual system by operating under Virginia laws that were intended to deliberately oppose the Supreme Court's decision. An example of these state laws was the establishment of the Pupil Placement Act. The responsibility of assigning children to schools was vested in the State Public Placement Board, rather than local school officials. Students were automatically assigned to the schools they had attended the previous year unless they applied to be assigned to another school. The board had sole discretion over what schools Virginia's students attended.

As of September 1964, New Kent County reported that neither black nor white students in the school district had applied to be reassigned. In March 1965, the plaintiff, Green, filed in District Court for injunctive relief against the school board. The plaintiff charged the school board with operating a dual school system. The school board wanted the case dismissed because black students had not taken advantage of the choice to be reassigned, offered through the State Public Placement Board. In August 1965, concerned about remaining eligible for federal funding, the school board developed a "freedom of choice" plan for school desegregation.

Through the "freedom of choice" plan, each year students in grades nine through twelve could choose to attend New Kent School or Watkins School. Students who did not declare a choice were assigned to the school they attended the previous year. Students in grades one through eight had to declare a school.

The court did not grant the injunction. Instead, it gave the school board time to modify the plan to focus specifically on the hiring and assignment of teachers and staff in a desegregated manner. The board made the modifications, and in June 1966 the District Court accepted the plan. Subsequently, the Court of Appeals for the Fourth Circuit affirmed the District Court's acceptance of the plan, and remanded it to the District Court. The Placement Board was disbanded in 1966 following the acceptance of the amended "freedom of choice" plan by the District Court.

When the case came to the U.S. Supreme Court in 1968, the school board argued that because students could attend any school they wanted, the plan complied with the requirements of *Brown II*. To expect the school board to do more would mean that the Fourteenth Amendment was interpreted as "universally requiring compulsory integration." The Supreme Court replied that opening the doors of schools was only the beginning of ending a dual system. It could not be considered the end of the process of abolishing a long-maintained segregated school system. The court wanted evidence of the exact actions the board had taken to completely dismantle the dual system. The school board's plan was to prove that "its proposed plan promises meaningful and immediate progress towards disestablishing state-imposed segregation." The court ruled that the "freedom of choice can have no place in such a plan." Such a plan did not meet the letter or the spirit of *Brown II*.

***Swann v. Charlotte-Mecklenburg Board of Education* (402 U.S. 1 [1971])** was a case based on the accountability of school officials and the span of power and discretion of federal courts with the jurisdiction to determine school districts' compliance to dismantle segregated public education. The Charlotte-Mecklenburg (North Carolina) school district, which incorporated the city of Charlotte and the county of Mecklenburg, served over 84,000 students during the 1968–1969 academic year, 29 percent of whom were black. Its 107 schools were situated across 550 square miles. By June 1969, there were 24,000 black students in the district; 86 percent attended schools in Charlotte. Sixty-six percent of those attending school in Charlotte were in 21 schools that were 99 percent to 100 percent black. The Supreme Court attributed this condition to a desegregation plan approved by the District Court in 1965, which included gerrymandering.

Citing the *Green* case, in September 1968 the plaintiff, Swann, requested relief of the continued segregated situation. The District Court conceded that the school board's actions were not in good faith, were discriminating, and that the gerrymandering maintained segregated schools.

In April 1969, the District Court ordered the school board to produce a plan that would desegregate teachers and students. Suggested plans to desegregate teachers and students were accepted by the court on an interim basis in June and August 1969. In addition, the court ordered the school board to produce another plan by November 1969. In November, the board requested an extension to develop the third plan. It wanted the extension until February 1970. The court denied the extension and the board submitted an incomplete plan. In December 1969 the court found the plan unacceptable, and appointed John Finger, an expert in educational administration, to develop a desegregation plan. Finger and the board each submitted plans on pupil assignment in February 1970.

The board's plan would: (1) close seven black schools and reassign the students, (2) revamp attendance areas, (3) unify the athletic program, (4) no longer use school transportation to maintain race divisions, (5) desegregate teachers and administrators, and (6) begin a school transfer system of majority-to-minority, sending majority students to minority schools.

The boundaries of the revamped attendance areas for the high schools would start at the center of Charlotte and move outward so that each attendance area was like a slice of pie. Each slice would include the city, suburbs, and rural areas. This pattern would reassign the black student population in the ten high schools. The result would be that black students would make up 17 percent to 36 percent of the student population in nine of the schools and 2 percent in one school.

The board plan restructured the twenty-one junior high school attendance areas. In twenty of the schools, black enrollment would range from 0 percent to 38 percent. In the remaining school, which was located in the black community, the black enrollment would be 90 percent. Elementary schools would not be affected by the desegregation plan. This meant that black students remained enrolled in the nine elementary schools they had always occupied. The percentage would be 86 percent to 100 percent, with similar percentages for whites in their elementary schools.

Finger's plan included the board's plan for high schools with one addition: An additional 300 black students would be reassigned to the all-white Independence High School, leaving their communities.

Finger maintained most of the redistricting proposed by the board, but augmented it with nine "satellite" areas. Blacks living in Charlotte would be assigned to distant, mostly white junior high schools. This would significantly desegregate "every junior high school in the system." Finger also proposed zoning, pairing, and grouping elementary schools. Using this method would mean that black elementary school populations throughout the district would range from 9 percent to 38 percent.

In February 1970, the District Court accepted the board plan with Finger's changes for the junior high and senior high schools. The court fully accepted Finger's plan for the elementary schools. In March 1970, the Court of Appeals accepted the District Court's decision concerning the faculty and the junior and high school desegregation plans, but did not accept the plan for elementary schools. The Court of Appeals believed that the plan would be burdensome on the elementary students. The case was sent back to the District Court for another plan to be developed. Until the District Court received and accepted a new plan, the Supreme Court ordered that the Finger plan for elementary schools be implemented.

Two new plans were submitted to the District Court. One plan was developed by the U.S. Department of Health, Education, and Welfare (HEW). It focused on grouping schools in adjoining areas. Four of the nine Charlotte school board members developed another plan. Their plan was similar to the Finger plan but would require less transporting of students. The other five board members refused to modify the original board plan. After reviewing the plans, in August 1970 the District Court decided that the board could use either the original Finger plan, the HEW plan, the plan developed by the four board members, or a new plan they would develop. The board decided to use the Finger plan while the case went to the Supreme Court, while continuing to contend that the plan was extreme.

The case was heard by the U.S. Supreme Court in October 1970. The court identified four questions concerning student assignment as a means to desegregate public schools: (1) What role do racial quotas play in school desegregation? (2) Do all racially identified schools have to be eliminated to achieve desegregation? (3) Should there be limits on what is considered reasonable in revamping attendance areas? (4) What is the appropriate use of the public school transportation system to remedy school segregation?

The court's responses to the four questions affirmed the District Court's judgment of August 1970. The court determined: (1) Racial quotas are a means to an end, and not an end in themselves. (2) The majority-to-minority transfer program is an acceptable component of a desegregation plan. The existence of a small number of one-race schools does not mean that a dual system is being maintained. However, the courts and school officials "should make every effort to achieve the greatest possible degree of actual desegregation." If some schools remain one race, it is the duty of the school board to provide evidence that it is not occurring as a vestige of a dual system, and the courts should closely examine these situations. (3) Gerrymandering is not acceptable. However, it is acceptable to group noncontiguous attendance areas. The court reasoned that while on a map it may appear to be excessive, it is possible that the actual travel time, given traffic and road conditions, may make these areas closer than they appear. It was not possible to predetermine a set ruling on the use of this strategy. This has to be determined by each school district. (4) Public school busing is not a new phenomenon in public school education. During the 1969–1970 school year, over 18 million students nationwide rode school buses. When considering the use of the public school transportation system the courts and boards must consider the age of the students and the length of travel time.

***San Antonio Independent School District v. Rodriguez* (411 U.S. 1 [1973])** calls into question state and local funding practices for public education. The case was initiated by a Hispanic couple who made the case a class action suit for all minorities and economically disadvantaged students who live in areas with low property tax bases. The Hispanic parents' child attended urban public schools in San Antonio, Texas.

In 1949, the Texas Minimum Foundation School Program was established. The foundation appropriated state and local contributions to provide money for teacher salaries, school operating expenses, and school transportation costs. The foundation was established to equalize the funding of public school education in Texas. The state contributes, from its general revenues, 80 percent of the funding for the foundation and the school districts contribute the other 20 percent. These funds were divided among the 254 county school districts based on the income the state received from each county. Originally, funding came from taxes on agriculture, mining, and manufacturing. As Texas became urbanized, school funding from the foundation was based on manufacturing and industrial property taxes. Personal property taxes were not originally a high priority in considering the distribution of foundation funds.

When Texas was primarily rural, its population and property wealth were generally distributed evenly across the state. At the time of this case, Texas was experiencing a growth in urban areas. Urban expansion was producing an increasing disparity in the distribution of the population and property wealth.

In 1968, Rodriguez filed suit against the Texas Board of Education, the Commissioner of Education, the Texas Attorney General, and the Bexar County Board of Trustees (San Antonio is located in Bexar County). In arguments before the District Court, comparisons were made between two of the seven metropolitan school districts in Bexar County—Edgewood Independent School District, the urban district in which Rodriguez lived, and Alamo Heights Independent School District.

The comparison served to illustrate a dual financial system for public education. Edgewood had 22,000 students and twenty-five schools. Because Edgewood was located in the inner city, commercial and industrial property were almost nonexistent. The majority of the population was Hispanic with about 6 percent black. The average assessed property value per student was $5,960, and the median family income was $4,686. Both were the lowest in the metropolitan area. The per-student annual expenditure was $356. Alamo Heights, on the other hand, was the richest district in the area. It had six schools and 5 thousand students. The population was mostly white, with 18 percent Hispanic and less than 1 percent black. The average assessed property value per student was above $49,000. The median family income was $8,001. The per-student annual expenditure was $594. The District Court decided that dual financing of public education did occur and concluded that Texas's system to fund public education did discriminate based on wealth.

Texas appealed to the U.S. Supreme Court. The court considered whether the Texas system to fund education was discriminatory based on class, and whether education is a fundamental right protected by the "equal protection of the laws" clause in the Fourteenth Amendment. Citing decisions in several cases in other states, the court reversed the judgment of the District Court, determining that while education is important, it is not in and of itself a fundamental right protected by the Fourteenth Amendment. The Supreme Court accepted that disparity of funding schools may exist, but it cannot be stated that the disparity exists because of preconceived "invidious" discrimination.

The Court added that the decision should not be seen as maintaining the status quo. The need for reform in the funding of public education was clear, it ruled. Yet this was something that was not the jurisdiction of the U.S. Supreme Court. Reform had to be addressed at the state level.

Regents of the University of California v. Bakke (**438 U.S. 265 [1978]**) was a case that brought into question the legality of admissions programs for people of color and introduced the concept of "reverse discrimination" in higher education.

In 1968, the medical school of the University of California at Davis opened with fifty students. In the first class, the only three people of color admitted were Asian. By 1971, the number of enrollees in the entering class had doubled.

In 1970, the medical school faculty developed an admissions program to increase the number of minority and disadvantaged students. The program was coordinated with the regular admissions program but had a separate admissions committee.

The regular admissions process required individuals to apply one year before the year they wanted to be admitted. The admissions committee screened each application. Applicants whose undergraduate grade point average (GPA) was below 2.5 were automatically excluded. Generally, one out of six applicants were interviewed. The interviewer and each of the four members of the admissions committee rated each interviewee on a scale of 1 to 100. A perfect score was 500. By 1974, an interviewer and five committee members rated the interviewees, making 600 a perfect score. Ratings included the interviewer's synopsis, the overall GPA, the GPA in science, the score on the Medical College Admissions Test, letters of recommendation, extracurricular activities, and additional personal information. The full committee reviewed the files and scores of all the applicants and offered admissions on a "rolling basis." The applicants were not necessarily admitted based on highest scores. The committee chairperson had the option of including individuals with "special skills," and had the option of placing individuals on a waiting list.

The special admissions program had a separate committee, on which the majority of the members were people of color. Beginning in 1973, applicants were asked to indicate on the application if they wanted to be considered as "economically and/or educationally disadvantaged." In 1974, the application form asked applicants if they wanted to be considered as a member of a "minority group." Minority groups were black, Chicano, Asian, and American Indian. The applications of individuals who identified themselves as a minority were sent to the special admissions committee. Although "disadvantaged" was not defined, the chairperson of the special admissions committee reviewed each application to determine if applicants' background reflected unfavorable economic or educational conditions.

Applications forwarded to the special committee were reviewed by the same admissions process as the applicants reviewed by the regular committee, with the exception that the applicants in the special program did not have to meet the minimum 2.5 GPA requirement. About one-fifth of all the applicants handled by the special committee were interviewed, and each interviewee was rated. Based on the rating, the special committee submitted its top applicants to the regular admissions committee. The regular admissions committee could not rate or compare the applicants from the special committee with those of the regular committee. However, the regular committee could refuse admission of a special candidate if specific course requirements were not met or there were "other specific deficiencies."

The special committee was allocated a specific proportion of slots each year, based on the potential overall class size. When the class size was fifty, eight slots were allocated and when the class size was 100, sixteen slots were allocated. Between 1971 and 1974, 63 people of color were admitted through the special program and 44 people of color were admitted through the regular program. The former admitted twenty-one blacks, thirty Chicanos, and twelve Asians. The latter admitted one black, six Chicanos, and thirty-seven Asians. A number of whites applied as economically and/or educationally disadvantaged, but none of them were offered admissions as a result of the process of the special program.

Bakke was a white male who applied to the medical school in 1973 and 1974. Both years he was reviewed through the regular admissions program, interviewed, and denied admission. In 1973, his interviewer noted that he is "a very desirable applicant to the medical school." Bakke had a rating score of 468 out of 500. Bakke's application was rejected because he applied late, and the regular committee did not accept any applicants who applied late with a rating below 470. Four special admissions slots were still open. Having been denied admission, Bakke wrote to the associate dean, who was also chair of the admissions committee, claiming that the special program operated as a racial and ethnic quota.

In 1974, Bakke submitted his application early. He received an overall rating of 94 from the student who interviewed him. His faculty interviewer was the associate dean and chair of the admissions committee, the same person to whom he had written the previous year when he was denied admission. The faculty interviewer noted that Bakke was "rather limited in his approach to the problems of the medical profession, and found disturbing Bakke's very definite opinions, which were based more on his personal viewpoints than upon a study of the total problem." The faculty interviewer rated him 86, his lowest rating that year. Bakke's overall committee rating was 549 out of 600. Bakke was refused admission again. The committee chair decided not to put Bakke on the waiting list. In the two years that Bakke applied, minorities were admitted through the special program with lower GPAs, Medical College Admissions Test scores, and committee rating scores than Bakke's.

After being denied admission in 1974, Bakke sued in the Superior Court of California. He wanted "mandatory, injunctive, and declaratory relief" to be admitted to the medical school. He claimed that he was being discriminated against because of his race and that it violated his equal protection under the law. The university filed a cross claim, stating that its special admissions program was legal. Superior Court found that the special program was a based on a racial quota because it held a specific number of slots specifically for minorities, and the university could not take race into consideration for admissions. Yet the court did not require that Bakke be admitted because he did not prove that he would have been admitted if a special program did not exist.

Both parties appealed the decisions of the Superior Court. The California Supreme Court took jurisdiction of the case directly from the Superior Court. The California Supreme Court acknowledged that the goal of the special program was admirable and addressed a special need of the state. However, it claimed that there were less "intrusive" ways to achieve the goal. The court held that the program denied non–minority applicants equal protection of the law, adding, "no applicant may be rejected because of his race, in favor of another who is less qualified, as measured by standards applied without regard to race." Since, according to the decision, the university had discriminated against Bakke, the university had to prove that without the special program he would have been denied admission anyway. The California Supreme Court ordered Bakke to be admitted.

The order to admit Bakke was stopped when the case went forward to the U.S. Supreme Court. The university contended that the decision of the California Supreme Court was inappropriate because white males, such as Bakke, are not a "discrete and insular minority requiring extraordinary protection from the majoritarian political process." The U.S. Supreme Court justices noted that it is possible to interpret the terms "discrimination" and "equal protection of the law" in many ways. To make this point they quoted Justice Oliver Wendell Holmes, "A word is not a crystal, transparent and unchanged, it is the skin of a living thought, and may vary greatly in color and content according to the circumstances and the time in which it is used."

For differing reasons, the justices affirmed part of the decision of the California Supreme Court and reversed part of it. Bakke was to be admitted because the university could not prove that Bakke would have been denied admission even if the special program had not existed. However, the special admissions program to the medical school was allowed to continue.

Freeman v. Pitts (503 U.S. 467 [1992]) was concerned with the relief of a school district from a court-ordered desegregation judgment. The plaintiff, Freeman, represented the DeKalb County School System (DCSS). The respondent, Pitts, represented black students and their parents.

DeKalb County is one of the counties that comprises metropolitan Atlanta. At the time of this case, 73,000 students were enrolled in kindergarten through twelfth grade. In about July 1968, black students and their parents filed a class action suit against DCSS in District Court. This class action was filed soon after the court's *Green* decision. Almost immediately after the suit was filed, DCSS began working with HEW to develop a final comprehensive desegregation plan. In 1969, the District Court accepted the plan. It was to be implemented at the beginning of the 1969–1970 academic year, and the court maintained jurisdiction.

The District Court's acceptance of the plan disallowed the freedom of choice plan, but accepted a neighborhood school plan. DCSS proposed, and HEW generally accepted, the neighborhood plan. The neighborhood plan meant the closing of all segregated black schools. Those black students were assigned to schools in other neighborhoods.

Occasionally, between 1969 and 1986, blacks asked the court to intercede in the implementation of the DCSS desegregation plan. DCSS was ordered in 1976 to do three things: first, to broaden its minority-to-majority program; second, to create a biracial committee that would be responsible for the minority-to-majority program and any revamping of attendance areas; and third, to assign teachers so that the racial ratio would resemble the racial makeup of the school district's student population. Between 1977 and 1979 the court approved an attendance area change and denied DCSS's request to limit the minority-to-majority program. DCSS was ordered in 1983 to expand the minority-to-majority program.

DCSS petitioned in 1986 to be removed from the authority of the court. It wanted the court to affirm that it was a unified school district and all vestiges of a dual system were abolished. The District Court noted that DCSS had made great gains in establishing a unified system. Its ruling was in two parts. A unified system existed, it ruled, in the areas of students' school assignments, transportation, physical facilities, and extracurricular activities. However, the court retained jurisdiction in the areas of teacher and principal assignments, resource allocation, and quality of education, finding that a dual system still existed. DCSS was told to remedy these areas.

The Court of Appeals ruled that the District Court could not retain jurisdiction in some areas and relinquish jurisdiction in others. The Court of Appeals held that all aspects of a unified system had to be met before a court could remove any jurisdiction. The Supreme Court rescinded the Court of Appeals's decision and remanded the case to the District Court. It concluded that the supervising court had the discretion to determine what areas it needed to continue to oversee.

United States v. Fordice (505 U.S. 717 [1992]) was a case focused on the definition of racially neutral institutions of higher education in states that had racially identifiable public higher education institutions. The case originated in Mississippi.

In 1848 Mississippi established the University of Mississippi for the higher education of whites. Four additional historically white post-secondary institutions were later established. They were: Mississippi State University in 1880, Mississippi University for Women in 1885, University of Southern Mississippi in 1912, and Delta State University in 1925. Three HBCUs were established in the state. Alcorn State University, 1871, was an agricultural college. Jackson State University, 1940, was established to train African American teachers to teach in African American public schools. Mississippi Valley State University, 1950, had the responsibility of training teachers for rural and elementary schools as well as vocational education.

Mississippi's higher education policies continued to operate on a dual system, in spite of the *Brown I* and *Brown II* decisions. James Meredith was the first black admitted to the University of Mississippi. He was admitted in 1962 by court order. Between 1962 and 1974, the dual higher education system was generally maintained. In those twelve years, one black student was admitted to each of the historically white institutions. Alcorn State had admitted five whites by 1968, and the other two HBCUs were totally black.

In 1969, to enforce Title VI of the Civil Rights Act of 1964, the U.S. Department of Health, Education, and Welfare (HEW) ordered Mississippi to develop a plan that would dismantle the dual system. The Mississippi Board of Trustees of State Institutions of Higher Learning submitted its plan. The plan was dependent on quotas for student enrollment, hiring faculty at the state institutions, and establishing remedial programs and special recruitment efforts. HEW rejected the plan because it did not do enough to dismantle the dual system in the areas of student recruitment and enrollment, faculty hiring, duplication of programs, and institutional funding methods. Thus, from HEW's standpoint the plan did not comply with Title VI. Despite HEW's decision, the board implemented its plan. The implementation of the plan was impeded by the Mississippi legislature, which did not fund the plan until 1978, and then with less than half of the money the board had requested.

In 1975, black citizens of Mississippi filed a suit arguing that the dual system violated the Fifth, Ninth, Thirteenth, and Fourteenth Amendments as well as Title VI of the 1964 Civil Rights Act. Subsequently, the United States, through HEW, filed its suit stating that Mississippi had not met the requirements of the equal protection of the laws clause of the Fourteenth Amendment or the requirements of Title VI. The parties were ordered by the District Court to develop a plan on which they could all agree. After twelve years the two parties were still not able to reach agreement on the remedy for voluntary desegregation.

In 1981, the board submitted mission statements for the eight public postsecondary institutions. The institutions were categorized as comprehensive, urban, and regional. University of Mississippi, Mississippi State, and Southern Mississippi were the comprehensive institutions. Their existing resources were the greatest and they had the broadest program offerings. These institutions would continue to offer doctorates and be the flagship institutions for certain fields of study. Jackson State would be the only urban school. Its research and degree mission was limited based on the needs of the urban setting. Alcorn State, Mississippi Valley, Delta State, and Mississippi University for Women were the regional institutions. In the board's plan "regional" had nothing to do with geography; regional institutions primarily offered undergraduate programs.

By 1985, the racial percentage of students in the eight institutions had not really changed. The percentage of black students at the HBCUs remained 92 percent to 99 percent. The percentage of white students at historically white schools was 80 percent to 91 percent.

By 1987, the black petitioners and HEW could not decide if the state had taken the necessary actions to abolish the dual system. This time the case went to the District Court for trial. The case focused on "admissions standards, faculty and administrative staff recruitment, program duplication, on-campus discrimination, institutional funding disparities, and satellite campuses." The plaintiffs contended that Mississippi continued to operate a dual system. The state contended that it made a good faith effort to abolish the dual system, and had established "race-neutral policies and practices" in student admission, faculty hiring, and procedures. In addition, Mississippi claimed just because institutions are racially identifiable does not mean that their existence is unlawful. In higher education, students can choose the institutions they want to attend based on their goals and the missions of the institutions. The District Court found that the state was making every effort to dismantle a dual system. The Court of Appeals concurred. The U.S. Supreme Court centered the case on whether Mississippi was meeting "its affirmative duty to dismantle its prior dual university system." The court acknowledged that students are not assigned to state universities as they can be assigned to precollege schools. Students in all states select and apply for admissions to public universities based on their educational objectives and the mission of the institutions.

The court disagreed that policies that appear to be racially neutral are necessarily racially neutral. It is possible to examine some policies and find vestiges of a *de jure* system. The court identified four areas that were traceable to a dual system, and remanded those areas to the District Court for remedy: (1) Admissions—The use of the American College Testing (ACT) Program was evidence of a dual system, and the initial purpose for using it was discriminatory. Mississippi citizens who were under twenty-one years old and applying for admission to a state university were required to take the ACT. Applicants scoring fifteen or higher on the ACT were automatically admitted to the five white universities. The Mississippi University for Women required a minimum score of eighteen. Applicants who scored fourteen or thirteen were automatically admitted to the three HBCUs. Given that as of 1985, 72 percent of the white secondary students scored fifteen or higher and 30 percent of blacks scored fifteen or higher, it is not surprising that the schools remained racially identifiable. In addition, using the ACT score as the sole determinant of automatic admission to a state institution is not the appropriate use of the examination. The association responsible for ACT "discourages use of ACT scores as the sole admissions criterion on the ground that it gives an incomplete 'picture' of the student applicant's ability to perform adequately in college." (2) Duplication of programs— The District Court defined "unnecessary duplication" of programs as those instances where two or more institutions are offering the same programs that are not core programs. Given that definition, the court decided that the "duplication at the bachelor's level of nonbasic liberal arts and sciences course work and all duplication at the master's level and above are considered to be unnecessary." The court found that 34.6 percent of the twenty-nine bachelor programs at HBCUs were unnecessarily duplicated by the white institutions, and 90 percent of the graduate programs at HBCUs were unnecessarily duplicated at the white institutions. It decided that this did not mean that these findings maintained a dual system. It stated that "elimination of unnecessary duplication would decrease institutional racial identifiability, effect student choice, and promote educationally sound policies." The Supreme Court justices could not determine whether the District Court had requested evidence on this issue. (3) Institutional Mission Statements— The Court of Appeals disagreed with the District Court, determining that the mission statements maintained racially identifiable postsecondary institutions and gave the HBCUs a limited educational arena. (4) Eliminating Institutions—Mississippi has eight institutions because of *de jure* segregation. The court acknowledged that the removal of duplicate programs and modification of admission policies could mean that some institutions would be eliminated. The fact that the majority of a student population is mostly black or white does not mean, in and of itself, that a dual system exists. What had to be carefully considered is "whether retention of all eight institutions itself affects student choice and perpetuates the segregated higher education system, whether maintenance of each of the universities is educationally justifiable, and whether one or more of them can be practically closed or merged with other existing institutions." To make this decision the policies and practices of the university system had to be considered in their entirety.

CONCLUSION

These U.S. Supreme Court cases, taken as a whole, illustrate what Gunnar Myrdal called "an American dilemma" (1944). The dilemma consists of three questions. First, what is to be done with people who were forcibly brought to these shores for the sole purpose of being free labor, more specifically chattel, for the economic benefit of whites? Second, with the social status of "slave" being illegal, how much of life, liberty, and the pursuit of happiness are African Americans to have under the constitutional status of citizen? Finally, to what extent are black citizens protected by the laws?

The selected Supreme Court cases portray the ebb and flow of legal opinions regarding African American education. Clearly, equality, equity, and quality in the education of African Americans were not going to be willingly granted by white society. Three observations can be made about these cases. First, novel means were used to block and impede the education of African Americans, specifically, and their constitutional rights as citizens of the United States, generally. The plans were either intended to not comply or to minimally comply with court mandates that benefited blacks. Second, once the plans began to be implemented, they were implemented in extremely small increments. Third, the interpretation of the equal protection of the laws clause in the Fourteenth

Amendment is dependent, in large part, upon white sensibilities concerning race in a given era.

Desegregation, which is the dominant issue in these court cases, is a complex topic for African Americans and an irritant for many whites. Beginning in 1955 with *Brown II,* it was obvious that blacks were to bear the brunt of the difficulties of school desegregation. The tangible and intangible effects of desegregation were not going to be equally shared across racial lines. Programs and plans implemented were designed to uproot black students. In some ways, desegregation became a punishment for blacks. Black schools were closed. Black children were transported to other schools. Black students were required to leave their neighborhoods.

For African Americans, desegregation has two decisive factors at its core. On one hand, desegregation was intended to provide blacks access to educational opportunities. However, even at the end of the twentieth century, the majority of the educational opportunities remained in predominantly white educational settings. Thus, to even approach the threshold of the broad spectrum of educational opportunities in the United States, blacks were required to function within white educational environments that generally did not affirm their cultural identity. As shown in Chapters 1, 3, and 4, blacks thrive academically, emotionally, and psychologically in educational settings that affirm them. Yet circumstances for full educational opportunities are not readily accessible. The historical and contemporary context of desegregation puts blacks in the dilemma of either/or. Either blacks have to decide to opt for better educational opportunities and forego, most of the time, a supportive and nurturing educational environment or blacks can elect to be in a supportive and nurturing educational environment and concede that there will be fewer educational opportunities.

A key problem with desegregation is that those who were to benefit, African Americans, were never involved in defining the concept of desegregation. Generally, the courts at all levels defined desegregation through their opinions. Subsequent state and school officials' perspectives on what desegregation *could be* forced blacks, from the beginning, to determine from within a narrowly defined context what they wanted to gain through desegregation. Desegregation became something that was done *to* blacks and not *for* blacks.

Most blacks believed that the *Brown v. Board of Education* decision (known as *Brown I*) would end *de jure* school segregation and the doctrines of equality, equity, and quality in education would be realized. However, this was not to be the case. *Brown I,* which removed the separate but equal doctrine in education, dealt with only the first barrier.

More than forty-five years after that decision, new forms of separate and unequal opportunities continue, as documented in earlier chapters of this book. These new forms include tracking and special education placement.

Ending the legalization of the separate but equal doctrine was easier than determining how it would be replaced. Voiding the doctrine could be done through a court mandate. It was a practice administrative in nature. However, something had to replace the doctrine. Its replacement, desegregation, which is based on changing the hearts and minds of people, continues to cause legal and societal consternation.

Desegregation was placed in the hands of courts along with state and educational institutional officials who had maintained *de jure* and *de facto* school segregation. For African Americans to truly benefit from school desegregation, the same systems that had denied blacks equality, equity, and quality in education for years must have, minimally, good faith and, optimally, a commitment to change. Repeatedly, the events that spawned these cases, beginning with *Brown II,* show that neither good faith nor commitment were or are forthcoming.

With over 50 percent of blacks living in inner cities, the *Rodriguez* case continues to be relevant. In an attempt to equalize funding for public school education, some states have changed their funding formulas. Yet the disparity in actual funds available to schools continues. Primarily the disparity is based on parents' ability to supplement budgets of schools with personal contributions to their children's schools, as noted by Ms. Henry in Chapter 3. Inner city children continue to have inadequately funded education and educational facilities. Davidson's, Harris's, and Henry's interviews in Chapters 1 and 3 provide examples of this disparity.

Whereas the decisions in *McLaurin* and *Sweatt* began to open the door for equal higher education access and opportunities, the *Bakke* case attempted to close those doors. The *Bakke* case is indicative of two issues embedded in the realities of African American higher education. First, affirmative action to redress long-held practices of discrimination is acceptable to whites in power only to a point. That point is when whites feel that they are being denied. Second, the opinion in this case was the handwriting on the wall for blacks seeking remedies to discrimination in higher education through the Supreme Court. The justices on the Supreme Court were changing and, in turn, the tide was changing. No longer were court opinions as decisively favorable to higher education desegregation as they had been in the past.

The *Bakke* decision was a compromise. Although allowing the minority admission program to continue, Bakke, who was never proven eligible to be admitted under any circumstance, was admitted through a court order. The compromise had several implications that would eventually bring the country to an era of anti–affirmative action. First, the Supreme Court had long held, as in *Green* and *Swann,* that quotas were a means to an end. Bakke based his case on challenging the legality of quotas. At the time of the *Bakke* case, those admitted through the minority admission program constituted only 8 percent of a total entering class. As a result of the court's decision, an increasing number of postsecondary institutions began eliminating programs that were taking affirmative actions for admitting people of color. Second, this case opened the floodgates for claims of reverse discrimination by white males. Having been the privileged group for centuries, now they were arguing that quotas and special admission programs denied them equal protection under the law. Third, assessment of qualified and unqualified students based on "standards" became an issue. Largely, being qualified was an intangible phenomenon in the minds of whites. When blacks met the "qualifications," they were still perceived as being less qualified in some other intangible ways, as noted in Davidson's, Henry's and Thomas's interviews in Chapters 1, 3, and 4 respectively. These qualifications are subtle and covert measures that stereotype blacks as inferior.

The *Fordice* case was doomed by the time it was heard by the Supreme Court. The justices were conservative and disregarded the letter and spirit of affirmative action. The court's decision was to create "racially neutral" institutions. The justices conceded that to achieve racially neutral institutions could mean that some institutions were eliminated. Racially neutral meant desegregated. African Americans remain concerned that public HBCUs will be eliminated by this order. If history is any indication of what happens in the name of quality education and desegregation, some if not all of Mississippi's HBCUs have a high probability of being eliminated, in whole or in part.

REFERENCES

Franklin, John Hope, and Alfred A. Moss, Jr. [1947] 1994. *From Slavery to Freedom: A History of African Americans.* 7th ed. New York: McGraw-Hill.

Myrdal, Gunnar. [1944] 1999. *An American Dilemma: The Negro Problem and Modern Democracy.* 2 vols. New Brunswick, NJ: Transaction Publishers.

Chapter Six

☙ Organizations, Associations, Schools, and Government Agencies

ACCREDITING ORGANIZATIONS

Following is directory information on the six regional accrediting agencies. These agencies are recognized by the U.S. Department of Education as the entities responsible for appraising the quality of education offered by elementary, secondary, and postsecondary institutions.

Middle States Association of College and Schools
3624 Market Street
Philadelphia, PA 19104
Telephone: (215) 662–5606; fax: (215) 662–5950
http://www.msache.org/
Accrediting Areas: Delaware, the District of Columbia, Maryland, New Jersey, New York, Pennsylvania, Puerto Rico, the U.S. Virgin Islands

New England Association of Schools and Colleges
209 Burlington Road
Bedford, MA 01730–1433
Telephone: (781) 271–0022; fax: (781) 271–0950
http://www.neasc.org/
Accrediting Areas: Connecticut, Maine, Massachusetts, New Hampshire, Rhode Island, Vermont

North Central Association of Colleges and Schools
30 North LaSalle Street, Suite 2400
Chicago, IL 60602
Telephone: (312) 263–0456, (800) 621–7440; fax: (312) 263–7462
http://www.ncacihe.org/
Accrediting Areas: Arizona, Arkansas, Colorado, Illinois, Indiana, Iowa, Kansas, Michigan, Minnesota, Missouri, Navajo Nation, Nebraska, New Mexico, North Dakota, Ohio, Oklahoma, South Dakota, West Virginia, Wisconsin, Wyoming

Northwest Association of Schools and Colleges
11130 NE 33rd Place, Suite 120
Bellevue, WA 98004
Telephone: (425) 827–2005; fax: (425) 827–3395
Accrediting Areas: Alaska, Idaho, Montana, Nevada, Oregon, Utah, Washington

Southern Association of College and Schools
1866 Southern Lane
Decatur, GA 30033–4097
Telephone: (404) 679–4501, (800) 248–7701; fax: (404) 679–4558
http://www.sacs.org/
Accrediting Areas: Alabama, Florida, Georgia, Kentucky, Louisiana, Mississippi, North Carolina, South Carolina, Tennessee, Texas, Virginia

Western Association of Schools and Colleges
c/o Mills College, Box 9990
Oakland, CA 94613–0990
Telephone: (510) 632–5000; fax: (510) 632–8361
http://www.wascweb.org/
Accrediting Areas: California, Commonwealth of the Northern Marianna Islands, Federated States of Micronesia, Hawaii, Republic of Palau, Republic of the Marshall Islands, U.S. territories of Guam and American Samoa

HIGHER EDUCATION ADVOCACY ASSOCIATIONS

The American Council on Education (ACE) is a national coordinating and advocacy association for higher education. As stated in its mission statement, "ACE is dedicated to the belief that equal educational opportunity and a strong higher education system are essential cornerstones of a democratic society." It has approximately 1,800 institutional members representative of a cross section of higher education institutions. Twice a month ACE publishes *Higher Education and National Affairs* (HENA). HENA provides timely information on higher education issues.

ACE Contact Information:
American Council on Education
One Dupont Circle, NW
Washington, DC 20036
Telephone: (202) 939-9300
http://www.acenet.edu

HENA Subscription Information:
Higher Education and National Affairs
American Council on Education
PO Box 191
Washington, DC 20005-0191
Telephone: (301) 604-9073

IMMERSION SCHOOLS AND SUPPLEMENTARY PROGRAMS

Two organizational forms of Afrocentric education are immersion schools and supplementary programs. Immersion schools fuse the public school district's curriculum with an African-centered education model. Supplementary programs are after-school and weekend activities that are offered by organizations to provide mentoring, tutoring, and cultural events. Following are two of the first immersion schools in the country, which are in Wisconsin, and a nationally recognized supplementary program.

Dr. Martin Luther King, Jr., African American
Immersion Elementary School
Milwaukee, WI
http://www.milwaukee.k12.wi.us/083.htm.

DuBois Learning Center
Kansas City, MO
http://www.duboislc.org

Malcolm X Academy
Milwaukee, WI
http://www.milwaukee.k12.wi.us/048.htm

MUSEUMS

The number of organizations specifically identified as museums is increasing. These museums are dedicated to the procurement, care, and display of artifacts related to the black experience, which includes aspects of African American education. All of the museums have educational programs.

California African American Museum
600 State Drive
Exposition Park

Los Angeles, CA 90037
Telephone: (213) 744–7535
http://www.caam.ca.gov/

DuSable Museum of African American History
740 East 56th Place
Chicago, IL 60637–1495
Telephone: (773) 947–0600
http://www.dusablemuseum.org

Museum of African American History
315 Warren Avenue
Detroit, MI 48201–1443
Telephone: (313) 494–5800
http://www.detroitnews.com/maah

National Civil Rights Museum
450 Mulberry Street
Memphis, TN 38103
Telephone: (901) 521–9699
http://www.midsouth.rr.com/civilrights/
Special Note: This website has an interactive tour, which highlights
some of the permanent exhibits.

NATIONAL ORGANIZATIONS

There is a network of numerous organizations that, through their missions and agendas, directly address or generally incorporate issues related to the education of African Americans. The organizations listed in
this chapter represent a microcosm of the entire network. Some of these
organizations offer conferences, fellowships, scholarships, and internship programs that further their missions.

Children's Defense Fund
25 E Street, NW
Washington, DC 20001
Telephone: (202) 628–8787
http://www.childrensdefense.org/

Congressional Black Caucus Foundation, Inc.
1004 Pennsylvania Avenue, SE

Washington, DC 20003
Telephone: (800) 784–2577 or (202) 675–6730
http://www.cbcfonline.org/index.html

National Association for the Advancement of Colored People
4805 Mount Hope Drive
Baltimore, MD 21215
Telephone: (410) 521–4939
http://www.naacp.org/

National Council of Negro Women, Inc.
633 Pennsylvania Avenue, NW
Washington, DC 20004
Telephone: (202) 737–0120
http://www.ncnw.com

National Urban League, Inc.
120 Wall Street
New York, NY 10005
Telephone: (212) 588–5300
http://www.nul.org

Office of Minorities in Higher Education,
American Council on Education
One Dupont Circle, NW
Washington, DC 20036
Telephone: (202) 939–9395
http://www.acenet.edu/About/programs/Access&Equity/OMHE/
home.html

100 Black Men of America, Inc.
http://www.100blackmen.org

Quality Education for Minorities Network
1818 N Street, NW, Suite 350
Washington, DC 20036
Telephone: (202) 659–1818
http://qemnetwork.qem.org/

Research Focus on Black Education, Special Interest Group,
American Educational Research Association
1230 17th Street, NW

Washington, DC 20036
Telephone: (202) 223–9485
http://www.aera.net

Southern Education Foundation
135 Auburn Avenue, NE
Atlanta, GA 30303
Telephone: (404) 523–0001
http://www.sefatl.org

ORGANIZATIONS ESTABLISHED TO ASSIST HBCUs

Four organizations and one office were established to assist specifically in complementing and empowering HBCU administration, faculty, and students. Three are nonprofit, one is governmental, and one is a professional development organization. Following is directory information.

National Association for Equal Opportunity
in Higher Education (NAFEO)
8701 Georgia Avenue, Suite 200
Silver Springs, MD 20910
Telephone: (301) 650–2440
http://www.nafeo.org

National HBCU Faculty Development Network
http://www.tsu.edu/hbcunet

Office for the Advancement of Public Black Colleges
1307 New York Avenue, NW
Suite 400
Washington, DC 20005–4701
Telephone: (202) 478–6049

United Negro College Fund (UNCF)
8260 Willow Oaks Corporate Drive
Fairfax, VA 22031
Telephone: (800) 331–2244
http://www.uncf.org

White House Initiative on HBCUs
Telephone: (202) 708–8667
http://www.ed.gov/offices/OPE/hbcu

PANHELLENIC ORGANIZATIONS

Black sororities and fraternities were established as affiliates for service to black communities and the development and advancement of black leadership. These organizations remain visible in African American communities because of the lifelong involvement of their members. While many members are initiated while in college, a substantial number of members are instated after graduating from college, through the graduate chapters.

The nine sororities and fraternities listed here have community service–oriented programs that focus on some combination of social change issues affecting black communities nationally and internationally. These issues include education, health, international development, economic development and sustainability, political consciousness, and involvement. Many members of the sororities and fraternities have essential roles in or are members of organizations and associations such as the ones listed previously. Multiple membership enables cross-fertilization of agenda setting, collaboration, and cooperation.

Alpha Kappa Alpha Sorority, Inc.
Founded in 1908 at Howard University
http://www.aka1908.org

Alpha Phi Alpha Fraternity, Inc.
Founded in 1906 at Cornell University
http://www.apa1906.org

Delta Sigma Theta Sorority, Inc.
Founded in 1913 at Howard University
http://www.dst1913.org

Iota Phi Theta Fraternity, Inc.
Founded in 1963 at Morgan State University
http://iotaphitheta.org

Kappa Alpha Psi Fraternity, Inc.
Founded in 1911 at Indiana University
http://www.kapsi.org

Omega Psi Phi Fraternity, Inc.
Founded in 1911 at Howard University
http://omegapsiphifraternity.org

Phi Beta Sigma Fraternity, Inc.
Founded in 1914 at Howard University
http://www.pbs1914.org

Sigma Gamma Rho Sorority, Inc.
Founded in 1924 at Butler University (Indiana)

Zeta Phi Beta Sorority, Inc.
Founded in 1920 at Howard University
http://www.zpb1920.org

PROFESSIONAL ASSOCIATIONS

African American professional organizations have components concerned with the education of African Americans. The following selected
organizations are examples of associations that advocate the advancement of African Americans through education and professional development. Some of the associations publish journals and sponsor conferences, fellowships, scholarships, and award recognition programs.

Association for the Study of African-American Life and History
7961 Eastern Avenue, Suite 301
Silver Spring, MD 20910
Telephone: (301) 587–5900
http://www.artnoir.com/asalh

Association of Black Sociologists
PO Box 1108
Montclair, NJ 07042–0360
http://members.aol.com/blacksociology

National Alliance of Black School Educators
2816 Georgia Avenue, NW
Washington, DC 20001
Telephone: (202) 483–1549 or (800) 221–2654
http://www.nabse.org

National Association for Multicultural Education
733 15th Street, NW, Suite 430
Washington, DC 20005
Telephone: (202) 628–6263
http://www.inform.umd.edu/NAME

National Black Child Development Institute
1023 15th Street, NW, Suite 600
Washington, DC 20005
Telephone: (202) 387–1281
http://www.nbcdi.org

National Black MBA Association, Inc.
180 North Michigan Avenue, Suite 1400
Chicago, IL 60601
Telephone: (312) 236–2622
http://www.nbmbaa.org

National Council for Black Studies, Inc.
The Ohio State University
1800 Canon Dr., 1030 Lincoln Tower
Columbus, OH 43210
Telephone: (614) 292–1035

National Society of Black Engineers
1454 Duke Street
Alexandria, VA 22314
Telephone: (703) 549–2207, Ext. 210
http://www.nsbe.org

RESEARCH CENTERS

There are over seventy research institutes across the country that further the study of African American culture and disseminate information on the social, cultural, political, and historical experiences of blacks. To enhance and enrich their research focus, several of these institutions offer undergraduate and graduate research fellowships, and publications. The following research institutions have exemplary resources for the study of African American education.

**Auburn Avenue Research Library on
African-American Culture and History**
101 Auburn Avenue, NE
Atlanta, GA 30303
Telephone: (404) 730–4001, Ext. 302
http://aarl.af.public.lib.ga.us/

Carter G. Woodson Institute for Afro-American and African Studies
University of Virginia
PO Box 400162
Charlottesville, VA 22904–4162
Telephone: (804) 924–3109
http://www.virginia.edu/~woodson/

Charles L. Blockson Afro-American Collection
Temple University
First Floor, Sullivan Hall
12th and Berks Mall
Philadelphia, PA 19122
Telephone: (315) 204–5197
http://www.library.temple.edu/blockson/

Frederick D. Patterson Research Institute
8260 Willow Oaks Corporate Drive
PO Box 10444
Fairfax, VA 22031–4511
Telephone: (703) 205–3570
http://www.patterson-uncf.org

John Henrik Clarke Africana Library
Cornell University Library
310 Triphammer Road
Ithaca, NY 14850–2599
Telephone: (607) 255–3822
http://www.library.cornell.edu/africana/

Joint Center for Political and Economic Studies
1090 Vermont Avenue, NW, Suite 1100
Washington, DC 20005–4928
Telephone: (202) 789–3500
http://www.jointcenter.org

Moorland-Spingarn Research Center
Howard University
Washington, DC 20059
Telephone: (202) 806–7240
http://www.founders.howard.edu/moorland-spingarn/

Schomburg Center for Research in Black Culture
515 Malcolm X Boulevard
New York, NY 10037–1801
Telephone: (313) 491–2200
http://www.nypl.org/research/sc/sc.html

W. E. B. DuBois Institute for Afro-American Research
Harvard University
12 Quincy Street
Cambridge, MA 02138
http://web-dubois.fas.harvard.edu/

Chapter Seven

❧ Selected Print and Nonprint Resources

This chapter provides an annotated listing of scholarly books, reports, and articles related to the ten topics discussed in Chapters 1 and 3 as well as selected research on HBCUs and interdisciplinary resources. Also included is directory information for journals, periodicals, television programs, videos, and Internet sites.

PRINT RESOURCES

Articles, Books, and Reports

The resources in this section will enhance and expand the reader's understanding of the topics discussed in the book concerning African Americans and American education.

Curriculum and Instruction

Banks, James A., and Cherry A. Banks, assoc. eds. 1995. *Handbook of Research on Multicultural Education*. New York: Macmillan Publishing Company.

The book presents historical, theoretical, and practical research on multicultural education. The parts of the book are: "History, Goals, Status, and Issues"; "Research and Research Issues"; "Knowledge Construction"; "Ethnic Groups in Historical and Social Science Research"; "Immigration Policy and the Education of Immigrants"; "The Education of Ethnic Groups"; "Language Issues"; "Academic Achievement: Approaches, Theories, and Research"; "Intergroup Education Approaches to School Reform"; "Higher Education"; and "International Perspectives on Multicultural Education."

———. 1999. *Multicultural Education: Issues and Perspectives*. 3d ed. New York: John Wiley and Sons.

The authors provide a practical overview of multicultural education. Chapter titles include: "Multicultural Education: Characteristics and Goals"; "Culture: Its Nature and Meaning to Educators"; "Classroom for Diversity: Rethinking Curriculum and Pedagogy"; "Ethnic Minorities and Educational Equality"; "Effective Schools: A Framework for Increasing Student Achievement"; and "Cultural Influences on Learning: Teaching Implications."

Banks, Reginald, Aaron Houge, and Terri Liddle Timberlake. 1996. **"An Afrocentric Approach to Group Social Skills Training with Inner-City African American Adolescents."** *Journal of Negro Education* 65, no. 4: 414–423.

In the article, the authors describe the results of a study comparing the effectiveness of an Afrocentric curriculum and a "culturally relevant" curriculum in the social development of African American youth ages ten through fourteen.

Dei, George Jerry Sefa. 1998. **"'Why Write Back?': The Role of Afrocentric Discourse in Social Change."** *Canadian Journal of Education* 23, no. 2: 200–208.

The article is the author's explanation of an Afrocentric curriculum as a means to equity in education.

Delpit, Lisa D. 1996. ***Other People's Children: Cultural Conflict in the Classroom***. New York: The New Press.

The author argues that the cultural miscommunications between teachers and African American students, and between African American parents and teachers, manifest themselves because of inaccurate classification of many African American students. Chapter titles include: "Language Diversity and Learning"; "Cross-Cultural Confusions in Teacher Assessment"; and "The Politics of Teaching Literate Discourse."

Ford, Donna Y. 1996. ***Reversing Underachievement among Gifted Black Students: Promising Practices and Programs***. New York: Teachers College Press.

Giftedness and underachievement, two topics that receive little attention as related to the education of African Americans, are discussed in terms of definitions, identification processes, and programs. Chapter titles include: "Gifted Students: Definitions, Theories, and Assessment"; "Underachievement: Definitions, Theories, and Assessment"; "Cultural Factors as Correlates of Underachievement"; "Psychological Factors as

Correlates of Underachievement"; "Schools Influences on Under-achievement"; and "Promising Practices, Paradigms, and Programs."

Foster, Michele. 1996. *Black Teachers on Teaching.* New York: The New Press.

Black teachers tell of the gains and losses in African American education over the past fifty years. Interviews are divided into three sections: "The Elders"; "The Veterans"; and "The Novices."

Grant, Carl A., and Gloria Ladson-Billings, eds. 1997. *Dictionary of Multicultural Education.* Phoenix, AZ: Oryx Press.

This is a resource book of over 150 articles defining factors related to multicultural education.

Hilliard, Asa G., III, Lucretia Payton-Stewart, and Larry O. Williams, eds. 1996. *Infusion of African and African American Content in the School Curriculum.* Chicago: Third World Press.

Recommendations are made on the inclusion of African and African American constructs in the curriculum. Chapter titles include: "The Cultural Base in Education"; "Curriculum and Cultural Identity"; "Future Directions for African and African American Content in the School Curriculum"; and "Curriculum Aids and Background Readings."

Hollis, Etta R., and Eileen I. Oliver. 1999. *Pathways to Success in School: Culturally Responsive Teaching.* Mahwah, NJ: Lawrence Erlbaum.

The book is designed to introduce curricular and pedagogical approaches that are culturally responsive for culturally diverse classrooms. Chapter titles include: "Becoming a Reflective Practitioner"; "Culturally Mediated Instruction in Mathematics: Strength and Barriers"; "'People Like Us': African American Children Respond to Self-Affirming Texts"; "Productive Science Teaching for Inner-City African American Students"; and "Sophistry, Aristotle, Contrastive Rhetoric, and the Student of Color."

Ladson-Billings, Gloria. 1997. *The Dreamkeepers: Successful Teachers of African-American Children.* Reprint. San Francisco: Jossey-Bass Publishers.

Through her lenses as an African American scholar, teacher, and parent, the author presents the varying styles and approaches of eight teachers who affirm the relevance of culture in the education of African American students. Chapter titles include: "A Dream Deferred"; "Seeing Color"; "Seeing Culture"; and "Culturally Relevant Teachers."

Oakes, Jeannie. 1985. *Keeping Track: How Schools Structure Inequality.* New Haven, CT: Yale University Press.

The author analyzes the patterns and practices of tracking based on data from approximately 300 classrooms. Chapter titles include: "The Distribution of Knowledge"; "Classroom Climate"; "Student Attitudes: The Legitimation of Inequality"; "Some Constitutional Questions"; and "The Search for Equity."

Perry, Theresa, and Lisa Delpit, eds. 1998. *The Real Ebonics Debate: Power, Language, and the Education of African-American Children.* Boston: Beacon Press.

The book revisits the 1996 Ebonics controversy in Oakland, California, and reveals the political, social, and educational outgrowth from it. The five parts of the book are: "Introduction"; "What Is Ebonics?"; "Classroom Implications"; "The Oakland Resolution"; and "Personal Essays."

Shulaa, Mwalimu J. 1994. *Too Much Schooling, Too Little Education: A Paradox of Black Life in White Societies.* Lawrenceville, NJ: Africa World Press.

The need and ways to imbue the education of African American children with their cultural reference points is emphasized in the book. Chapter titles include: "Education and Schooling: You Can Have One without the Other"; "Outthinking and Outflanking the Owners of the World: An Historiography of the African-American Struggle for Education"; "The Search for Access and Content in the Education of African-Americans"; "Educating for Competence in Community and Culture: Exploring the Views of Exemplary African-American Teachers"; "Afrocentric Transformation and Parental Choice in African-American Independent Schools"; "The Rites of Passage: Extending Education into the African-American Community."

Smitherman, Geneva. 1999. *Talkin That Talk: Language, Culture, and Education in African America.* New York: Routledge.

As an African American linguist, the author analyzes and discusses the interrelation among language, culture, and African American education. The six parts of the book are: "Ebonics, Language Theory, and Research"; "Language and the Education of African Americans"; "Language and Culture"; "Language Policy, Politics, and Power"; "Columns"; and "The Struggle Continues."

Welch, Olga M., and Carolyn R. Hodges. 1997. *Standing Outside on the Inside: Black Adolescents and the Construction of Academic Identity*. Albany: State University of New York.

Based on a six-year longitudinal study of African American students in two urban high schools, the authors analyze and discuss the results of academic achievement and precollege enrichment. Chapter titles include: "Precollege Enrichment for African American Adolescents and the Construction of Identities: Is There a Relationship?"; "Diffusing the Rumors of Inferiority: Creating a Climate of Excellence for Inner-City, College-Bound Students"; and "Equal Access to Excellence: Shifting the Center and Reconstructing Knowledge."

Williams, Belinda, ed. 1996. *Closing the Achievement Gap: A Vision for Changing Beliefs and Practices*. Alexandria, VA: Association for Supervision and Curriculum Development.

This book contains an investigation and analysis of factors that affect urban student academic achievement and the need for urban school reform. Chapter titles include: "Bridging the Achievement Gap in Urban Schools: Reducing Educational Segregation and Advancing Resilience-Promoting Strategies"; "Cultural Values in Learning and Education"; "Educating Teachers to Close the Achievement Gap: Issues of Pedagogy, Knowledge, and Teacher Preparation"; "Closing the Achievement Gap: Opportunity to Learn, Standards, and Assessment"; and "Teacher Engagement and Real Reform in Urban Schools."

Education and Poverty

Attles, Henrietta S. Evans. 1997. *The Effects of Homelessness on the Academic Achievement of Children*. Rev. ed. New York: Garland.

Through this study, the influence of homelessness on the achievements of homeless children based on their results on the California Achievement Test is examined, and recommendations are provided. The "Review of Literature" chapter includes: "Political Implications of the Problem of Homelessness"; "Socioeconomic Implications of Homelessness"; "Shelters and Welfare Hotels"; "Psychological Implications of Homelessness"; and "Educational Implications of Homelessness."

Ellsworth, Jeanne, and Lynda J. Ames, eds. 1998. *Critical Perspectives on Project Head Start: Revisioning the Hope and Challenge*. Albany: State University of New York Press.

A discussion of Head Start as a program for social change and its interactions with the communities it serves and with social service agencies. Chapter titles include: "A Lost Legacy: Head Start's Origins in Community Action"; "Beyond Busywork: Crafting a Powerful Role for Low-Income Mothers in Schools or Sustaining Inequalities?"; "Personal Growth in Head Start"; "Developmentalism Meets Standardized Testing: Do Low-Income Children Lose?"; and "Inspiring Delusions: Reflections on Head Start's Enduring Popularity."

Kozol, Jonathan. 1988. *Rachel and Her Children: Homeless Families in America*. New York: Crown.

Homeless children's living and schooling environments are examined. Chapter titles include: "The Mood of Resignation"; "Stereotypes"; "Distancing Ourselves from Pain and Tears"; and "One Childhood: No Second Chance."

———. 1991. *Savage Inequalities: Children in America's Schools.* New York: Crown.

The author illustrates how the education system does not address the educational needs of poor children.

———. 1996. *Amazing Grace: The Lives of Children and the Conscience of a Nation*. New York: HarperPerennial.

Based on interviews with parents, children, and community people in the South Bronx, the author tells the story of life in one of the poorest communities in the United States.

Mills, Kay. 1999. *Something Better for My Children: How Head Start Changed the Lives of Millions of Children*. New York: Penguin.

The book is a review of the author's visits to Head Start centers in diverse settings across the United States. Chapter titles include: "The First Day of School at Watts Towers Center"; "Mississippi: The Fight for Control"; "Fort Belknap, Montana: A Powwow to Preserve a Culture"; "Montgomery County, Maryland: Head Start in a Suburban School System"; "Where Are They Now?"; and "Getting Men Involved, Getting Communities Involved."

Orfield, Gary, and Elizabeth H. DeBray, eds. 1999. *Hard Work for Good Schools: Facts, Not Fads, in Title I Reform.* Cambridge, MA: The Civil Rights Project, Harvard University.

This volume is a collection of research that explores factors needing to be considered for Title I programs to be more effective in achieving their purpose. Chapter titles include: "Strengthening Title I: Designing a Policy Based on Evidence"; "Instruction, Poverty, and Performance; Older Students Also Need Major Federal Compensatory Education Resources"; and "Overcoming the Cognitive Wall: Accelerating the Learning of Title I Students after Third Grade."

Educational Governance

Sarason, Seymour Bernard. 1995. *Parental Involvement and the Political Principle: Why the Existing Governance Structure of the Schools Should Be Abolished.* San Francisco: Jossey-Bass.

The author presents alternatives to the current local and state governance of education institutions and systems. Chapters include: "Consideration of Power"; "Sources of Resistance"; "Beyond the Political Principle"; and "Changing the System."

Wirt, Frederick M., and Michael W. Kirst. 1997. *The Political Dynamics of American Education.* Berkeley, CA: McCutchan.

The macropolitical and micropolitical aspects of education are examined. Chapter titles include: "Conflict, Politics, and Schools"; "School Policy Access: Boards, Elections, and Referenda"; "Local School Boards, Politics, and the Community"; "The State Political Process"; "Federal Aid"; and "The Politics of Education Standards."

Educational Ideology

Goodlad, John I., and Pamela Keating, eds. 1995. *Access to Knowledge: The Continuing Agenda for Our Nation's Schools.* New York: Henry Holt.

The nineteen essays in this book address the structure of education and the challenges of achieving equality, equity, and quality education in American schools. Chapter titles include: "Common Schools for the Common Weal: Reconciling Self-Interest with the Common Good"; "Equal Access to Quality in Public Schooling: Issues in the Assessment of Equity and Excellence"; and "Educators for a Truly Democratic System of Schooling."

Gutmann, Amy. 1999. *Democratic Education.* Rev. ed. Princeton, NJ: Princeton University Press.

The author examines the theory of education and related educational policies in America. Chapter titles include: "Dimensions of Democratic Participation"; "The Limits of Democratic Authority"; "Distributing Higher Education"; and "The Primacy of Political Education."

House, Ernest R. 1999. **"Race and Policy."** *Education Policy Analysis Archives* 7, no 16. (A peer-reviewed scholarly electronic journal: http://epaa.asu.edu/epaa/v7n16.html.)

The author discusses the relationship between race and the formulation and implementation of education policies that influence schooling experiences of students. The sections of the article are: "Our National Identity"; "The Formative Process"; "Education Policy"; "The Education of Blacks in the South, 1860–1935"; "Chicago Desegregation, 1967"; "Chicago Retention, 1998"; and "The Current Educational System."

Kohl, Herbert. 1995. *I Won't Learn from You: And Other Thoughts on Creative Maladjustment.* New York: The New Press.

Through five essays, the author examines public education and its potential for social and political activism. Chapter titles include: "Excellence, Equality, and Equity"; "Uncommon Differences: On Political Correctness, Core Curriculum, and Democracy in Education"; and "Creative Maladjustment and the Struggle for Public Education."

Educational Opportunities

American Council on Education. 1999. *Making the Case for Affirmative Action in Higher Education: What You Can Do to Safeguard Affirmative Action on Campus and in Your Community.* Washington, DC: American Council on Education.

The book traces the legal actions related to and implications of affirmative action and provides suggestions on political activism that can be taken in support of affirmative action. The sections are: "Threats to Affirmative Action"; "Affirmative Action Works"; "Answering the Critics"; "Legal Issues"; "What You Can Do"; and "ACE and Affirmative Action."

Brown, William G., and Derek Bok. 2000. *The Shape of the River: Long-Term Consequences of Considering Race in College and University Admissions.* Princeton, NJ: Princeton University Press.

The authors discuss affirmative action in higher education based on their analysis of data on the educational and employment attainment of graduates of selected institutions. Chapter titles include: "Historical Context"; "Academic Outcomes"; "Employment, Earnings, and Job Satisfaction"; "Diversity: Perspective and Realities"; and "Informing the Debate."

Fritzberg, Gregory J. 1999. *In the Shadow of "Excellence": Recovering a Vision of Education Opportunity for All.* San Francisco: Caddo Gap.

The author discusses how federal, state, and local education policies have impeded educational opportunities for segments of the American population, and makes recommendations. Chapter titles are: "The Recent Neglect of Equality of Opportunity in American Educational Policy"; "Less Than Equal: The Chronic Victims of Inequality of Educational Opportunity"; "Opportunities of Substance: Revisiting Equality of Opportunity as a Moral Ideal"; and "Opportunities to Learn: The Manifestations of Equality of Opportunity in American Educational Policy."

Howe, Kenneth R. 1997. *Understanding Equal Education Opportunity: Social Justice, Democracy, and Schooling.* New York: Teacher College Press.

The author reviews educational and societal issues that influence educational opportunity. Chapter titles include: "A Radical Liberal Framework"; "Multiculturalism"; "Segregation"; and "Testing."

Lowe, Eugene Y., ed. 1999. *Promise and Dilemma: Perspectives on Racial Diversity and Higher Education.* Princeton, NJ: Princeton University Press.

The book contains essays and responses to essays by educators with various views on affirmative action. Chapter titles include: "Promise and Dilemma: Incorporating Racial Diversity in Selective Higher Education"; "A Threat in the Air: How Stereotypes Shape Intellectual Identity and Performance"; "Problematics of Affirmative Action: A View from California"; and "What a University Can Learn and Teach about Conflict and Differences: Comments on the Essay."

McQuillan, Patrick James. 1997. *Educational Opportunity in an Urban American High School: A Cultural Analysis.* Albany: State University of New York Press.

The author examines how administrators, teachers, and students have varying definitions of educational opportunity, and how those definitions influence what occurs in an urban high school.

Higher Education

Anderson, Charles W. 1996. *Prescribing the Life of the Mind: An Essay on the Purpose of the University, the Aims of Liberal Education, the Competence of Citizens, and the Cultivation of Practical Reason.* Madison: University of Wisconsin Press.

The author explains ways that universities can reconcile themselves with their aims and address external expectations. Chapter titles include: "What Do We Expect a University to Do?"; "Competence: What Can We Know? What Are We Entitled to Teach?"; "The Core of the Curriculum"; and "The Governance of the University."

Bloom, Allan. 1988. *The Closing of the American Mind: How Higher Education Has Failed Democracy and Impoverished the Souls of Today's Students*. New York: Simon and Schuster.

The author contends that the twentieth century social and political crisis was actually an intellectual crisis from which universities remained distant and aloof. The three sections of the book are: "Students"; "Nihilism American Style"; and "The University."

Kors, Alan Charles, and Harvey A. Silverglate. 1999. *The Shadow University: The Betrayal of Liberty on America's Campuses*. New York: HarperCollins.

The authors contend that the environment at postsecondary institutions embodies the antithesis of social, political, and intellectual liberties. Chapter titles include: "Free Speech in a Free Society"; "What Is Academic Freedom?: The Moral Reality of Political Correctness"; "Individual Identity: The Heart of Liberty"; "Double Standards: Some Are More Equal than Others"; and "The Rules of Civilization."

Miller, Richard E. 1998. *As If Learning Mattered: Reforming Higher Education*. Ithaca, NY: Cornell University Press.

The author discusses the resistance to change in higher education. Chapter titles include: "Thinking with Students: Deliberations on the History of Educational Reform"; "'Education for Everybody': Great Books and the Democratic Ideal"; "Cultural Studies for the Masses"; and "Distance Education and the Open University's Ideal Student."

Nussbaum, Martha Craven. 1998. *Cultivating Humanity: A Classical Defense of Reform in Liberal Education*. Cambridge, MA: Harvard University Press.

The author demonstrates how classical education in the Western tradition embraces multiculturalism. Chapter titles include: "Socratic Self-Examination, Citizens of the World, the Study of Non-Western Cultures" and "African American Studies."

Historically Black Colleges and Universities

The majority of the research involving HBCUs consists of comparisons with historically white institutions. Research specifically on HBCUs is sporadic. Dissertations provide some of the most consistent research on these institutions. Following are selected articles, reports, and dissertations about HBCUs.

Carroll, Evelyn CJ. 1982. **"Priorities in Philanthropic Support for Private Negro Colleges and Universities, 1930–1973"** Ph.D. diss., University of Michigan. (UMI No. 8214970.)

Fennell, Reginald. 1997. **"Health Behaviors of Students Attending Historically Black Colleges and Universities: Results from the National College Health Risk Behavior Survey."** *Journal of American College Health* 46: 109–117.

Gray, William H., III. 1997. **"The Case for All-Black Colleges."** *The ERIC Review, 5,* no. 3: 21–23.

Haynes, Leonard L., III. 1997. **"A Century of Success: Historically Black Colleges and Universities, America's National Treasure—Annual Report/The African American Education Data Book. Volume I: Higher and Adult Education."** *Journal of Negro Education* 66, no. 1: 94–96.

Payne, Ilene D. 1995. **"The Viewpoint of Historically Black Colleges/Universities (HBCU) Presidents: Four Viability Issues for HBCUs in a Pluralistic Society."** Ph.D. diss., The Union Institute, 1995. Abstract in *Dissertation Abstracts International* 56: 10A.

Ponder, Anna K. 1998. **"Empowering Difference: Politics, Particularism, and the Protection of Parallel Institutions."** Ph.D. diss., Yale University. Abstract in *Dissertation Abstracts International* 59: 5A.

Price, Sherrell M. 1995. **"Black Students' Perceptions at Historically Black Colleges and Universities Concerning Faculty, Staff, and Various Aspects of the Institutions that Contribute to the Overall College Experience."** Ed.D. diss., University of Alabama. Abstract in *Dissertation Abstracts International* 57: 2A.

Robinson, Yolanda A. 1997. **"The Federal Commitment to Historically Black Colleges and Universities: The Dollars and Sense of Title III of the Higher Education Act of 1965."** Ph.D. diss., Claremont Graduate School. Abstract in *Dissertation Abstracts International* 58: 3A.

Rowland, Terri Y. 1997. **"Institutional Advancement Initiatives of Historically Black Colleges and Universities: A Multicase Study of African**

American Higher Education." Ed.D. diss., North Carolina State University. Abstract in *Dissertation Abstracts International* 58: 6A.

Thomas, Arthur E., and Green, Robert L. 1993. **"Historically Black Colleges and Universities: An Irreplaceable National Treasure."** *Central State University News* (June).

Originally written for the 1993 Presidential Peer Conference of the National Association for Equal Opportunity in Higher Education, this article is in the Appendix. Written by Arthur E. Thomas, president emeritus of Central State University in Ohio, and Robert L. Green, professor at Michigan State University, it provides a historical and contemporary accounting of HBCUs, and over thirty bibliographic entries.

Wagener, Ursula Elizabeth, and Michael T. Nettles. 1998. **"It Takes a Community to Educate Students."** *Change* 30, no. 2: 18–25.

Wenglinsky, Harold. 1997. *Students at Historically Black Colleges and Universities: Their Aspirations and Accomplishments*. Princeton, NJ: Policy Information Center Educational Testing Service.

Wesley, Vinetta L. 1997. **"Leadership at Historically Black Colleges and Universities: Impact on Student Outcomes."** Ed.D. diss., Peabody College for Teachers of Vanderbilt University. Abstract in *Dissertation Abstracts International* 58: 4A.

White House Initiative on Historically Black Colleges and Universities. 1999. **"Historically Black Colleges and Universities for the 21st Century: Annual Report of the President's Board of Advisors on Historically Black Colleges and Universities."** ERIC ED428626.

Interdisciplinary Resources

Anderson, Claud. 1994. *Black Power, White Wealth: The Search for Power and Economic Justice*. Bethesda, MD: PowerNomics Corporation of America.

The author traces the history of economic disparity between blacks and whites, and suggests solutions. Chapters include: "The Nature of the Problem"; "Impediments to Empowerment and Economic Justice"; "Why Whites Chose to Enslave Blacks"; "White Bridges to Wealth and Power"; and "Becoming Political and Economically Competitive in America."

Asante, Molefi Kete. 1997. *The Afrocentric Idea.* Rev. ed. Philadelphia: Temple University Press.

The book defines and analyzes Afrocentric thinking. Chapters include: "Rhetorical Conditions as a Conceptual Field"; "African Foundations in Nommo"; "African American Orature and Context"; and "The Search for an Afrocentric Method."

Beauboeuf-Lafontant, Tamara, and D. Smith Augustine, eds. 1996. *Facing Racism in Education.* Cambridge, MA: Harvard Educational Review.

The book contains essays by a variety of authors who examine the implications of racism in the education of children of color. Chapters include: "Reflections of a Black Social Scientist: Some Struggles, Some Doubts, Some Hopes"; "The Silenced Dialogue: Power and Pedagogy in Educating Other People's Children"; "Racelessness as a Factor in Black Students' School Success: Pragmatic Strategy or Pyrrhic Victory?"; "Cultivating a Morality of Care in African American Adolescents: A Culture-Based Model of Violence Prevention"; "Because You Like Us: The Language of Control"; and "Talking about Race, Learning about Racism: The Application of Racial Identity Development Theory in the Classroom."

Blassingame, John W., ed. 1971. *New Perspectives on Black Studies.* Urbana: University of Illinois Press.

The editor provides a collection of articles by authors who provide the history of black studies and with varying views on the need and significance of black studies. Chapters include: "What Should Be the Role of Afro-American Education in the Undergraduate Curriculum?"; "Ghetto and Gown: The Birth of Black Studies"; "Black Studies: Bringing Back the Person"; "Black Studies: Trouble Ahead"; "A Charade of Power: Black Students at White Colleges"; "The Road to the Top Is through Higher Education, Not Black Studies"; and "Black Studies: An Intellectual Crisis."

Boyd, Herb, and Robert L. Allen, eds. 1995. *Brotherman: The Odyssey of Black Men in America—An Anthology.* New York: Ballantine Books.

A collection of essays, stories, and poems by nationally and internationally known black men, this anthology chronicles the black male experience. The sections of the book are: "Forefathers"; "A Son in the Family"; "Relationships"; "Trouble Man"; "Black Magic"; and "Sankofa: Past as Prologue."

Breggin, Peter R., and Ginger Ross Breggin. 1998. *The War against Children of Color: Psychiatry Targets Inner City Youth.* Monroe, ME: Common Courage Press.

The authors, a physician and a researcher, present their investigation into the excessive use of medications with inner city children and the implications for their education and lives. Chapters include: "Born to Be 'Disruptive'? Diagnosing and Drugging America's Children and Youth"; "Current Federal Programs for the Biomedical Control of Children and Youth"; "Racial Guinea Pigs? Victims of Genocide?: Science and the African American"; and "Ending Biomedical Child Abuse."

Comer, James P. 1995. *School Power: Implications of an Intervention Project*. New York: Simon and Schuster.

The author provides ways for educators to draw on the theories of education and behavioral and social sciences to address issues in schooling. Chapters include: "The School Program"; "The Mental Health Program"; "The Parent Program"; "Teachers, Teaching, and Curriculum"; and "Pre-Service and In-Service Education."

Douglass, Frederick. [1845] 1999. *The Frederick Douglass Papers: Series Two: Autobiographical Writings. Vol. I*. Edited by John W. Blassingame, John R. McKivigan, and Gerald Fulkerson. New Haven, CT: Yale University Press.

In these essays written by Frederick Douglass seven years after escaping slavery, he provides an account of his life and his views of the differing worlds of slavery and freedom.

Gibbs, Spencer C. 2000. *Above Our Heads: The Making of a Morehouse Man*. New York: Hamilton House.

The author chronicles his four years at Morehouse College, describing what this school does to produce some of the black male leaders in the United States.

Giddings, Paula. 1996. *When and Where I Enter: The Impact of Black Women on Race and Sex in America*. Reprint. New York: William Morrow and Co.

The author provides a history of black women in America. Chapters include: "Casting of the Die: Morality, Slavery, and Resistance"; "'To Be a Woman, Sublime': The Ideas of the National Black Women's Club Movement (to 1917)"; "A Search for Self"; "Dress Rehearsal for the Sixties"; and "The Women's Movement and Black Discontent."

Hacker, Andrew. 1995. *Two Nations: Black and White, Separate, Hostile, Unequal*. New York: Ballantine Books.

The author examines the continued racial gulfs in America and their impact on society and people. Chapters include: "Race and Racism: Inferiority or Equality?"; "Being Black in America"; "White Responses: Right and Left, Guilt and Sex"; "Education: Ethnicity and Achievement"; "Segregated Schooling: Voluntary and Imposed"; and "What's Best for Black Children?"

Harding, Vincent. 1981. *There Is a River: The Black Struggle for Freedom in America.* San Diego, CA: Harcourt Brace and Company.

The author provides an in-depth account of African American history from capture in Africa through the end of the Civil War. Chapters include: "American Bondage, American Freedom: Shaping the Struggle"; "Rebels, Resistants and Others: Building the River's Power"; "Strange River in Canaan: The Paradoxical Search for Freedom in the North"; "The Blood-Red Ironies of God: Civil War, Black Freedom, and the Dialectics of Transformation"; and "Black Hope, Black Soldiers, and Black Codes: The Clashing Versions of Justice."

hooks, bell, and Cornel West. 1991. *Breaking Bread: Insurgent Black Intellectual Life.* Boston: South End Press.

The book presents interviews and dialogues between the two authors on various aspects of black intellectualism. Chapters include: "Black Men and Women: Partnership in the 1990s"; "The Dilemma of the Black Intellectual"; and "Black Women Intellectuals."

Jones-Wilson, Faustine C. 1977. *The Changing Mood in America: Eroding Commitment?* Washington, DC: Howard University Press.

Using Gunnar Myrdal's *An American Dilemma* as the conceptual framework, the author examines the climate in the United States for equal opportunity for African Americans, raising issues that remain relevant in the twenty-first century. Chapters include: "The Changing Mood in the Dominant Society since 1969"; "The Changing Tone of the Federal Government since 1969"; "The Changing Mood in Education"; and "The Changing Mood and the Future."

Kozol, Jonathan. 2000. *Ordinary Resurrections: Children in the Years of Hope.* New York: Crown Publishers.

The author provides insight into the "miracles" that can occur in the lives of children living in New York's South Bronx, one of the most economically deprived communities in the United States, in spite of continued societal general indifference toward their circumstances and potential as participants in society.

Marable, Manning. 1996. *Beyond Black and White: Transforming African-American Politics.* New York: Verso Books.

The author examines the dynamics of the status of African Americans through the lenses of politics, black leadership, and race. Chapters include: "Race and Class in the U.S. Presidential Election of 1992"; "Affirmative Action and the Politics of Race"; "Clarence Thomas and the Crisis of Black Political Culture"; "Education, Faith and the Promise of Equality"; "Black Intellectuals in Conflict"; "African-American Empowerment in the Face of Racism: The Political Aftermath of the Battle of Los Angeles"; "The Divided Mind of Black America: Race, Ideology and Politics in the Post–Civil Rights Era"; and "History and Black Consciousness: The Political Culture of Black America."

Myrdal, Gunnar. [1944] 1999. *An American Dilemma: The Negro Problem and Modern Democracy.* 2 vols. New Brunswick, NJ: Transaction Publishers.

This two-volume study, which remains relevant today, is considered a landmark comprehensive study on the status of African Americans and race relations in the United States. The sections in Volume 1 are: "The Approach"; "Race"; "Population and Migration"; "Economics"; and "Politics." The sections in Volume 2 are: "Justice"; "Social Inequality: Social Stratification"; "Leadership and Concerted Action"; "The Negro Community"; and "An American Dilemma."

Sarat, Austin. 1996. *Race, Law, and Culture: Reflections on* **Brown v. Board of Education.** New York: Oxford University Press.

The essays contained in this volume use the *Brown* decision as a framework to analyze race, law, and culture in American education. Chapters include: "*Brown* in Context"; "From *Brown* to *Casey:* The U.S. Supreme Court and the Burden of History"; "Social Engineers or Corporate Tools?"; "*Brown v. Board of Education* and the Conscience of the Black Corporate Bar"; and "Cultural Imperialism, White Anxiety, and the Ideological Realignment of *Brown.*"

Taylor, Robert Joseph, James S. Jackson, and Linda M. Chatters, eds. 1997. *Family Life in Black America.* Newbury Park, CA: Sage.

The contributors provide an examination of the varying family structures and interactions among African Americans. Chapters include: "Life Stress and Psychological Well-Being among Married and Unmarried Blacks"; "Families, Unemployment, and Well-Being"; "Child Rearing, Social Support, and Perceptions of Parental Competence among African American

Mothers"; "Strategies of Racial Socialization among Black Parents: Mainstream, Minority, and Cultural Messages"; "Instrumental and Expressive Family Roles among African American Fathers"; and "Changes Over Time in Support Network Involvement among Black Americans."

Washington, Linn. 1998. *Black Judges on Justice: Perspectives from the Bench.* New York: The New Press.

Fourteen black federal, state, and local jurists share their experiences in and insights on the U.S. justice system in relation to African Americans. The sections are: "Opening Argument"; "The Front Line"; "The Pioneers"; "The Future"; and "Closing Argument."

West, Cornel. 1994. *Race Matters.* New York: Vintage Books.

The author provides a critique of racism in America, characterizing it as xenophobia. Chapters include: "Nihilism in Black America"; "The Pitfalls of Racial Reasoning"; and "Beyond Affirmative Action: Equality and Identity."

School Reform

Clinchy, Evans, ed. 1997. *Transforming Public Education: A New Course for America's Future.* New York: Teachers College Press.

A variety of issues on education reform is discussed through the theme of education transformation. Chapter titles include: "Reframing the School Reform Agenda: Developing Capacity for School Transformation"; "Art and Imagination: Reclaiming a Sense of the Possible"; "The End of the Federally Driven Standards Movement in U.S. School Reform?"; "Listening to Voices on the Inside: Beyond the Conservative-Liberal-Radical Debate to a Common Vision for Schools in Our Multiethnic Society"; and "Reinventing Schools—From the Bottom Up."

Hirsch, E. D., Jr. 1999. *The Schools We Need: And Why We Don't Have Them.* New York: Random House.

The author offers an explanation for why school reform has not produced the expected and needed education outcomes. Chapter titles include: "Introduction: Failed Theories, Famished Minds"; "Intellectual Capital: A Civil Right"; "Reality's Revenge: Education and Mainstream Research"; and "Test Evasion."

Kohn, Alfie. 1999. *The Schools Our Children Deserve: Moving beyond Traditional Classrooms and "Tougher Standards."* Boston: Houghton Mifflin.

The author examines the effects of education reform that are dependent on tougher standards, and provides alternatives. Chapter titles include: "Tougher Standards Versus Better Education"; "Getting Motivation Wrong: The Cost of Overemphasizing Achievement"; "Getting School Reform Wrong: The Arrogance of Top-Down Coercion"; and "Education at Its Best: The Way Out."

Paris, David C. 1995. *Ideology and Educational Reform: Themes and Theories in Public Education*. Boulder, CO: Westview Press.

The premise of this book is that due to three conflicting views of the aims and purposes of public schools, education reform has not occurred. Chapter titles include: "The First Triangle: The Problems of Education Reform"; "The Common School Theme: Moral Education and the 'Tie that Binds'"; "Schools, Scapegoats, and Skills: Educational Reform and the Economy"; and "The Future of Educational Reform: Political Choices and School Culture."

Sarason, Seymour B. 1996. *Revisiting "The Culture of the School and the Problem of Change."* New York: Teacher College Press.

Twenty-five years after the first publication of the book, the author reexamines university and school relations and principals, teachers, and school environments as they relate to school reform. The two parts of the book are: "Part I—The Culture of the School and the Problem of Change" (this was the original book) and "Part II—Revisiting: 25 Years Later."

Timpane, P. Michael, and Lori S. White, eds. 1998. *Higher Education and School Reform*. San Francisco: Jossey-Bass.

The authors examine the need for a collaborative relation between higher education institutions and school systems for reform in precollege education. Chapter titles include: "'Something, But Not Very Much': School-University Partnerships in Historical Perspective"; "The Role of State Policy Systems in Fostering Separation or Collaboration"; and "School Improvement and Higher Education."

Schooling Experiences

Anyon, Jean. 1997. *Ghetto Schooling: A Political Economy of Urban Educational Reform*. New York: Teacher College Press.

Focusing on Newark, New Jersey, the author explains school reform from the perspective of urban school needs through a historical and contemporary examination. Chapter titles include: "Cities, Urban Schools, and Current Visions of Educational Reform"; "Social Class, Race, and Educational Reform at Marcy School"; "Pauperization of the City and Its Schools: 1945–1960"; and "Class, Race, Taxes, and State Educational Reform: 1970–1977."

Comer, James A., and Alvin F. Poussaint. 1992. ***Raising Black Children: Two Leading Psychiatrists Confront the Educational, Social, and Emotional Problems Facing Black Children.*** New York: Plume/Penguin.

The authors ask and answer questions on the unique parenting concerns for black children to succeed educationally, socially, and emotionally. Chapter titles include: "America and the Black Child"; "The Preschool Child—Ages Two to Four"; "The School Age Child—Ages Five to Eight"; "The Black Child in School—An Overview"; "The Elementary School Child—Ages Nine to Twelve"; and "Adolescence."

Curry, Constance. 1995. ***Silver Rights: The Story of the Carter Family's Brave Decision to Send Their Children to an All-White School and Claim Their Civil Rights.*** San Diego, CA: Harcourt.

The author recounts the personal experiences of a family of black children experiencing desegregation of a school system in Mississippi. Chapter titles include: "We Thought They Meant It"; "Take Care of My Kids"; "Advancement for Colored People"; "I've Got Needs"; and "She Wouldn't Let Us Say We Wished We Had Never Been Born."

Fordham, Signithia. 1995. ***Blacked Out: Dilemmas of Race, Identity, and Success at Capital High***. Chicago: University of Chicago Press.

The author examines black community culture in relation to African American achievement and attainment. Chapter titles include: "Schooling and Imagining the American Dream: Success Alloyed with Failure"; "Teachers and School Officials as Foreign Sages"; "School Success and the Construction of 'Otherness'"; "Retaining Humanness: Underachievement and the Struggle to Affirm the Black Self"; and "Reclaiming and Expanding Humanness: Overcoming the Integration Ideology."

Hale, Janice E. 1994. ***Unbank the Fire: Visions for the Education of African American Children***. Baltimore: Johns Hopkins University Press.

Using her family's history, the author illustrates the importance of the infusion of African American culture into the educational experiences of African American children. The two parts of the book are: "Understanding African American Children in the Context of Their

History" and "Educating African American Children in the Context of Their Culture."

Kozol, Jonathan. [1967] 1985. *Death at an Early Age: The Destruction of the Hearts and Minds of Negro Children in the Boston Public Schools*. New York: Plume.

The author describes educational conditions of 1964 Boston (Massachusetts) Public Schools as experienced by African Americans.

Lipman, Pauline. 1998. *Race, Class, and Power in School Restructuring*. Albany: State University of New York.

The author investigates the impact of school reform on the education of African American children. Chapter titles include: "The Education of African Americans and School Restructuring"; "Teachers' Beliefs about African American Students"; and "Conclusion: Restructuring in Social Context."

Shujaa, Mwalimu J. 1996. *Beyond Desegregation: The Politics of Quality in African-American Schooling*. Thousand Oaks, CA: Corwin Press.

The author examines school desegregation from a historical, philosophical, and political context in relation to African American communities and the schooling of African American students. Chapter titles include: "Reclaiming Historical Visions of Quality Schooling: The Legacy of Early Twentieth-Century Black Intellectuals"; "The Brown Decision Revisited: Mathematizing a Social Problem"; "Cultural Ignorance and School Desegregation by District-Level School Administrators"; "Before and After School Desegregation: A Community Narrative"; and "All-Black School: Inherently Unequal or a Culture-Based Alternative?"

Smith, Willy DeMarcell, and Eva Wells Chunn, eds. 1991. *Black Education: A Quest for Equity and Excellence*. New Brunswick, NJ: Transaction.

The book is a collection of papers commissioned by the National Urban League. The sections of the book are: "Commentaries"; "Perspective and Analysis"; "Selected Issues"; "Spectrum on Desegregation"; "Strategies for Academic Excellence"; and "Special Reports."

Vernon-Feagans, Lynne. 1996. *Children's Talk in Communities and Classrooms*. Oxford, England: Blackwell Publishers.

The author examines the initial school experiences of rural African American children and an early intervention strategy. Chapter titles include: "Poverty, Language, and Early Intervention"; "The Communities, Families, and Schools"; "Language Use Out of School"; and "Tutorial Interaction between Teacher and Child."

Schooling Options

Ascher, Carol. 1991. *School Programs for African American Males*. New York: ERIC Clearinghouse on Urban Education.

This monograph discusses the issues of schooling experiences of young black males and provides descriptions of seventeen programs and an extensive bibliography.

Bush, Lawson V. 1997. **"Independent Black Institutions in America: A Rejection of Schooling, an Opportunity for Education."** *Urban Education* 32, no. 1: 98–116.

In this article the author presents the historical context for independent African American schools and reasons for their continued existence.

Lomotey, Kofi. 1992. **"Independent Black Institutions: African-Centered Education Models."** *Journal of Negro Education* 61, no. 4: 455–462.

This article discusses the focus of African-centered education and the origins and purpose of the Council of Independent Black Institutions (CIBI).

Warfield-Coppock, Nsenga. 1992. **"The Rites of Passage Movement: A Resurgence of African-Centered Practices for Socializing African American Youth."** *Journal of Negro Education* 61, no. 4: 471–483.

The article discusses a study conducted on rites of passage programs and its findings.

Testing

Fischer, Claude S., Michael Hout, Martin Sanchez Jankowski, Samuel R. Lucas, Ann Swidler, and Kim Voss. 1996. *Inequality by Design: Cracking the Bell Curve Myth*. Princeton, NJ: Princeton University Press.

Reexamining the findings in *The Bell Curve*, the authors refute the conclusions that intelligence is innately endowed. Chapter titles include: "Why Inequality?"; "Understanding 'Intelligence'"; "The Rewards of the Game: Systems of Inequality"; and "Enriching Intelligence: More Policy Choices."

Fraser, Steven, ed. 1995. *The Bell Curve Wars: Race, Intelligence, and the Future of America*. New York: Basic Books.

This is a compilation of nineteen articles that dismantle the conclusions drawn in *The Bell Curve*. Article titles include: "Cracking Open the IQ Box"; "Race, IQ, and Scientism"; "The Source of *The Bell Curve*"; "Back to the Future with *The Bell Curve*: Jim Crow, Slavery, and G"; "Has There Been a Cognitive Revolution in America? The Flawed Sociology of *The Bell Curve*"; "Scientific Truth and the American Dilemma"; and "Equality: An Endangered Faith."

Hernstein, Richard J., and Charles Murry. 1995. *The Bell Curve: Intelligence and Class Structure in American Life*. New York: Simon and Schuster.

The authors contend that intelligence is innate and hierarchical in nature in the context of race/ethnic groups. Chapter titles include: "Cognitive Class and Education, 1900–1990"; "Ethnic Difference in Cognitive Ability"; "Ethnic Inequalities in Relation to IQ"; "Social Behavior and the Prevalence of Low Cognitive Ability"; "Raising Cognitive Ability"; and "The Leveling of American Education."

Hilliard, Asa G., III, 1996. *Testing African American Students*. Chicago: Third World Press.

The author disputes the accuracy of standardized test results as measurements of African American children's abilities. Chapter titles include: "Psychometrics and African American Reality: A Question of Cultural Antimony"; "Standardized Tests and African Americans: Communication and Language Issues"; "The Impact of Testing on African Americans"; and "It's Time to Examine the Examiners."

Milofsky, Carl. 1989. *Testers and Testing: The Sociology of School Psychology*. New Brunswick, NJ: Rutgers University Press.

The author examines how school psychologists define their purpose and role in urban and suburban settings, and the influence of those definitions on how they fulfill their professional responsibilities. Chapter titles include: "Intelligence Testing and Race in the Public Schools"; "Activism versus Formalism in School Psychology"; "Work Orientation and Testing Patterns"; and "How Organization Affects Psychologists' Work Orientation."

Qualls, Audrey L. 1998. **"Culturally Responsive Assessment: Development Strategies and Validity Issues."** *Journal of Negro Education* 67, no. 3: 296–301.

The author argues that reliable and valid assessment is only as relevant as the cultural premise of the curricula.

Sacks, Peter. 1999. *Standardized Minds: The High Price of America's Testing Culture and What We Can Do to Change It.* Cambridge, MA: Perseus.

The author examines the reliance of education and other sectors on standardized testing, and the appropriate use of assessment. Chapters include: "Inventing Intelligence: The Origins of Mental Measurement"; "Babes in Test Land: The Sorting Begins"; "Crime and Punishment: How the Accountability Machine Hurts School Children"; and "Do No Harm: Stopping the Damage to American Schools."

Sandoval, Jonathan H., Craig L. Frisby, Kurt F. Geisinger, Julia Ramos-Grenier, and Janice Dowd Scheuneman, eds. 1998. *Test Interpretation and Diversity: Achieving Equity in Assessment.* Washington, DC: American Psychological Association.

This book is intended to instruct test interpreters on how to avoid bias in test score interpretations with diverse populations. Chapter titles include: "Psychometric Issues in Test Interpretation"; "Critical Thinking in Test Interpretation"; "Culture and Cultural Differences"; "High-Stakes Testing in Education"; "Poverty and Socioeconomic Status"; and "Test Interpretation in a Diverse Future."

Journals

The Black Scholar
This journal contains articles that examine black culture and political thought, and issues in the United States and Africa. The website is http://www.theblackscholar.org.

The Crisis
This is the premier publication of the National Association for the Advancement of Colored People (NAACP). It was founded by W. E. B. DuBois in 1910. It presents national and international events and issues that affect the lives of nonwhites nationally and internationally, and the past and present achievements of these people. The website is http://www.naacp.org/crisis.

Journal of Blacks in Higher Education
JBHE publishes scholarly papers on issues affecting blacks in higher ed-

ucation as well as providing governance, policies, and practices in colleges and universities. The website is http://www.jbhe.com.

Journal of Negro Education

This is a refereed scholarly publication that was founded in 1932 at Howard University. Its mission is to disseminate information on the education of black people, to analyze current and proposed policies and practices related to the education of black people, and to serve as a catalyst for research about black education. The website is http://jne.law.howard.edu.

Souls

This journal is published quarterly and sponsored by the Institute for Research in African-American Studies at Columbia University. It is an interdisciplinary publication that presents the contemporary issues and various ideologies related to African Americans. The website is: http://www.columbia.edu/cu/iraas/souls.

Periodicals

There are approximately 200 black newspapers in the United States. These newspapers are black owned and operated. They are published in the fifty states and the District of Columbia. The papers, mostly published weekly, are a source of information on political, economic, social, and educational issues of concern to blacks locally, nationally, and internationally. In many cities, these papers are distributed at black churches. The following website lists the black newspapers and contacts by state: http://www.aasm.com/pubs.html.

Black Issues in Higher Education

This is a newsmagazine that is published biweekly. It provides information on higher education issues that affect African Americans as well as other people of color. The website is http://www.blackissues.com.

NONPRINT RESOURCES

Internet

The number of websites focused specifically on African American culture and consumer interests is increasing. The following websites were selected because of their highlighted focus on news, issues, and events concerning the African American community. They include chat rooms.

The Black World Today
http://www.tbwt.com

BlackFamilies.com
http://www.blackfamilies.com

NetNoir, Inc.
http://www.netnoir.com

Television

Information on program topics can be accessed through the websites.

Black Entertainment Television Network (BET)
This is the first black-owned cable television network in the United States. Its mission is to meet the needs and interests of African Americans. It offers three news and public affairs programs. The website is: http://www.betnetworks.com.

BET News

Monday through Friday, 11:00 P.M. (EST). A thirty-minute news program of national and international news from an African American perspective.

BET Tonight with Travis Smiley

Monday through Friday, 11:30 P.M. (EST). A thirty-minute program that focuses on news, issues, and trends. Viewers can call in to speak with guests.

Lead Story

Sunday, 10:30 A.M. (EST). A thirty-minute program that examines and analyzes national and international news and events of the week.

Teen Summit

Saturday, 1:00 P.M. (EST) and 5:00 P.M. (EST). This one-hour program provides a forum for teenagers to discuss issues affecting them with guests. This program is part of the Cable in the Classroom series.

Tony Brown's Journal

A half-hour weekly discussion program on PBS. The website is: http://www.tonybrown.com/journal.htm.

Black Issues Forum

A half-hour weekly public service program on PBS through the University of North Carolina Television. Check local television listings for day and time. The website is http://link.unctv.org/bif.

Videos

Across the River: Saving America's Inner Cities

Five aspects of inner city development are presented. One aspect is school programs that boast a 94 percent graduation rate in an area where the dropout rate is usually 40 percent.

Length: 57 minutes
Source: Films for the Humanities and Sciences
PO Box 2053
Princeton, NJ 08543–2053
(800) 257–5126

Affirmative Action and Reaction

Law professor Lani Guinier examines the issues concerning affirmative action. Professor Guinier received national attention when President Clinton nominated and then withdrew her nomination for assistant attorney general for civil rights.

Length: 26 minutes
Source: Films for the Humanities and Sciences
PO Box 2053
Princeton, NJ 08543-2053
(800) 257-5126

Affirmative Action under Fire: When Is It Reverse Discrimination?

Based on the 1989 New Jersey high school case concerning the employment of a black teacher and a white teacher, Cokie Roberts moderates a debate between the president of the NAACP and the director of litigation from the Institute of Justice.

Length: 22 minutes
Source: Films for the Humanities and Sciences

PO Box 2053
Princeton, NJ 08543-2053
(800) 257-5126

African-Americans: Marching to Freedom

ABC News anchor Peter Jennings illustrates the rise of black political consciousness from the Civil Rights movement in the 1960s through the Million-Man March in 1995.

Length: 54 minutes
Source: Films for the Humanities and Sciences
PO Box 2053
Princeton, NJ 08543-2053
(800) 257-5126

American Apartheid

This program examines and questions the real and perceived status and condition of African Americans.

Length: 37 minutes
Source: Films for the Humanities and Sciences
PO Box 2053
Princeton, NJ 08543-2053
(800) 257-5126

Autobiography of Miss Jane Pittman

The 110-year-old fictional character traces her life from slavery through the birth of the Civil Rights movement. The movie is based on the novel by Ernest J. Gaines. Suggested age level is senior high school and college.

Length: 110 minutes
Source: Instructional Media Services
1291 Hickory Street, Suite E
Pewaukee, WI 53072
(262) 691-1200

Awakenings 1954–1956

The American social system of segregation, by Jim Crow in the South and by tradition and routine in the North, is described. The far-reaching influences of these practices on the education, employment, and economics of African Americans are examined. This is the first program in the *Eyes on the Prize* series.

Length: 60 minutes
Source: PBS Video

Customer Support Center
1320 Braddock Place
Alexandria, VA 22314-1698
(800) 344-3337

Black America and the Education Crisis
Syndicated columnist Juan Williams moderates a town meeting to discuss test scores, academic performance, and Ebonics.

Length: 45 minutes
Source: Films for the Humanities and Sciences
PO Box 2053
Princeton, NJ 08543-2053
(800) 257-5126

Black History: Lost, Stolen or Strayed
The distortions of the historical roles and contributions of African Americans is examined through narration by Bill Cosby. Suggested age levels are grades six and up.

Length: 60 minutes
Source: Wisconsin Reference and Loan Library
AV Booking/Circulation Department
2109 S. Stoughton Road
Madison, WI 53716-2899
(608) 224-6169

Black Is My Color—The African American Experience
African American history is explored beginning with abductions from Africa and continuing through to modern discriminatory practices.

Length: 16 minutes
Source: Instructional Media Services
1291 Hickory Street, Suite E
Pewaukee, WI 53072
(262) 691-1200

BreakThrough: The Changing Face of Science in America
This video presents contemporary scientists who are people of color. The scientists chronicle their academic and educational paths and the scientific work in which they are engaged.

Length: Six 60-minute programs
Source: PBS Video
Customer Support Center

1320 Braddock Place
Alexandria, VA 22314-1698
(800) 344-3337

By River, By Rail: History of Black Migration

Poet Maya Angelou, NAACP President Kweisi Mfume, and others de-scribe the impact of blacks' migration North on African American fami-lies, and the challenges and disappointments that accompanied it.

Length: 22 minutes
Source: Films for the Humanities and Sciences
PO Box 2053
Princeton, NJ 08543-2053
(800) 257-5126

Divided We Stand

Genetic studies that are used to prove the racial superiority of whites to blacks are examined. This is a BBC Production that is part of the *In the Blood* series.

Length: 49 minutes
Source: Films for the Humanities and Sciences
PO Box 2053
Princeton, NJ 08543-2053
(800) 257-5126

Evaluating Preschool Education

The efficacy of High Scope, a program that began in Michigan and is similar to Head Start, is presented by following 123 black participants over a period of twenty-five years.

Length: 25 minutes
Source: Films for the Humanities and Sciences
PO Box 2053
Princeton, NJ 08543-2053
(800) 257-5126

The Fateful Decade: From Little Rock to the Civil Rights Bill

The desegregation of Central High School in Little Rock, Arkansas, is ex-amined.

Length: 27 minutes
Source: Films for the Humanities and Sciences
PO Box 2053

Princeton, NJ 08543-2053
(800) 257-5126

Fighting Back 1957–1962
The reactions of Southern elected officials to the *Brown v. Board of Education* decision are presented. This is the second program in the *Eyes on the Prize* series.

Length: 60 minutes
Source: PBS Video
Customer Support Center
1320 Braddock Place
Alexandria, VA 22314-1698
(800) 344-3337

Inspirations
Hosted by the late Arthur Ashe and produced by ABC News, this program presents means being used by blacks to collaboratively address issues in low-income black communities across the country. The issues include child care, urban violence and crime, housing, teenage pregnancy, and community development. This is the fifth program in the series *In Search of the Dream: A Story of the African American Experience.*

Length: 47 minutes
Source: Films for the Humanities and Sciences
PO Box 2053
Princeton, NJ 08543-2053
(800) 257-5126

The Keys of the Kingdom 1974–1980
The program examines the victories and defeats of antidiscrimination laws and affirmative action. This is the seventh program in the *Eyes on the Prize II* series.

Length: 60 minutes
Source: PBS Video
Customer Support Center
1320 Braddock Place
Alexandria, VA 22314-1698
(800) 344-3337

Legislating Morality: Affirmative Action and the Burden of History
This program explores the implications of affirmative action. Roy Innis, chairman of the Congress on Racial Equality; Ward Connerly, regent of

the University of California and the author of the Civil Rights Initiative, an anti–affirmative action movement; and Charles Willie, professor of education at Harvard, are featured.

Length: 29 minutes
Source: Films for the Humanities and Sciences
PO Box 2053
Princeton, NJ 08543-2053
(800) 257-5126

Liberty

"To what extent should African Americans strive to maintain their unique cultural heritage, and to what degree should they seek to become assimilated into the hegemonic culture?" is the question posed to U.S. Representative Charles Rangel of New York and psychologist Kenneth B. Clark. This is the sixth program in the series *In Search of the Dream: A Story of the African American Experience.*

Length: 46 minutes
Source: Films for the Humanities and Sciences
PO Box 2053
Princeton, NJ 08543-2053
(800) 257-5126

The Matter with Me

The two worlds—black and white—of a twelve-year-old black boy are seen through his eyes. The suggested grade levels are kindergarten through eighth grade.

Length: 15 minutes
Source: Instructional Media Services
1291 Hickory Street, Suite E
Pewaukee, WI 53072
(262) 691-1200

Race and Psychiatry

Focus is given to the issues of racism in mental health care and the response by some blacks to provide alternatives.

Length: 25 minutes
Source: Films for the Humanities and Sciences
PO Box 2053
Princeton, NJ 08543-2053
(800) 257-5126

Reweaving the Web: Building Communities to Nurture All Children

A panel examines the impact of economics on families and family values, and the need for intergenerational bonding.

Length: 30 minutes
Source: South Carolina Educational Television
Early Childhood Training Videos
1101 George Rogers Blvd.
Columbia, SC 29211
(803) 737-3308
ecnp@scetv.org

The Road to Brown—The Man Who Killed Jim Crow

The history of segregation and the legal strategies that were the catalysts for the Civil Rights movement are presented through the work of attorney Charles Hamilton Houston, who is known as "the man who killed Jim Crow."

Length: 56 minutes
Source: California Newsreel
149 Ninth St.
San Francisco, CA 94103
(415) 621-6196

Saviors

This video examines the federal government's role in legislating and enforcing rights for African Americans. It discusses *Brown v. Board of Education of Topeka,* assesses the Supreme Court's role in civil rights, and evaluates presidents Ronald Reagan's and George Bush's records on civil rights. This is the fourth program in the *In Search of the Dream: A Story of the African American Experience* series.

Length: 47 minutes
Source: Films for the Humanities and Sciences
PO Box 2053
Princeton, NJ 08543-2053
(800) 257-5126

☞ Appendix: Historically Black Colleges and Universities: An Irreplaceable National Treasure

Arthur E. Thomas and Robert L. Green

> *"If Historically Black Colleges and Universities did not exist in their present form, it would be necessary for the supporters of Black educational excellence to re-invent them."*
>
> —*Lerone Bennett, Jr.*

EDITOR'S NOTE: This paper was prepared by Arthur E. Thomas, then president of Central State University, and Robert L. Green, then professor of education at Cleveland State University. It was presented at the 1993 Presidential Peer Conference of the National Association for Equal Opportunity in Higher Education. Thomas served as chair of the NAFEO board of directors for 1993. He is chairman of the organization's International Committee and a former member of the board of directors.

At no other time in the nation's history have Historically Black Colleges and Universities been better prepared to train and graduate the hundreds of thousands of African-American students who attend Black institutions of higher learning. Ironically, however, just when Historically Black Colleges and Universities (HBCUs) are now poised to provide the African-American community and the nation with even greater educational benefits than ever before, the Black college system is being threatened by forces that would fundamentally harm, if not destroy, the character and quality and the strength of Black institutions of higher learning.

Coming as they do at this point in the history of Black colleges, these threats to the existence of HBCUs represent the ultimate in injury and insult. After decades of painstaking efforts, sacrifice, and scrambling and scraping for only the minimal resources allotted to keep these institutions viable and effective, after some 150 years of fighting against the rampant racism that was the cause for HBCUs to be established in the first place—after enduring and surviving all manner of social and racial mistreatment and yet emerging from all this as highly respected educational institutions, Black colleges are now confronted by the injustice of proposals to phase them out of existence.

The Supreme Court in a June 1992 decision ruled in the Ayers vs. Fordice case that the state of Mississippi was guilty of having maintained a dual and discriminatory system of higher education that deprived Black colleges of proportionately equal resources. The Court further ruled that the state of Mississippi must take the necessary steps to equalize state funds appropriated to both its predominantly White and Black colleges. In response to this ruling, the *Mississippi* Board of Trustees of State Institutions of Higher Learning has made the deplorable proposal that one of Mississippi's three Black universities (Mississippi Valley State) be eliminated and that another Black college (Alcorn State University) be merged with the predominantly White Mississippi State University. This merger would, in effect, mean that Alcorn State would lose its administrative authority as well as its unique identity to function as a Black institution of higher learning. This proposal for closing and merger has dire implications, not only for Black colleges in Mississippi but for the entire system of HBCUs.

Despite the various administrative and fiscal reasons being given to justify these proposals to merge or close African-American schools, the conclusion is inescapable that race and racism are major motives underlying these proposals. In far too many cases, the very same ones who now want to close HBCUs are the same ones who throughout the history of this country have done all in their power to keep Black colleges separate and highly unequal. Having failed through both legal and extralegal means to break the determination of the African-American college system to support higher education for African-American youth, these opponents of Black advancement now hope to accomplish the same negative, racially hostile aims under the guise of fiscal necessity.

Some might doubt these charges of racism. But why is it (as is true in the present case) that throughout the history of our nation it is the African-American community that suffers the harshest impact from the social restructuring that takes place? From urban renewal to expressway construction, to reapportionment, to school integration, to name a few recurrent social changes, it is the African-American community that has invariably borne the severest impact. And why now, it must be asked, is it only African-American educational institutions that must bear the brunt of the proposed changes? Why is it not being proposed that White institutions in Mississippi (and other states) be closed? More importantly, with all the objective, statistical data showing the absolutely critical role of Black colleges to the educational advancement of the African-American community, how could any concerned, fair-minded person propose the closure of a single Black institution of higher learning? Regrettably, for both African Americans and the wider community, there are too many involved in the decision-making process who are not concerned or fair-minded.

Not fairness but racism also appears to be a major factor in the timing of these proposals to close Black schools. Now that Black colleges and universities have become even more competitive with the larger and better-funded White schools and now that HBCUs are attracting greater and greater numbers of top-ranked African-American students, many Historically White Colleges and Universities (HWCUs) perceive Black colleges as a serious threat. Within the various individual states and across the nation these White schools are being forced to compete as never before for limited funds and for a select number of high-profile African-American students. Opponents of Black colleges see in the proposed mergers and closures a convenient and legally supported opportunity to do all they can to eliminate and undermine the increasingly stronger challenge represented by HBCUs.

These proposals for closing Black schools must also be seen as a form of retaliation against African-American citizens for having the audacity to demand that HBCUs in Mississippi, Alabama, Louisiana, and other states be provided with funding proportionately equal to that provided to White state schools. How dare African Americans demand equality of treatment, various decision-makers in these states appear to be saying. How dare African-American educators and the African-American community petition for the equality of funding that has been their legal right but that has been routinely and systematically denied them since the original legislation establishing state-supported colleges in 1862 (1). And when African Americans do dare to request a fair share of resources, it is not equal treatment they receive but rather retaliation in the form of threats and proposals to begin the wholesale destruction of Black institutions of higher learning. These threats of mergers and closures are all too consistent with a history of institutional racism that has been implemented to keep African Americans undereducated, subordinate and "in their place."

These opponents of Black colleges seek to undermine HBCUs and in so doing undermine the African-American community's most consistent source for the nurturing of outstanding African-American leaders. With fewer Black colleges and universities, the African-American community would be deprived of invaluable centers of critical, independent thought. The shaping of the social and political outlook of African-American youth would then increasingly be dominated by institutions and individuals potentially antagonistic to the larger aspirations of the African-American community. Such a situation represents a grave danger. For as the pioneering African-American historian and educator Carter G. Woodson long ago observed:

> "When you control a man's thinking, you do not have to worry about his actions. You do not have to tell him to stand here or go yonder. He will find his 'proper place' and stay in it. You do not need to send him to the back door. He will go without being told. In fact, if there is no back door, he will cut one for his special benefit. His education makes it necessary." (2)

In response to the argument above, there are many as noted earlier, who believe that since African Americans now have the opportunity to attend HWCUs, there is no longer a need for Black colleges. Yet it would never occur to these same people to suggest that since people of Irish descent have wider educational options today, Notre Dame can or should be closed or that since Jews have freer educational choices, Brandeis and Yeshiva Universities can or should be closed. Nor is it ever suggested that the Black schools in the various states in question should be kept open while White schools in these states be closed.

More than twenty years ago, the great African-American educator Dr. Benjamin Mays spoke about similar efforts to close Black schools. His insightful remarks deserve to be quoted at length.

> "It is discouraging and disturbing to me that there are indications of a subtle move afoot to abolish Black colleges. Prior to Emancipation and since, thousands of White writers have taken pride in their determination to brand Negroes as inherently inferior. Something similar has occurred regarding Black colleges since 1954. Writers have pounced on the Negro colleges, not with the purpose of helping them, but rather, it seems of destroying them. Numerous critics have made a crusade of tearing Black colleges apart, but no group of White colleges has been selected and set aside as targets for annihilation. White liberals and White conservatives alike have participated in this tragedy . . ." (3)

Dr. Mays's words ring ominously true today.

Many of those who do not see the importance of maintaining a strong HBCU system are, understandably, not aware of the marked differences that can exist in the educational experiences of African Americans who attend Black colleges as opposed to those who attend White colleges. Yet, for large numbers of African-American students there are, unfortunately, still qualitative differences between the learning environments and outcomes on White and Black campuses. To cite only one illustrative example of these differences, Harvard for its 1992–93 freshman class enrolled fewer than 100 African Americans. (4) The average size HBCU enrolls 10 to 15 times more freshmen each year. If our society had to rely on only the accomplishments of such schools as Harvard to supply the desperate need for Black doctors, scientists, and engineers, the plight of the African-American community, and of race relations, would be far worse than it is today and would be so for decades to come.

In contrast to other schools, HBCUs have both a historical and an institutional commitment to maintaining and promoting the educational progress of African-American and other low-income students. Consequently, until Harvard produces as many BAs as Hampton or Howard, until Cornell enrolls and graduates as many African Americans as Central State or Clark Atlanta universities, until Stanford graduates as many Black students as Shaw and Spelman, until the University of Mississippi produces as many African-American BAs as Jackson State University, there should not be even a suggestion of closing a Black college or university. Rather, the focus of inquiry should be on Historically White Colleges and Universities and on the reasons why to this day they do not do nearly as well as Historically Black Colleges and Universities in educating and graduating African-American students.

The fact that White colleges in general are far less effective than HBCUs in graduating African-American students is the central issue that should be kept uppermost in the minds of those who might question whether there continues to be a need for Black institutions of higher learning. Such persons are likely to ask: 1) Are not all of our colleges open to all students, regardless of race? 2) Is it not our goal to establish a color-blind, integrated society?

The answer to both of these questions is yes, but as will be shown in this paper a great number of White colleges and universities continue to employ practices and policies that have a negative, color-conscious impact on African American students. On the other hand, the cultivation by HBCUs of well-educated, well-trained young African Americans who can go out and make a meaningful contribution to society and who can therefore interact with other groups and races on the basis of mutual respect is one of the surest means of creating the foundation for achieving our common goal of a color-blind, integrated society. This is the crucial service and function that Black colleges continue to perform in our society. It is a function that no other educational institutions have shown the capacity to perform as successfully as HBCUs.

For the evidence clearly shows that throughout the history of America no other institutions, whether private or public, technical or professional, two-year or four-year, small college or major university—none of these have done as much to prepare and educate African-American students as have Historically Black Colleges and Universities—None. This fact, this undeniable truth is the message that must be spread more widely among the general public, black and white. It is especially imperative that HBCUs' record of excellence be made better known to political decision-makers at both the state and federal levels.

This task of increasing our public relations efforts and enhancing our public profile is crucial if Historically Black Colleges and Universities are to overcome the mounting threats to their very existence. We can emerge victorious from the present dangers but we must work in unity and with great diligence if we are to achieve success. Encouragement can be taken from the fact that lessons of success can be found throughout the history of HBCUs. In a fundamental sense our current problems are nothing new, because Black colleges from their inception have had to struggle to maintain themselves in an atmosphere of hostility and opposition.

HISTORICAL OVERVIEW OF BLACK COLLEGES

The first Black colleges (Cheyney, Lincoln, and Wilberforce universities) were established in the North well before the Civil War and the abolition of slavery. It is important to note that these institutions were organized in response to the widespread discrimination and resistance on the part of Northern Whites to African Americans obtaining basic and advanced learning experiences. (5) It was the African American's universal demand and thirst for knowledge that spurred White and Black missionaries, Northern philanthropists, and the Freedmen's Bureau to found and support Black colleges. (6)

From the very beginning Black colleges were determined to provide their students with the kind of comprehensive higher education they would need to be able to return to their communities as effective, contributing teachers, scientists and leaders. (7) As of 1865 only 28 known African Americans had received BAs from American colleges. (8) However, by the turn of the century, HBCUs had already produced more than 2,000 four-year college graduates. In other words, in a period of approximately 40 years HBCUs produced almost 100 times more BAs than Historically White Colleges and Universities had produced in the roughly 200 years that African-Americans had been in the United States. Despite this remarkable success, however, there were influential voices, both North and South, who questioned the value or the need for African Americans to receive a higher education. In the decade following the Compromise of 1876 the federal government abandoned the egalitarian ideals of Reconstruction and, in consequence, abandoned African-American hopes for equality of treatment. One key outgrowth of this abandonment was a prevailing agreement between Northern and Southern Whites that higher or liberal education was fundamentally not appropriate for Blacks. It was generally agreed instead that industrial education was the only suitable and necessary education for a backward and subordinate race of people. (9) The same kind of resistance to Black educational advancement can be seen today in the great difficulty many HBCUs have in getting approval for comprehensive undergraduate programs and for the establishment of graduate programs. (10)

All those concerned about or involved with Black educational development are well aware of the classic confrontation and debate between W.E.B. DuBois and Booker T. Washington over the relative educational needs and options of Black people. (11) What is perhaps not as well known is that it was not only DuBois and his circle who opposed the subservience implied in the dominant industrial-education-only philosophies of the day. Most significantly, it was the presidents and faculty of most Historically Black Colleges who steadfastly refused to yield to an ideology of subordination. On the contrary, these administrators and teachers worked both covertly and overtly to expand the spiritual and intellectual horizons of young African-American minds. It was these HBCU administrators who defied current opinions and gave practical expression to the ideas of DuBois and others. It was our predecessors who made the determination to provide both industrial and technical *and* liberal arts training to African-American students. And it was from this determination that our HBCUs were able to produce the doctors, nurses, lawyers, architects, teachers, and other skilled professionals so desperately needed to serve the African-American community. (12) This same determination to provide African-American students today with the widest and best possible educational opportunities was unanimously expressed at the March 1993 18th annual conference of the association of colleges and universities that make up the National Association for Equal Opportunity in Higher Education (NAFEO).

Just as was the case in 1890, so today in 1993 HBCU presidents find themselves opposed to much current thinking in educational circles. In fact there are striking parallels between the opposition of our predecessors to the dominance of industrial education and our strong opposition today to the continually increasing placement of African Americans in community colleges rather than in four-year institutions. (13) The parallel nature of our situation today with that of 1890 was a point strongly emphasized in the first annual report of the President's Board of Advisers on Historically Black Colleges and Universities (PBA). (14)

It can be seen, then, that the present troubles of HBCUs are in many respects only current versions of old problems. And as Tollett rightly points out, there has been a continued ebb and flow in the support provided for Black educational development. He further notes, "As one observes the state of Blacks in the United States over historical time, it generally can be assessed in terms of how well the society has regarded and treated them educationally." (15) When consideration is given to the cutbacks in state funding that so many of Black colleges have recently faced, to the increased ratio of loans to scholarships, to the decreasing number of Black males in college, and when consideration is given to the ominous threats to Black colleges in Mississippi and other states, what emerges is an all too vivid and alarming picture of the distressed state of African-American education in our society today.

The great irony in these circumstances is that while there are those who advocate a reduced role for Black colleges in the higher education system, it might well be argued that the need for the contributions of HBCUs has never been greater. Given the universal agreement about the imperative need for a more skilled workforce in the immediate future and given the large percentage of undereducated and underskilled in the African-American community, we would think that our state and national leaders would be doing all they could to bolster the position of Black colleges. Given these needs for maintaining the economic strength of the country, and the political muscle in the world arena, it would seem unthinkable that our state and national leaders would be doing anything to harm the unquestionably best source for producing highly skilled and trained African Americans. As is well known, however, state and national leaders are doing just such harm.

INDISPENSABLE CONTRIBUTIONS OF HISTORICALLY BLACK COLLEGES AND UNIVERSITIES

Despite the long record of accomplishment, African-American institutions of higher learning are continually threatened and challenged to justify their existence and their worth. As Blake states, "Attacking historically Black Colleges' capacity to produce baccalaureates is a tactic that has been consistently employed to maintain the inequality of Blacks in higher education . . ." (16) Indeed it is a deplorable commentary on our society that these threats to the existence of Black colleges are not at all new. As already mentioned in the PBA report, emphasis was given to the broad parallels between our problems today and those faced by Black colleges in the 1890s. In the more recent past Green wrote some 25 years ago about the necessity of not only maintaining but also strengthening

Black institutions of higher learning. (17) Over this same period he has analyzed and written about the related difficulties African-American students have had in being admitted to and in graduating from predominantly White schools. (18) As is all too apparent from Green's work, the issues of access, retention and graduation for minority students remain essentially unchanged. This is why NAFEO must become a more assertive agent of change.

Those associated with HBCUs are intimately familiar with the great record of achievement of Black colleges. But for probably most of the general public, the outstanding contributions of HBCUs are an untold story. The same applies for many of the state and national legislators who at this very hour are considering the fate of these schools. As a consequence, one of the most urgent tasks of NAFEO and its individual members must be to become better publicists. It is incumbent upon HBCUs, for example, to discover and invent ways to make more widely known such facts as:

1. HBCUs in 1990 accounted for only about 17 percent of Black student enrollment but produced 27 percent of all BAs earned by Blacks. That is better than 1 in every 4 BAs earned by African-American students. (19)
2. In 1990 HBCUs trained and graduated:
   • 44 percent of the Black students who were awarded BAs in the physical sciences
   • 41 percent of the BAs to Blacks in mathematics
   • 38 percent of the BAs to Blacks in computer sciences
   • 38 percent of the BAs to Blacks in life sciences
   • 37 percent of the BAs to Blacks in education
   • 25 percent of the BAs to Blacks in engineering. (20)
   • The majority of African-American lawyers, teachers, and dentists in the country today received their baccalaureate degrees from Black institutions of higher learning. (21)
   • Overall, African-American colleges have produced up to 70 percent of all Black college graduates. (22)

In addition to their achievements in producing undergraduates, HBCUs have a major and growing impact on the development of African-American Ph.D.s. From 1986 to 1988, for example, 9 of the top 10 schools identified as the baccalaureate origin of Black Ph.D.s were historically Black colleges. (23) Relatedly, Blacks who attend HBCUs as undergraduates are more likely to persist and earn graduate degrees, including Ph.D.s, in higher numbers than Blacks who attend historically White schools. (24) Most significantly, as more HBCUs obtain Ph.D.-granting authority, the percentage of HBCU Ph.D.s has risen quickly and substantially. In fact, the proportion of Blacks earning their Ph.D.s from HBCUs increased from 3 percent in 1976–77 to 12 percent by 1989–90. Overall, the number of degrees conferred by HBCUs during this period increased by an impressive 214 percent. (25)

The above cited examples are only some of the more illustrative facts about what African-American schools routinely accomplish. These are the same kinds of facts that Dr. Edward Fort, Chancellor of North Carolina A&T University, and Dr. Elias Blake, president of the Benjamin E. Mays Resource Center, and others provided to that important House Subcommittee meeting on HBCUs in 1988. These are the same kinds of facts that have to be made known to the general public. These are the same kinds of facts that have to be made widely known in both Houses of Congress. These decision-makers need this information in order for them to realize, to clearly see, that no Ivy League schools, no PAC-10 schools, no Big Eight or Big Ten either, no public or private colleges or universities have done nor can they do what HBCUs have been committed to doing and consistently doing from the beginning: training, molding, and graduating in record numbers African-American youth who have become outstanding American citizens.

Historically Black Colleges and Universities are so successful in their mission because they have been at this work now for some 150 years. From the earliest beginning fight up until today HBCUs have had an unvarying commitment to providing Black youth with a first-rate higher education. And during this century and a half of educating, Black colleges have measured and evaluated the pedagogical methods and procedures most likely to promote the skill development and the personal and professional success of African-American youth. This is why they are the best at what they do. In fact, because of their consistent success in training those typically rejected by other institutions, Black colleges are ideally suited to develop graduate programs, both M.A. and Ph.D., in developmental education. HBCUs are proven experts in this field.

THE UNIQUE ROLE OF HBCUs IN HIGHER EDUCATION

The achievements of Black schools are inseparably linked to the overall learning environment in which African-American students are placed. Despite the very definite but still uneven and inconsistent progress that has been made in race relations, there are still many Black students who require a more nurturing learning environment than that provided at predominantly White universities. HBCUs provide these more supportive, nurturing environments, what Tollett calls "psycho-socially congenial settings." (26) In these more congenial academic settings, Black students know they will not have to contend with any forms of institutional racism. They know they can devote their energies to learning and not have to be concerned with defending themselves from the racial attacks that have been occurring more and more frequently on predominantly White campuses all over the nation. (27)

What is perhaps most important is that these Black students know that they will be taught and advised by instructors and administrators who believe in them and their ability to learn and who will hold high expectations for their academic success. This factor of belief is what from their very beginnings has distinguished HBCUs from Historically White Colleges and Universities. HBCU students did not have to overcome individual and institutional resistance in order to be admitted to Black colleges. No one had to picket or protest, or petition to get into Black colleges. Just the opposite. HBCU personnel sought these students out, encouraged them, welcomed them, and most of all, believed in their ability to succeed.

Black colleges and universities have historically steadfastly maintained their belief in their students' abilities while others have said that these students lacked either innate ability or sufficient preparation to succeed. There has developed an extensive body of literature that indicates that the beliefs and expectations of administrators and teaching staff play a major role in shaping behavioral outcomes. (28) From the HBCUs positive beliefs and expectations has evolved the complex of institutions and instructional strategies designed to best further the educational development of a large strata of African-American students.

In his essay "The Case for Black Colleges," Tollett identifies a number of unique functions served by HBCUs. (29) Several of these have already been discussed, but one important function that should not be overlooked is the leadership role performed by Black colleges and their graduates. In discussing the importance of Black leadership development, the great scholar and former president of Central State University Dr. Charles H. Wesley made this pertinent observation: "A college program of quality will be more than the traditional presentation of that material in a routine manner. Such a program will give opportunity for students to work with ideas and develop their relations to spiritual, moral, and social problems." (30)

As Tollett points out, the very existence of HBCUs "as visible and viable institutions or organizations gives some sense of pride and identity to other Blacks, particularly those who are deprived and disadvantaged." (31) Just as important, the varied administrative leaders and educators at HBCUs provide Black students with working models of success that the students can readily identify with and draw inspiration from. As Dr. Shirley Lewis said recently, these African-American teachers and administrators represent "touchable role models" for young African-American students. (32) This accessibility, as Dr. Johnnetta Cole, President of Spelman College, notes, "is what role modeling is in its ultimate and most penetrating expression." (33) Being surrounded by such a wide array of Black models is surely one of the key factors behind HBCUs' outstanding record of leadership development.

BLACK LEADERS AND HISTORICALLY BLACK COLLEGES AND UNIVERSITIES

Developing the capacity for leadership among African Americans is arguably the single most important function of Black colleges. It can only be imagined how bleak the circumstances of the African-American community and the society would be today without these pioneers, these caregivers, these trendsetters and barrier-breakers, these community and national leaders. It can be said with certainty, though, that without these HBCU-nurtured leaders critical pools of talent and ideas would be lost to both the African-American community and the nation.

In contrast to Black colleges, organizations in the larger society provide few opportunities for African Americans to practice and develop leadership skills. (34) On the other hand, the principal administrators at Black colleges and universities are African Americans and virtually all student events and organizations are led by young African Americans. These experiences often denied Blacks at predominately White institutions provide invaluable opportunities that most of these African Americans would not otherwise have to develop their leadership abilities. And the results of these leadership experiences are reflected at every realm and strata of our society.

Volumes would be required to name the many illustrious African-American graduates of HBCUs, but any such representative list would surely include: the Rev. Dr. Martin Luther King Jr., Thurgood Marshall, Spike Lee, Jessye Norman and Leontyne Price, Alice Walker, Ralph Ellison and Toni Morrison, Marva Collins and Marian Wright Edelman, Andrew Young, Douglas Wilder, and Jesse Jackson. One could go on and on naming such outstanding African Americans. Nor should it be forgotten that the unfortunately and recently deceased Richard Lewis, head of the largest Black-owned company in the nation (Beatrice Foods), was a product of a Black college. The same is true of Joshua Smith, a Central State graduate, and the owner of the computer firm MAXIMA, Inc., the ninth largest African-American business in the country.

This representative sampling of names makes clear the major impact that HBCU graduates have had and continue to have on every facet of American life, and no mention has been made of athletics. But just imagine how much less gold America's Olympic teams would bring home in the Summer Olympics without all the HBCU-trained athletes in track and field. Just the mention of names like Buck Buchanan and Walter Payton is enough to indicate that the character and quality of professional football would not be what it is today without HBCU players. And even yet today the greatest Black quarterback and one of the greatest quarterbacks ever to play in the NFL is a product of the Black college system.

As notable as are HBCUs' development of leaders in the sports field, it is the HBCUs' development of leaders in the struggle for social justice that remains their most enduring legacy. Our nation would be far more segregated and far more unjust socially without the untold sacrifices and heroic defiance of African-American students from African-American colleges. It was four Black students from North Carolina A&T who began the sit-in movement. This tactic quickly became an integral part of the entire desegregation movement for equal accommodations. SNCC, cultivated and supported by Dr. Martin Luther King, Jr., was by and large a Black-college organized and led student movement. The HBCUs were the wellspring of the Black culture awareness and Black self-appreciation movements that thrive yet today. The all-important voter registration drives, from which all of our society is still benefitting, would have been virtually impossible without the mass involvement and input of Black college staff and students.

Putting aside for the moment the many other contributions of HBCUs, the nation owes a great debt of gratitude and an obligation of sustained and substantive support to HBCUs for the instrumental role they played in bringing about one of the greatest periods of democratic expansion in the history of this country. As Tollett has aptly put it, Historically Black Colleges and Universities "have done so much, so well, with so little." (35)

Leadership development opportunities, readily accessible role models, psycho-socially congenial settings, positive and nurturing learning environments—these are some of the principal attributes that account for the high degree of success of HBCUs in educating African-American students. This is not to say that Historically White Colleges and Universities cannot provide these benefits. Far too often though, and particularly within the last five to ten years, fewer and fewer White colleges appear to be able or willing to provide the kind of positive learning environment that promotes Black educational success.

CURRENT TRENDS AT HISTORICALLY WHITE
COLLEGES AND UNIVERSITIES

One of the most obvious and most negative trends among HWCUs is the steady erosion of the affirmative admissions policies of the 60s and early 70s. This regressive approach is undoubtedly one of the key reasons for the overall decline in Black student college enrollment since the high mark period of 1976. (36) When this educational conservatism is combined with the increased hardship of low-income students having to assume higher and higher loan burdens, a clear picture develops of the institutional barriers placed in the way of Black educational progress. (37)

The numbers clearly show the harmful results of these negative policies: Since 1976 African Americans have dropped from 76 percent of parity for college-going 18 to 24 year olds to 61 percent of parity in 1990. (38) From 9.4 percent in 1976, Blacks accounted for only 8.9 percent of total college enrollment in 1990. This decline is reflected at every level of higher education, undergraduate and graduate, two-year and four-year enrollment. (39) During this period African-American females have shown occasional gains, but these gains have been heavily offset by the decline in completing degrees by African-American males at all levels in the 1980s. (40)

Only a few of the dismal figures on Black College enrollment have been cited. What these figures show, however, is that as White colleges move away from the affirmative policies of HBCUs, they are abandoning the methods that Black colleges have shown to be most successful in retaining and graduating African-American students. As NAFEO has consistently maintained, the race-neutral policies that so many HWCUs have been implementing can only have a negative, race-specific impact on Black college applicants. When most urban students receive inadequate elementary and secondary education, when most African-American youth grow up feeling the effects of some forms of institutional and societal racism, institutions of higher education cannot then turn around and demand that these youth begin to compete for placement on the same basis as students who have had the benefit of much better early preparation and opportunity.

It is HBCUs' recognition of prevailing unequal social conditions and their accordingly establishing the necessary compensatory and remedial policies that set Black colleges apart from most HWCUs. The history of the success of Black colleges has demonstrated the crucial importance of using multi-criteria in admissions standards. African-American institutions of higher learning know firsthand the rewards and benefits of looking past a student's present ACT or SAT score and seeing the motivation of a potential graduate. HBCUs know from repeated experiences that with the appropriate remediation and encouragement, the uncertain student prospect of today will be tomorrow's Black doctor, or scientist, or teacher.

HWCUs experienced these same kinds of successes when in the 60s and 70s they took an affirmative approach to admissions and the need for remediation. As they move away from these practices, they are abandoning the surest methods known for increasing the number of Black graduates. Despite the largely negative trend, however, some quarters of academia do recognize the educational gains that are derived from applying the affirmative institutional practices of HBCUs. For example, in 1991 the American Association for the Advancement of Science conducted a study entitled "Investing in Human Potential: Science and Engineering at the Crossroads." One pertinent conclusion of the study was that HBCUs offer a good example of providing access and then of retaining Blacks in the sciences and engineering. The study goes on to state that the example of HBCUs is one that the "larger and better-funded institutions should follow." One author of the study states, "The difference between HBCUs and predominately White institutions in retaining minority students in science and engineering was often that between cultivating and weeding." (41) These conclusions are similar to those reached by a 1987 report by the National Academy of Sciences and the National Science Foundation on the under-representation of minorities in science and engineering. The report concluded that a major factor in low minority representation in these fields was the insufficient number of remedial programs at universities. Similarly, Dr. L. Jay Olivia, Chancellor of the New York University system, recently stated that HBCUs, "with their strong tradition of undergraduate teaching, can give us all greater insight into issues bearing on the education of minority students." (42)

Unfortunately, there are too few administrators at HWCUs (and too few state and national decision-makers) who feel as Dr. Olivia does. This is not to say that there has not been real progress made at White colleges regarding minority issues. The broader acceptance of the need for multicultural programs and the calls for cultural diversity on campuses are positions to be applauded. On the other hand, however, we must question how such cultural diversity can be achieved when these same schools are instituting policies that severely decrease the number of their African-American students?

Significantly enough, the distance between the spoken support for and the actual practice of diversity is reflected not only in the student enrollments at White colleges but also in the composition of their college faculty. As Wilson notes, "Despite all the mandates, people of color collectively are only 11.5 percent of the faculty (at HWCUs)." More specifically, African Americans account for only 2 percent of the faculty at predominantly White schools. (43)

When Black high school seniors have to confront the prospect of being isolated on a White campus because of the increasing barriers being placed on Black student enrollment, or confront the increases in racial and ethnic violence on White campuses, or the very small number of Black faculty at HWCUs, it is hardly surprising that more and more of these Black students are choosing to go to Black colleges. Enrollment rose 16 percent at HBCUs between 1976 and 1990, with the majority of this increase coming between 1986 and 1990. This percentage increase exceeded that for all other institutions. (44) Reflective of the continually growing popularity of HBCUs is the fact that in 1990 Black colleges were the top 6 choices of Black high school seniors who took the SAT and overall 10 of their top 15 choices were Black schools. (45)

CULTURAL DIVERSITY ON HBCU CAMPUSES

Equally noteworthy is the fact that not only Black students, but White students as well are coming to HBCUs in greater and greater numbers. At present 19 percent of student enrollment at HBCUs is non-Black. What's more, between 1976 and 1980 White student enrollment at HBCUs increased by 60 percent. (46) Just as notable, and in sharp contrast to HWCUs, 33 percent of the faculty at Black colleges are non-Blacks, and most of them are White. (47)

These figures suggest that while the administrators of many other schools are talking about it, administrators of HBCUs are emphatically putting into practice the concepts of cultural and racial diversity—both for student enrollments and faculty placements. As is true of other accomplishments by Black colleges, however, the success of HBCUs in achieving cultural diversity on their campuses is too often overlooked by the media and the general public. The fact is, Black colleges and universities should be the models held up to other schools on how to achieve campus environments more reflective of the society in which we live. It should be pointed out too, that HBCUs have established cultural diversity at their institutions without all the conflict and violence that has continually plagued other institutions of higher learning.

It is critical to note in this context that the cultural diversity that has been taking place at HBCUs clearly demonstrates that scholarships and other race-specific programs targeted for African Americans can and do work effectively while still providing for the educational progress of Whites. The very same formula can be applied with comparable effectiveness at predominantly White schools. This point is crucial to understand because it will take the combined efforts of both HBCUs and HWCUs to bring the number of college-educated

African Americans up to parity levels. (48) This point is of such significance because there is hardly another issue more important to the African-American community than the substantial and long-term increase in the numbers of its college-educated population.

THE CRUCIAL ROLE OF HIGHER EDUCATION
FOR AFRICAN AMERICANS

A college degree is arguably the African American's single best weapon in the fight against poverty, inequality, and discrimination. College-educated African Americans 25 to 34 with four or more years of college in 1990 earned 98 percent of the median annual income of comparable Whites. (49) For the period 1975 to 1988 the earnings of college graduates on their first jobs increased from 132 percent to 180 percent of the earnings of high school graduates entering the work force. Notably, the ratio of earnings of Black college graduates to high school graduates increased faster than for Whites. (50) By contrast the median income for Black families overall was only 58 to 60 percent of that of Whites. (51)

The impact of a college degree on income becomes of paramount importance when we consider the role of income on family structure in the African-American community. Convincing research shows that for Black males in particular income levels play a decisive part in the formation of Black families. Simply put, the higher the income level of African-American males, the more likely they are to form stable, two-parent families. Conversely, the lower the income level, the less likely are African-American males to form stable families. (52) The problems that stem from the disarray of contemporary Black family life can hardly be overstated. It need hardly be added that these are problems that affect both the African-American community and the nation.

How many of these problems could be swiftly eradicated if the nation used the billions that have gone for building more prisons, for increasing police forces, and for waging the War on Drugs and instead invested these monies in expanding educational opportunities for African Americans? The horrible mayhem and destruction that occurred last year in the Los Angeles upheaval and the eruption of prison violence that has recently taken place in Lucasville, Ohio, and in Jackson, Michigan, are the tragic but inevitable results that will continue to occur as long as our society places greater emphasis on putting young African-American men in prison than it does in putting them in college. Yet, would it not be far more cost effective to send young people to college for roughly $6,000 to $10,000 a year compared to the $25,000 and more a year it costs to house a single prisoner? Would it not be more economical and more just to invest in education as a proven means of solving many of today's problems and as a proven means of salvaging the futures of many of those trapped by lives with few options? And how many more benefits would derive to our social and economic well-being, Black and White, from having hundreds of thousands more college-educated, productive young African-American men and women? Just as critical, how will the nation expect to meet the ever-expanding work force demands for highly trained minorities without a strong Black college system?

NAFEO and its member schools firmly state that it will be impossible to meet the work force demands for the year 2000 and beyond without the major contributions of thriving, well-supported Historically Black Colleges and Universities. This is true because Black colleges are the unchallenged leaders in training and graduating African-American youth.

HBCUs: A RECORD OF CONTINUING EXCELLENCE

In one important category after another Black institutions of higher learning lead all others in training and graduating African-American students. A summary by "Black Issues in Higher Education" of data from the National Center for Education Statistics shows the following for the 1988–89 school year:

- The top ten schools for conferring Black BAs are all HBCUs. There is only one White school among the top fifteen.
- Black colleges represent the first nine of the top ten schools producing African Americans with BAs in the all-important Engineering/Computer Science/Math category.
- HBCUs represent eight of the top ten schools in the production of African Americans with Business degrees.
- Nine of the top ten producers of Black BAs in the Life Sciences are HBCUs.
- Three of the top five producers of African Americans with medical degrees are HBCUs. (53)

Furthermore, the data show that Black institutions—namely Howard and Clark Atlanta Universities—have surpassed all HWCUs in the production of African Americans with Ph.D.s. (54)

These statistics vividly show the truth of William Gray's recent statement to the effect that Historically Black Colleges and Universities are not just "ethnic assets but national assets." (55) This is exactly how Black colleges and universities should be regarded, as a national asset, a national treasure. Rather than being applauded for their legacy of enduring accomplishments, however, and rather than being rewarded for their unmatched success in furthering the cause of education in the African-American community, the system of HBCUs is being punished and threatened with great danger.

AYERS V. FORDICE

The potential outcome of this case represents one of the single greatest threats to the function, the mission, and the existence of Black institutions of higher learning. Not only are Alcorn State and Mississippi Valley State faced with closure in Mississippi, but similar desegregation cases are being waged in Alabama, Louisiana, Maryland, and Tennessee. (56) If Black schools in any of these states are allowed to be closed, NAFEO, the individual states, and the entire nation will suffer incalculable losses—losses that are not being seriously enough considered by those legislators who would close Black schools. The reasons given for the proposed merger or closure of HBCUs are often couched in financial terms. However, we should not overlook anti-Black bias and racial motivations behind these efforts. Alcorn and Mississippi Valley State are among the top 50 schools in the nation in producing African-American BAs. (57) Just as important, these two universities are also among the top 41 schools nationwide in graduating African Americans in the Engineering/Computer Science/Math category. Have the Mississippi decision-makers given any serious thought to how they can possibly make up for the 300 to 400 BAs that Alcorn and Mississippi Valley State generate each year? Or how they will make up for the hundreds of African-American computer scientists and engineers who are now successfully contributing to the state's social and economic structure?

There is a bitter irony in the fact that Mississippi is the leading state in the effort to close Black schools. This is the state that throughout its history has been notorious for its cruelty and brutal mistreatment of African Americans. Even during slavery, slaves were terrorized into obedience with the threat of being sold into slavery in Mississippi. This is the state that Dr. King in his "I Have A Dream" speech singled out as "a desert state sweltering with the heat of injustice and oppression." (58) This is the state that was always among the leaders in lynching African Americans and burning down their places of worship. This is the state that the Civil Rights Movement viewed as the heart and soul of the Southern system of oppression and injustice. This is the state that etched in the minds of the nation the names Chaney, Schwerner and Goodman, Emmett Till, and Medgar Evers as symbols of Mississippi's violent opposition to racial equality and justice. Now Mississippi is once again in the forefront of a movement that would just as certainly destroy Black lives as did all the other historic acts of violence against the African-American community.

Richard Wright in his classic autobiography "Black Boy" says this of the obstacles placed in the way of his boyhood ambitions in Mississippi: "I was building up in me a dream which the entire educational system of the South had been rigged to stifle. I was feeling the very thing that the state of Mississippi had spent millions of dollars to make sure that I would never feel . . . I was beginning to dream dreams that the state had said were wrong, that the schools had said were taboo." (59) Do the decision-makers of Mississippi and other states realize that in the contemplated closing of Black colleges that they are (just as did the politicians and administrators of Richard Wright's day) placing in great jeopardy the hopes and dreams, the aspirations for betterment of tens of thousands of African Americans and other low-income youth?

We of NAFEO think not. We, however, fully realize the terrible social and human loss that will likely result if these schools are closed. Therefore, with all of the resources at our disposal, with all of our powers of persuasion and protest, NAFEO must resolutely say "NO!" to any of the proposed mergers or closures. It should be made clear, as the earlier discussion on diversity shows, that Black colleges are not opposed to integration on their campuses. However, HBCUs want to be just as emphatic in declaring that *integration* should not mean *disintegration*. History shows all too well what happened to Black elementary and high schools and Black teachers and administrators as a result of these last few decades of public school integration. (60) Consequently, while welcoming diversity, Black colleges must insist upon maintaining all of the administrative and educative policies that make them distinctive (and distinctly successful) as Historically Black Colleges and Universities.

The watchword, in fact, should be *multiply,* not *merge.* The success of Black colleges—so important to the well-being of the nation—should be expanded, not reduced. The crisis in urban education, the shortage of African-American teachers, the crisis of the African-American male, the shortage of college-trained minority workers—the surest way to help solve all these social problems is through the expanded output of Black colleges. This is so because more than any others Black colleges have proved themselves to be the most successful in responding to these problems. It is this message of irreplaceable success that must be put fully before the nation.

SUMMARY AND CONCLUSION

Those who would reduce the number and strength of Black colleges would be crippling one of the few institutions in the nation that is consistently providing inspiration and positive role models for African-American youth. In addition to service to the African-American community, Black colleges and universities help to strengthen the fabric of the entire society, Black and White, through production of teachers, health professionals, legal scholars, and scientists.

For these reasons, our society can ill-afford to diminish the role of HBCUs. In doing so, the nation would be diminishing one of the strongest beacons of hope held out to the African-American community.

The tragedy of Los Angeles in 1992 and similar urban explosions in recent decades reflect the destructive consequences of communities dominated by hopelessness and despair. Black colleges and universities represent a positive, meaningful alternative to such despair. In fulfilling this crucial role, Black institutions of higher learning have earned and deserve the support of all Americans.

REFERENCES

1. Hoffman, Charlene M., Thomas D. Snyder, Bill Sonnenberg, 1992. Historically Black Colleges and Universities. 1976–90. U.S. Department of Educa-

tion, National Center for Educational Statistics. Washington, DC: U.S. Government Printing Office.

2. Woodson, Carter G., 1933. The Mis-Education of the Negro. Washington, DC: The Associated Publishers, Inc.

3. Mays, Benjamin E., 1971. Born to Rebel. New York: Charles Scribner's Sons.

4. The Chronicle of Higher Education, 9/30/92.

5. Hill, Susan T., 1984. The Traditionally Black Institutions of Higher Education, 1960 to 1982. Washington, DC: U.S. Department of Education.

6. Bullock, Henry A., 1967. A History of Negro Education in the South. Cambridge: Harvard University Press.

7. Bowles, Frank, and Frank A. DeCosta, 1971. Between Two Worlds. New York: McGraw-Hill.

8. Johnson, Charles S., 1969. The Negro College Graduate. New York: Negro University Press.

9. McPherson, James M., 1975. The Abolitionist Legacy. Princeton University Press.

10. The 1992 First Annual Report of the President's Advisory Board on Historically Black Colleges and Universities (PAB), 1992. Washington, DC: The National Association for Equal Opportunity in Higher Education.

11. Bennett, Lerone, Jr., 1966. Before the Mayflower. Chicago: Johnson Publishing Co., Inc. This classic work has a very dramatic and insightful analysis of the Washington-DuBois educational debate.

12. For a discussion of HBCUs during this period, see the 1992 PBA Report.

13. Thomas, Arthur E., 1992. The Vital Role of Central State University in the Ohio System of Higher Education. Wilberforce, Ohio: Central State University. This paper contains an extended discussion of the essential role that four-year HBCUs have played and continue to play in the struggle to achieve educational parity for African-Americans.

14. 1992 PBA Report.

15. Tollett, Kenneth S., 1989. Universal Education, Blacks and Democracy: The Expansion and Contraction of Educational Opportunities. W. A. Van-Horne and T. V. Tonnesen (Eds.), Race, Twentieth Century Dilemmas Twentieth Century Progress. Milwaukee: The University of Wisconsin System Institute on Race and Ethnicity.

16. Blake, Elias, Jr., 1991. Is Higher Education Desegregation a Remedy for Segregation but not Educational Inequality? A Study of the Ayers vs. Mabus Desegregation Case. The Journal of Negro Education, Vol. 60, No. 4.

17. Green, Robert L., 1967. Why the Rush to "Upgrade" Negro Colleges? Southern Education Report, July-August.

18. Green, Robert L., 1971. Minority Group Students at Predominantly White Universities: Need and Perspectives. Educational Journal. Vol. 92, September-October, University of Wisconsin.

19. Hoffman, Charlene M., Thomas D. Snyder, Bill Sonnenbert, 1992. Historically Black Colleges and Universities, 1976–90. U.S. Department of Edu-

cation, National Center for Educational Statistics. Washington, DC: U.S. Government Printing Office.

20. Ibid.

21. Jaynes, Gerald D., and Robinson M. Williams, Jr. (eds), 1989. A Common Destiny: Black and American Society. Washington, DC: National Academy Press.

22. Hoffman, Charlene M., Thomas D. Snyder, Bill Sonnenbert, 1992. Historically Black Colleges and Universities, 1976–90. U.S. Department of Education, National Center for Educational Statistics. Washington, DC: U.S. Government Printing Office.

23. Blake, 1991.

24. Inroads. May, 1990. Washington, DC: The National Association for Equal Opportunity in Higher Education.

25. Hoffman, et al., 1992.

26. Tollett, Kenneth S., 1991. Social and Political Issues Concerning Historically Black Colleges: The Case for Black Colleges. Washington, DC: Howard University.

27. Forum. National Institute Against Prejudice & Violence, March 1992, Vol. 6, No. 1. (See also, U.S. News & World Report, 4/19/93).

28. Lezotte, Larry W., 1983. School Learning Climate and Student Achievement. Tallahassee, Florida: SSTA; Ellison, N. M., Smith, J. D., Green, R. L., 1987. Access, Excellence, and Student Retention: A Leadership Commitment. Higher Education: Significant and Contemporary Concerns. Cleveland, Ohio: Info-Tech, Inc. Expectations.

29. Tollett, 1991.

30. Charles H. Wesley, quoted in Goggins, Lathardus, 1987. Central State University: The First One Hundred Years. Wilberforce, Ohio: Central State University.

31. Tollett, 1991.

32. Black Issues in Higher Education, 8/27/92.

33. Cole, Johnnetta B., 1993. Conversations. New York: Doubleday.

34. Tollett, 1991; Blake, 1991.

35. Tollett, 1991.

36. Koretz, Daniel, 1990. Trends in Postsecondary Enrollment of Minorities. Santa Monica, California: The Rand Corporation.

37. Blake, Elias, Jr., 1990. Financial Aid and the Drive Toward Parity of African Americans in Higher Education: Will It Take More Money? Advisory Committee on Student Financial Assistance. Washington, DC: Howard University.

38. Ibid.

39. Carter, Deborah, Reginald Wilson, 1991. Minorities in Higher Education. 10th Annual Report. Washington, DC: American Council on Education.

40. Morgan, Frank, 1992. Racial/Ethnic Trends in Degrees Conferred by Institutions of Higher Education: 1980-81 through 1989–90. National Center for Educational Statistics. Washington, DC: U.S. Department of Education.

41. Black Issues in Higher Education, 5/7/92.

42. Ibid., 9/24/92.

43. Wilson, Reginald, 1992. Minorities in Higher Education, 11th Annual Report. Washington, DC: American Council on Education.

44. Hoffman, et al., 1992.

45. Education Week, 5/8/91.

46. Hoffman, et al., 1992.

47. 1992 PBA Report.

48. Ibid.

49. National Center for Education Statistics, 1992. The Condition of Education 1992. Washington, DC: U.S. Government Printing Office.

50. Edsall, Thomas Byrne, with Mary E. Edsall, 1991. Chain Reaction: The Impact of Race, Rights, and Taxes on American Politics. New York: W.W. Norton.

51. Ibid.

52. Green, Robert L., and Denise L. Wright, 1991. African-American Males: A Demographic Study and Analysis. Cleveland: Cleveland State University.

53. Black Issues in Higher Education, 5/7/92.

54. Ibid.

55. Ibid., 8/27/92.

56. Ibid., 11/5/92.

57. Ibid., 5/7/92.

58. The Words of Martin Luther King, Jr., Selected by Coretta Scott King, 1992. New York: Newmarket Press.

59. Wright, Richard, 1937. Black Boy. New York: Harper Collins Publishers, Inc.

60. See Bell, Derrick A., Jr., 1973. Race, Racism and American Law. Boston: Little, Brown and Company.

61. Black Issues in Higher Education, 12/31/92.

◆ Glossary

Ability tests—Examinations given before instruction, intended to determine the academic aptitude of students.

Abolitionist—A person opposed to slavery in the United States.

Access—Availability of needed and desired services and resources without prejudice.

Accountability—The requirement by public officials and taxpayers that school personnel report to them and demonstrate that monetary appropriations for education yield the expected educational outcomes.

Accreditation—The process used to determine whether specified educational standards are met and the nature of educational programs that can be offered by education institutions. *See also* Regional accreditation

Achievement tests—Standardized tests that purport to measure the knowledge and/or skill attainment of an individual. An individual's test score is compared to the test's standard or norm.

Affirm—The ruling when a higher court agrees with the judgment of a lower court.

Affirmative action—Programs and policies that are designed to redress past discrimination and prevent current discrimination that is based on race, color, religion, gender, or national origin.

African American—The term used for people of African descent who are born in the United States and who have ancestral lineage in the United States system of slavery. Also refers to people of African descent who live in the United States and its territories.

Afrocentric curriculum—Subject matter covered in a class or course of study that is grounded in the history, experiences, traditions, contributions, and thought of people of African descent. *See also* Eurocentric curriculum; Multicultural curriculum

Amendment—Changes or revisions made to a law.

Amici curiae—The English translation is "friend of the court." A person or persons, frequently representing an organization, who is allowed to present in a legal case a particular point of view that has the potential of setting a legal precedent.

Amicus brief—The English translation is "friendly brief." A presented point of view that serves the same purpose as amici curiae, except it is written.

Appeal—To ask a higher court to review the decision of a lower court.

Appellant—The person who asks a higher court to review a case.

Appellate—The court that hears an appeal.

Assessment—The process used to determine the potential for learning or whether expected learning occurred.

Black—*See* African American. For the purposes of this book, the terms are used interchangeably.

Brief—A summary of previous cases, laws, and legal precedents related to the current legal matter before a court. Usually it is used as a guide by the attorney arguing a matter before a court.

Busing—The primary method used to achieve desegregation of schools, whereby students are transported to specific schools to eliminate racial separation.

Competency test—Examinations that purport to determine whether minimum skills and/or knowledge have been achieved.

Criterion-referenced test—An examination that is designed to determine whether an individual has achieved the expected level of mastery of a skill or subject. The individual's score is compared to the predetermined criteria.

Culture—The shared perceptions, experiences, beliefs, knowledge, values, norms, and social forms of a group of people.

Curriculum—A course of study for a grade level or discipline.

De facto segregation—Separation of people by race through practices and traditions but without the support of laws.

De jure segregation—Separation of people by race that is sanctioned by laws.

Demonstration of new topics—Instructional methods used to introduce new skills and concepts to a student.

Desegregation—The plans and processes developed and implemented to eliminate racial separation in school districts, housing, or public facilities.

Discrimination—The practices and traditions of an organization or society of unequally or unfairly limiting the opportunities and participation of an individual or group in the organization or society.

Docket—A court's calendar of cases to be heard.

Drill and practice—Repetitive rote instructional methods that reinforce a student's understanding and development of skills and concepts that have been taught.

Enculturation—Processes and procedures used by an older generation of a society to teach a younger generation the traditions, values, and customs of the culture. Schools are one social institution that is used for enculturation.

Equality in education—The same instructional resources are available to all within a school system.

Equity in education—The exercise of fairness or impartiality in the accessibility of educational opportunities whereby all students in the school can develop their potential.

Eurocentric curriculum—Subject matter covered in a class or course of study that is grounded in the history, traditions, contributions, and thought of people of Western European descent. *See also* Afrocentric curriculum; Multicultural curriculum

Expulsion—Permanent removal of a student from a school or school system.

Gerrymandering—Altering school or voting districts in way that will benefit one group or party over another.

Gun-Free Act of 1994—Federal legislation mandating that all states have a law requiring local school districts to expel students for a minimum of one year for bringing weapons to school. States that do not comply can lose federal funding.

Head Start—Federally funded preschool programs established to strengthen the school and learning readiness of children ages three through five whose combined family income is below the federal index of poverty.

Historically Black Colleges and Universities (HBCUs)—Postsecondary institutions established to educate African Americans specially.

Independent black schools—Precollege private education institutions that are owned and operated by African Americans.

Injunction—A court order that a person or persons either stop or start doing something.

Intelligence Quotient (IQ) tests—Standardized, norm-referenced examinations that purport to measure the cognitive endowment of students. *See also* Norm group

Interdisciplinary—Connections one makes among the theories and knowledge bases of two or more disciplines to understand the breadth and scope of a topic.

Judgment—The official court decision about a legal case.

Jurisdiction—Executive, legislative, judicial, or administrative legal right to exercise official authority.

Land-grant institutions—Land given to states by the federal government through the Morrill Acts of 1862 and 1890 for the building of state agricultural or mechanical colleges.

Learning games—Educational activities for students to demonstrate mastery of skills or concepts.

Mandamus—A court order of an individual, organization, or government agency to take action to correct what is legally wrong or improper.

Multicultural curriculum—Subject matter covered in a class or course of study that is grounded in the history, experiences, traditions, thoughts, and contributions of multiple racial and ethnic groups. *See also* Afrocentric curriculum; Eurocentric curriculum

Norm group—A randomly selected group of individuals who are tested and whose range of scores establishes the scoring standards of performance when the test is used for the general population. The test developers select the norming group.

Norm-referenced test—A test that purports to compare individual or group test results to the test results of a norm group.

People of color—Racial and ethnic groups that are not of European descent.

Quality in education—Standards used to determine that the highest levels of instructional staff, instructional resources, and achievement are acquired and attained.

Racism—The power of one racial group to exclude individuals or racial groups from societal rights. Exercise of the exclusion is based solely on race.

Regional accreditation—Approval by one of the six regional accrediting agencies of education institutions that have met predetermined standards. The six regional accrediting agencies are the closest entity in the United States to national quality control of education. The agencies appraise the quality of education offered at the elementary, secondary, and postsecondary levels. The six agencies are recognized by the United States Department of Education. *See also* Accreditation

Remand—The process of a higher court sending a case back to a lower court for the lower court to address.

Respondent—A person who is being sued. Also called the defendant.

Reverse—A higher court's rejection of the decision of a lower court.

School climate—An intangible sense or feeling that people have about the atmosphere of a school. Responses to the following types of questions determine the school climate: Do people feel they belong or do they feel alienated? Is there a sense of trust or distrust among individuals in the school? Is there a sense of ease or tension in the interactions?

School culture—The behaviors, values, and assumptions that people make about each other and their roles in a school.

School environment—The internal and external forces, practices, and procedures in which education occurs.

Schooling—The systematic interplay among education regulations, academics, the school environment, culture, and climate.

Segregation—Separation of people based on race by laws or customs.

Simulations and applications—Educational activities used when a student has mastered a skill or concept and can engage in independent activities to demonstrate higher-level thinking and conceptualization of the skill or concept. Higher-level thinking and conceptualization skills include comparing and contrasting, critiquing, synthesizing, analyzing, and evaluating.

Socialization—The teaching and development of skills for appropriate interactions and behaviors between and among individuals. For example, in school students are taught to raise their hands to be called on by the teacher so everyone can have a turn to speak instead of everyone speaking at one time.

Special education—Instructional programs, usually individualized, designed and implemented for students whose learning and/or behavioral needs cannot be appropriately met in a general instructional setting.

Standardized test—An examination that purports to be an objective measurement of achievement or skills possessed and that it is administered, scored, and interpreted in a uniform manner regardless of where it is taken. Examples of standardized tests are the Scholastic Achievement Test (SAT), the Graduate Record Examination (GRE), the Iowa Test of Basic Skills, and the Stanford Achievement Test (SAT). *See also* Norm group

Suspension—Temporary removal of a student from a school.

Talented tenth—A term coined by Dr. W.E.B. DuBois, a black educator and author, to describe the portion of the African American population that needed to be developed intellectually and as leaders for African Americans to progress as a people.

Teacher certification—State issued credentials that recognize an individual as being professionally qualified and competent to teach according to state professional teacher standards. Teacher standards vary from state to state.

Territories—Areas under the jurisdiction of the federal government that are not states.

Tracking—The permanent placement of students in a program of study based on students' perceived ability to learn. Tracking placement is based on test scores and teacher judgments.

Universal education—A societal principle based on the belief that all citizens are entitled to an education. In the United States, the concept is embedded in the belief that a democratic society requires enlightened citizens who assume responsibility for the advancement of all aspects of society.

Western curriculum—*See* Eurocentric curriculum.

Whites—People of European descent.

Zero tolerance—School district policies that require immediate and severe punishment for all infractions of discipline codes, regardless of the seriousness of the behavior.

•◦ Index

ABC Board. *See* Alcohol Beverage Control Board
Ability grouping, 63–64, 78
Ability tests, 65
Ability to learn, 75
Abolitionist Society, 47
Access, 145
   to HBCUs, 137–139
Accountability, teacher
Accreditation, regional, 4–5
   agencies, 5
   and HBCUs, 145
   organizations, 201–202
ACE. *See* American Council on Education
Achievement, 23–25, 82–83
   and socioeconomic status, 6, 37–38
Achievement scores, 10
Achievement tests, 65
ACT Program. *See* American College Testing Program
ACT scores, 267
Adams cases, 131–133
Adams v. Califano, 131–133
Adib Shakir, 143
Administration of Children and Family, 8
Admission, college
   and affirmative action, 6–7, 199–200, 265, 267
   and race-conscious policies, 57
   requirements for, 10
Affirmative action, 6–7, 53, 56, 57, 138–139

   and admission, college, 6–7, 199–200, 265, 267
   and Executive Order 8802, 6–7
   and Executive Order 11246, 54
   and executive orders, 174
   in higher education, 41–42
   See also Anti-affirmative action
African American Enterprise Casebook, Volume I, 151
African American Enterprise Casebook Teaching Notes, Volume I, 151
African Free School, 47
African Methodist Episcopalian (AME) Church, 49
African-centered education, 62, 88, 203
After-school activities, 105, 203
   and busing, 87
   at International Preparatory Institute, 104
Alabama, 132
   HBCUs in, 255
   HBCUs in, closing of, 271
Alabama A&M University, 110, 171
Alabama National Guard, 53
Alabama State University, 110
Albany State University, 114
Albright, Robert, 155–156
Alcohol Beverage Control (ABC) Board, 154
Alcorn College, 50
Alcorn State University, 118, 194, 195, 254, 271
Allen, Richard, 49
Allen University, 122–123

Allen, Walter R., 20
Alpha Kappa Alpha Sorority, Incorporated, 207
Alpha Phi Alpha Fraternity, Inc., 207
AME Church. *See* African Methodist Episcopalian Church
American Association for the Advancement of Science, 267
American College Testing (ACT) Program, 196
American Council on Education (ACE), 14, 55, 56, 202
  and affirmative action, 57
  Office of Minorities in Higher Education, 205
American Negro Academy, 51
Anderson, James D., 20
Anti-affirmative action
  and admission, college, 200
  and Civil Rights Initiative, 56–57
  in higher education, 41–42
  impact of, on HBCUs, 143–144
  and Proposition 209, 56
  See also Affirmative action
Apartheid
  liberal and meritocratic, 42
A-Plus Plan, 72–73
Aptitude tests, 82
Arkansas, 132
  and desegregation, 53, 183
Arkansas Baptist College, 112
Asante, Molefi Kete, 20, 62
Assassinations
  by police, 143
Assessment programs, 82
Assessment, student
  and admission, college, 200
Assimilation, 34
Association for the Study of African-American Life and History, 51, 208
Association for the Study of Negro Life and History, 51
Association of Black Sociologists, 208

"Atlanta Compromise" speech (Washington), 50
Atlanta Parent, 90
Atlanta University, 52
Auburn Avenue Research Library on African-American Culture and History, 209
Ayers v. Fordice, 54–55, 254, 271–273
Ayers v. Waller, 54–55

Banks, James A., 20
Barber-Scotia College, 119
Basic skills, 10
Behavior problems, 79–80, 83–84
Bell curve, 65–68
The Bell Curve: Intelligence and Class Structure in American Life (Herrnstein and Murray), 67–68
Bell, Terrel H., 10
Benedict College, 123
Benjamin E. Mays Resource Center, 262
Bennett College, 119–120
Berea College, 49
Bethune-Cookman College, 113
Bethune, Mary McLeod, 39
Binet, Alfred, 67
Binet test, 67
Biotechnology
  in North Carolina, 158–160, 161
"Black Boy" (Wright), 272
Black Caucus, 140
Black Codes, 50, 174
Black history, 74
Black history week/month, 35, 39
"Black Issues in Higher Education," 170
Black Mississippians' Council on Higher Education, 55
Black studies, 53
  origin of, 35
Blake, Elias, 262
Blakey, William, 143
Blue, Dan, 158

Bluefield State College, 127, 130–131
Boarding schools, 51
Bond, Horace Mann, 18, 65
Bowen, William, 141
Bowie State University, 117
Brainwashing, 34
Brown, Charlotte Hawkins, 51
Brown I. See Brown v. Board of Education (1954)
Brown II. See Brown v. Board of Education (1955)
Brown v. Board of Education (1954), 52–53, 54, 64, 73, 130, 132, 145, 181–182, 183, 184, 194, 198–199
Brown v. Board of Education (1955), 183–184, 194, 198, 199
Buchanan, Buck, 265
Bullock, Henry Allen, 19
Bush administration, 142
Bush, George, 137
  and Executive Order 12677, 135
Bush, George W., 56–57
Bush, Jeb
  and One Florida Initiative, 56–57
Busing, 6, 54, 87, 187, 188
  and behavior problems, 84

California
  and anti-affirmative action ballot, 56
  people of color in, 42
  and reverse discrimination, 190–193
California Achievement Test, 12
California African American Museum, 203
Caring
  and minority teachers, 85
Carter G. Woodson Institute for Afro-American and African Studies, 210
Carter, Jimmy
  and Executive Order 12232, 55, 135

Central State University, 121, 133, 139, 143, 171
  funding for, 141–142
Chancy, 272
Charles L. Blockson Afro-American Collection, 210
Charleston School for Free Negroes, 48
Charter schools, 42–43
Chavis, John, 47–48
Cheyney University of Pennsylvania, 48
Cheyney State University, 122, 133
Children's Defense Fund, 8, 204
CIBI. *See* Council of Independent Black Institutions
Citizenship
  and Thirteenth amendment, 174
Civil rights
  and Thirteenth amendment, 174
Civil Rights Act of 1964, 53
  Title IV, 175–176
  Title VI, 55, 131, 133, 176, 194–195
Civil Rights Bill, 73
Civil Rights Initiative, 56–57
Civil Rights Movement, 68, 272
Civil War
  teachers during, 49
Claflin College, 123
Clark Atlanta University, 114, 271
Clark, Kenneth, 52, 182
Clinton administration, 140, 142
Clinton, William Jefferson, 8–9, 137
  Executive Order 12876, 135–136
Coleman, James, 5–6, 37–38, 54
Coleman Report, 5–6, 37–38, 54
College admission. *See* Admission, college
College Board's Advanced Placement Program, 23–24
College degrees
  and income, 269
College-Level Academic Skills Test, 11

Collins, Marva, 264
Colorado, 156
  and school disciplinary action,
    27
Commission on Institutions of
    Higher Education of the North
    Central Association of
    Colleges and Schools, 165
Competency tests, 65
Competition
  and uniforms, 95
Compliance to dismantle, and
    school segregation
  and *Swann v. Charlotte-*
    Mecklenburg Board of
    Education, 185–188
Comprehensive Assessment
    Program National
    Achievement Test, 12
Comprehensive Test of Basic Skills,
    12
Compromise of 1876, 258–259
Computer(s), 72
  access to, 86
  exposure to, 36
  literacy, 24–25, 24(table)
  for mathematics instruction,
    24–25
Concordia College, 110
The Condition of Education 1996, 7
Confidence building, 74
Congress
  and Elementary and Secondary
    Education Act, 9
  and Fourteenth Amendment, 174
  and HBCUs, 262
Congressional Black Caucus
    Foundation, Inc., 204–205
Conley, Robert T., 166
Connecticut
  free blacks in, education for, 48
  and schools for blacks, laws
    against, 48
Connerly, Ward, 41, 42, 56, 57
Constantine, Jill M., 129

Constitutional amendments
  and slavery, 174–175
  and voting rights, 175
  See also particular amendments
Control, 68, 140
Coppin State College, 117
Cost-of-living differences
  and funding, 70
Council of Independent Black
    Institutions (CIBI), 88
Crandall, Prudence, 48
Criminal convictions
  and voting rights, 175
Criminality
  and IQ scores, 67
Crummel, Alexander, 51
Cultural bias
  and test scores, 66
  and testing, 65
Cultural diversity, 70–71, 267–268,
    268–269, 272
Cultural heritage
  and HBCUs, 145–146
Cultural identity, 198
Cultural repository
  HBCUs as, 171
Culture
  and public schooling, 60–61
  and school curriculum, 80
Culture, school, 59
Culture, U.S., 38
Curriculum, 61–63
  development, at HBCUs, 160–161
  multicultural education, 62–63
  state vs. national, 3

Darwin, Charles, 66
Davenport, Vivien
  interview with, 89–101
Davidson, Douglas V.
  interview with, 32–43
De facto segregation, 175
De jure segregation, 175, 183
Defense contractors
  and federal funds, 174

Delany, Martin R., 17
Delaware, 56, 132
   and desegregation, 181, 183, 184
Delaware State University, 112
Delpit, Lisa, 22
Delta Sigma Theta Sorority, Inc.,
   207
Delta State University, 194, 195
Democratic expansion, 265
Desegregation, 6, 36, 60, 84–85
   and Arkansas, 53
   and *Brown v. Board of Education*
     (1954), 181–183
   and *Brown v. Board of Education*
     II (1955), 183–184
   and court decisions, 198–200
   and *Green v. County School Board*
     of New Kent County, 184–185
   and HBCUs, 131–133
   and legislative acts, 175–177
   and Massachusetts, 54
   and Mississippi, 53, 55
   and public schools, 55–56
   and teachers, 53
   and teachers, black vs. white,
     39–40
   and tracking, 64
   See also Segregation
Desegregation judgment, court-
   ordered
   and *Freeman v. Pitts,* 193–194
Detention. *See* Disciplinary action
Dillard University, 116
Disciplinary action, 26–28, 83–84,
   104
   at International Preparatory
     Institute, 98–99
Disciplinary practice, 61
Discipline problems
   and Montessori schools, 76
Discriminated groups
   and testing, 65
Discrimination, 70
   and affirmative action, 6–7
   and Connecticut, 48

   and Kentucky, 49
   and Maryland, 54
   and Massachusetts, 48
   and public funds, 52
   and schooling, 60–61
   against teachers, 53
Disintegration
   vs. integration, 272
Dr. Martin Luther King, Jr. African
   American Immersion
   Elementary School, 203
Doctoral programs
   access to, 167–169, 170
"Doll" study, 52
Dominant groups
   and testing, 65
Douglass, Frederick, 39
Dred Scott decision, 49
Dropouts, 28–29, 41
Drug fetal syndrome, 79
DuBois Learning Center, 203
DuBois, W. E. B., 17, 39, 51, 259
Duke, David, 66
Duke University, 158
DuSable Museum of African
   American History, 204

Eastern Europeans
   and eugenics, 67
Economic opportunity
   and educational opportunity,
     5–7
Economics
   and parental involvement,
     87
Edelman, Marian Wright, 264
Education
   control of, 2–5
   and eugenics, 66
   field of, 36–37
   ideology of, 1–2
   and poverty, 7–9, 23
   and slavery, 47
   and sociology, 33–35
   status and condition of, 22–29

Education attainment
and educational opportunity, 5–7
and income, 30–31, 31(table), 41,
73–74, 266
and tracking, 64
Education reform movement, 9–12
Educational conservatism, 265
Educational opportunity, 5–7
and desegregation, 198
and tracking, 64
See also Equal educational
opportunity
Educational standards, 2
Educator professionalism, 9
Edward Waters College, 113
Eisenhower, Dwight D., 53, 138
Elders, Jocelyn, 144
Elementary and Secondary Education Act (ESEA) of 1965, 7, 175
Title I, 6, 8–9, 24, 176
Elizabeth City State University, 120,
158
Ellison, Ralph, 264
Emancipation
and education, 16
and HBCUs, 108
Emancipation Proclamation, 50
Employment
and affirmative action, 6–7
and postsecondary degrees,
29–30
Employment practices,
discriminatory
and federal funding, 174
Engineering, 267
Enrollment
and affirmative action, 174
in HBCUs, declines in, 266
Environment, school, 59
nonsupportive, 87
Equal educational opportunity
and HBCUs, 107
in Oklahoma, 179–180
in Texas, 180–181
See also Educational opportunity

"Equal Employment Opportunity,"
174
Equal protection, 200
and Fourteenth Amendment, 174
and *Plessy v. Ferguson,* 178–179
Equality, educational, 1–2, 78, 86,
88, 197
and HBCUs, 145–146
and segregation, 60
Equality of Educational Opportunity
(Coleman), 5–6, 37–38, 54
Equity, educational, 1–2, 60, 78, 86,
88, 197
and HBCUs, 145–146
ERIC Clearinghouse on Urban
Education, 131
ESE. *See* Exceptional Student
Education
ESEA. *See* Elementary and
Secondary Education Act of
1965
Eugenicists, 67–68
Eugenics, 66, 67–68
Evers, Medgar, 272
Excellence for All Children Act of
1999, 8–9
Exceptional Student Education
(ESE), 78
Executive Order 8802, 6–7, 174
Executive Order 11246, 54, 174
Executive Order 12232, 55, 135
Executive Order 12677, 135
Executive Order 12876, 135–136
Executive orders, 174. *See also*
particular orders
Experiences
and testing, 82
Expulsion. *See* Disciplinary action
Extracurricular activities, 104

Facilities, equitable separate, 178
Faculty, college
of HBCUs, interview with,
147–157
Fair treatment, 74

Farrakhan, Louis, 21
Faubus, Orval, 53
Fayetteville State University, 120,
    158
FCAT. *See* Florida Comprehensive
    Assessment Test
Federal agencies
    and HBCUs, 136
Federal funding
    and defense contractors, 174
    and discrimination, 176
    and discriminatory employment
        practices, 174
    and HBCUs, 176–177
    See also Funding
Federal government
    and education, control of, 3–4
Federal resources
    for HBCUs, 140–141
Fifteenth Amendment, 50, 175
Fifth Amendment, 195
Financial resources
    and HBCUs, 130
Finch, Charles S., III, 169
Finger, John, 186–187
Fisk University, 124, 171
Florida, 78, 132, 133
    A-Plus Plan in, 72–73
    and anti-affirmative action
        ballot, 56
    and desegregation, 183
    education reform in, 10–12
    people of color in, 42
    and school disciplinary action, 27
Florida A&M University, 113, 146
Florida Board of Regents
    and One Florida Initiative, 57
Florida College Entry-Level
    Placement Test, 11
Florida Comprehensive Assessment
    Test (FCAT), 11–12, 72–73
Florida Department of Education,
    11, 12
Florida Educational Leadership
    Exam, 12

Florida Memorial College, 113–114,
    171
Florida Statewide Assessment
    Program, 10–12
Florida Supreme Court
    and anti-affirmative action
        proposal, 56–57
Florida Teacher Certification
    Examination, 12
Florida Writing Assessment
    Program, 11
Fort, Edward, 262
Fort Valley State College, 114
Fourteenth Amendment, 50, 52–53,
    174–175, 182, 185, 195,
    197–198
Fox, Linette P.
    interview with, 147–157
Francis, Norman, 146
Frederick D. Patterson Research
    Institute, 210
Free blacks
    schools for, 47–48
Freedman Bureau, 49, 50
Freedom of choice
    and *Green v. County School Board
        of New Kent County*, 184–185
Freeman v. Pitts, 193–194
Funding, 69–70, 199
    cutbacks in education, 55
    for HBCUs, 55, 141–142, 255
    for higher education, 14–15
    at International Preparatory
        Institute, 95
    and *San Antonio Independent
        School District v. Rodriguez*,
        188–190
    and Teacher Education Redesign,
        15
    See also Federal funding

Galton, Francis, 66–67
General intelligence, 67
"The General Intelligence Factor,"
    (Gottfredson), 68

Genetics, 66
George W. Watkins Schools, 184–185
Georgia, 132
    and desegregation judgment,
        court-ordered, 193–194
Gerrymandering, 186, 188
G-factor, 67, 68
*The G-Factor: The Science of Mental
    Ability* (Jensen), 67
GI Bill, 14
Gifted classes, 75
Gifted education, 78
Goodman, 272
Gordon, Robert, 67
Gottfredson, Linda, 68
Grade retention, 28–29
Grade Ten Assessment Test, 11
Graduates
    of HBCUs, increase in number of,
        149–150
Graduation requirements
    high school, 10
Grambling State University, 116, 171
Grant, Carl A., 62
*Green v. County School Board of New
    Kent County*, 184–185, 186,
    193, 200
Gun-Free Schools Act of 1994, 28

Hale-Benson, Janice E., 19
Hamner, Charles, 158, 162
Hampton University, 126, 146, 171
Hampton, Virginia, 49
Hangings, 143
Hanna, John P., 137–138
Harrington, Michael, 7
Harris, Andrea, 158
Harris, Edward M.
    interview with, 69–77
Harris, Sarah, 48
Harris-Stowe State College, 119
Harvard, 256–257
The Harvard Educational Review, 68
Harvey, William, 146
"HBCU Capital Financing," 177

HBCU Initiative. *See* The Union
    Institute HBCU Initiative
HBCUs
    access to, 137–139
    accomplishments of, 128–129,
        270–271
    and anti-affirmative action
        movement, impact of,
        143–144
    challenges to, 129–131, 140–142,
        164
    contributions of, 260–263
    and cultural heritage, 145–146,
        171
    curriculum development at,
        160–161
    definition of, 109–110
    and desegregation, 131–133
    enrollment in, 51, 55, 266
    and equal educational
        opportunity, 107
    faculty of, interview with,
        147–157
    federal resources for, 140–141
    and funding, 55, 141–142,
        176–177, 255
    graduates of, 149–150, 264–265
    history of, 108–109, 139, 258–260
    and HMU Program Initiative,
        157–165
    and leadership development,
        255–256
    and leadership role models,
        142–143
    list of, 110–127
    mergers and closings of, 200
    mission of, 137–140, 145–146
    need for, 144
    in North Carolina, 163–164
    organizations assisting, 134–136,
        206
    and post-baccalaureate degree
        attainment, 129
    presidents of, 32–43, 146–147
    private, 161

and program assistance, 156–157
proposals to merge or close,
253–258, 271–273
and racial identification, 163–164
and racism, 141–142
and racist white media
propaganda, 145
and regional accreditation, 145
role of, 137–140, 149–150,
262–264
and The Union Institute HBCU
Initiative, 165–171
and United Negro College Fund,
52
vs. HWCUs, 255–257, 258,
265–268, 271
White House Initiative on, 55,
135–136
*See also particular colleges and
universities*
Head Start, 7, 8, 23, 54
Headmaster
private school, interview with,
89–101
HENA. *See* Higher Education and
National Affairs
Henderson, John, 146
Henry, Janice B.
interview with, 77–88
*Hereditary Genius: An Inquiry into
Its Laws and Consequences*
(Galton), 66–67
Heredity
and intelligence, 66–67
Heritage
need to hold on to, 85–86
Herman, Alexis, 144
Herrnstein, Richard, 67
HEW. *See* U.S. Department of
Health, Education, and
Welfare
High School Competency Test, 11
High schools
and diplomas, 29, 35–36
and graduation requirements, 10

Higher education, 13–16
Higher Education Act
Title III, 177
Higher Education Act of 1965, 109,
176
Higher Education Act of 1998,
176
Higher education advocacy
associations, 202–203
*Higher Education and National
Affairs,* 202
Higher Education and National
Affairs (HENA), 203
Hill, Tony, 57
Hilliard, Asa G., III, 22
Historical identification and
preservation of HBCUs, 130
Historical racial identification
and HBCUs, 163–164
Historical repository
HBCUs as, 171
Historically Minority Universities
Bioscience and Biotechnology
Program Initiative. *See* HMU
Program Initiative
Historically White Colleges and
Universities. *See* HWCUs
History, U.S., 35, 38
HMU Program Initiative
director of, interview with,
157–165
establishment of, 157–159
goals, 160
mission of, 159–160
and North Carolina
Biotechnology Center, 162
successes and challenges of,
163
Holloway, Ernest, 146
Holmes, Hamilton, 53
Holmes, Oliver Wendell, 192
Homework
at International Preparatory
Institute, 97
hooks, bell

House Subcommittee meeting on HBCUs (1988), 262

"How Much Can We Boost IQ and Scholastic Achievement?" (Jensen), 68

Howard University, 50, 52, 112–113, 128, 171, 271

Humphries, Frederick, 144, 146

Hunter-Gault, Charlayne, 53

Huston-Tillotson College, 125

HWCUs
    trends at, 266–268
    vs. HBCUs, 255–257, 258, 265–268, 271

IDEA. *See* Individuals with Disabilities Education Act

Illiteracy, 41

Immersion schools, 104–105, 203

Immigrants
    and public schools, 38

Improving America's Schools Act, 8
    Title 1, 71–72

"Improving America's Schools Act of 1964," 176

Income
    and college degrees, 269
    and education attainment, 30–31, 31(table), 41, 73–74, 266

Indentured servants, 47

Indifference, 63

Individuals with Disabilities Education Act (IDEA), 26, 129
    amendments of 1997, 129

Industrial education, 108, 259

Inner-city populations
    and charter schools, 42–43

Institute for Independent Education, 88

Institute of Minority Economic Development, 158

Instruction
    organizational design of, 63–64
    style of, 63–64, 81

Instructional personnel, 2

Integration, 272
    compulsory, 185

Intelligence
    and testing, 64–65. *See also particular tests*

Intelligence Quotient tests. *See* IQ tests

Interdenominational Theological Center, 114

International Preparatory Institute (IPI)
    achievement assessment at, 96–97
    admission procedures at, 95, 103
    curriculum at, 92–93
    disciplinary action at, 98–99
    extracurricular and after-school activities at, 104
    and funding, 95
    and graduates, success of, 99
    headmaster at, interview with, 89–101
    history of, 90–91
    homework at, 97
    parent of student at, interview with, 101–104
    parental involvement at, 97–98, 102–103
    philosophy and mission of, 91–92
    teaching staff, 93–95
    testing at, 96–97

Internet
    and HBCUs, 131

"Investing in Human Potential: Science and Engineering at the Crossroads," 267

Iota Phi Theta Fraternity, Inc., 207

Iowa Test of Basic Skills, 12, 96–97

IPI. *See* International Preparatory Institute

IQ scores
    and criminality, 67

IQ tests, 65, 67

Jackson, Jesse, 137, 144, 264
Jackson State University, 118, 194
James, George G. M., 18
Jarvis Christian College, 125
JCSU. *See* Johnson C. Smith
    University
Jensen, Arthur, 67
Jews
    and eugenics, 67
Jim Crow laws, 175
John Henrik Clarke Africana Library,
    210
Johns Hopkins University, 67
Johnson, Andrew, 174
Johnson C. Smith University (JCSU),
    120, 147–157
    interdisciplinary courses at, 150
    program funding at, 153–155
    students at, 152–153
    teaching challenges at, 150–152
    and United Negro College Fund,
    155–156
Johnson, Lyndon B., 6–7, 7, 53, 73
    and Executive Order 11246, 54,
    174
Joint Center for Political and
    Economic Studies, 210
Jordan, Vernon, 144
The Journal of Negro Education, 52
The Journal of Negro History, 51

Kansas, 49
    and *Brown v. Board of Education*
    (1954), 52–53
    and desegregation, 181, 183, 184
Kappa Alpha Psi Fraternity, Inc., 207
Kennedy, John, 53
Kentucky, 132, 133
    and discriminatory practices, 49
Kentucky State University, 116, 133,
    171
King, Martin Luther, Jr., 73, 264, 265,
    272
Knowledge, 63
    access to, 86

Ku Klux Klan, 66

Labeling, 70, 75
Land-grant institutions, 49, 50,
    134–135
Lane College, 124
Langston University, 122, 146, 171
Laws
    against discriminatory practices,
    49
Leadership development, 263–264,
    265
    and HBCUs, 255–256
Leadership role models, 264–266
    and HBCUs, 142–143
Learning disabilities, 82
Lee, Spike, 264
Legislative acts
    and desegregation, 175–177
    See also particular acts
LeMoyne-Owen College, 124
Level playing field, 41, 42
Lewis, Richard, 264–265
Liberal apartheid, 42
Liberal arts, 259
    and HBCUs, 108–109
Libraries, public
    access to, 86
Lincoln University, 119, 122, 130
Literacy, 41, 50, 51
    and voting rights, 175
Livingstone College, 120
Locke, Alain, 51
Locke, Gary, 56
Louisiana, 132
    and HBCUs, 255, 271
    and separate but equal doctrine,
    177–179
Lucy, Autherine, 53
Lynching, 272
Lyons, Professor, 156

Majority-to-minority transfer
    program, 186, 188
Malcolm X, 19, 143, 145

Malcolm X Academy, 203
Mallory, Bill, 141
Manumission Society, 47
Marable, Manning, 22, 169
Marshall, Thurgood, 52–53, 73, 144, 145, 264
Maryland, 54, 132, 133
and desegregation, 183
and HBCUs, closing of, 271
Maryland Eastern Shore, 146
Massachusetts
and desegregation, 54
and discriminatory practices, 48, 49
Mathematics instruction
computer use for, 24–25
Mays, Benjamin, 256
McLaurin v. Oklahoma State Regents, 179–180, 199
McLin, C. J., Jr., 141
Media propaganda, racist white, 145
Meek, Kendrick, 57
Meharry Medical College, 50, 124, 128
Meredith, James, 53, 194
Meritocratic apartheid, 42
Mfume, Kweisi, 144
Michigan, 270
and school disciplinary action, 27
Michigan State University, 137–138
Middle States Association of College and Schools, 5, 201
Miles College, 111
Minimal education, 13
Minorities
and literacy, 41
Minority admission program, 200
Minority populations, 42
"Minority Science and Engineering Improvement Program," 177
Minority teachers
number of, decrease in, 85
The Mis-Education of the Negro (Woodson), 34, 52, 88
Mislabeling, 26

Mississippi, 132
and desegregation, 53, 55
and HBCUs, 200, 254, 255, 271–273
and racial neutrality, 194–197
Mississippi Board of Trustees of State Institutions of Higher Learning, 254
Mississippi State University, 194, 195, 254
Mississippi University for Women, 194, 195
Mississippi Valley State University, 118, 194, 254, 271
Missouri, 132
Moité, Derrick L.
interview with, 101–104
Montessori schools, 76, 78
Moorland-Spingarn Research Center, 210
Morals orientation
and charter schools, 43
Morehouse College, 114–115
Morehouse School of Medicine, 115
Morgan State University, 117, 146
Morrill Act of 1862, 49
Morrill Act of 1890, 50, 135
Morris Brown College, 115
Morris College, 123, 167
Morrison, Toni, 264
Multicultural education curriculum, 62–63
Multicultural programs, 267
Multiculturalism
and charter schools, 43
Murray, Charles, 67
Museum of African American History, 204
Museums, 203–204

NAACP. *See* National Association for the Advancement of Colored People
NAFEO. *See* National Association for Equal Opportunity in Higher Education

Nakaboo, Arch, 158
NASULGC. *See* National Association
of State Universities and
Land-Grant Colleges
*A Nation at Risk: The Imperative for
Educational Reform*, 9–10
National Academy of Sciences,
267
National Advisory Council, 169
National Alliance of Black School
Educators, 208
National Association for Equal
Opportunity in Higher
Education (NAFEO), 54, 109,
134, 206, 259, 266, 270, 271,
272
National Association for
Multicultural Education,
208
National Association for the
Advancement of Colored
People (NAACP), 51, 52, 131,
205
National Association of State
Universities and Land-Grant
Colleges (NASULGC), 133–134
National Black Child Development
Institute, 209
National Black MBA Association,
Inc., 209
National Center for Education
Statistics, 7, 109, 170
National Civil Rights Museum, 204
National Commission on Excellence
in Education, 10
National Commission on Higher
Education Issues, 14
National Council for Black Studies,
Inc., 209
National Council of Negro Women,
Inc., 205
National curriculum, 3
National Education Association
(NEA), 53
National Guard, 53

National HBCU Faculty
Development Network, 134,
206
National Science Foundation, 267
National Society of Black Engineers,
209
National Teacher Examination, 37
National Urban League, Inc., 51, 205
NEA. *See* National Education
Association
Neighborhood schools, 84
New England Association of Schools
and Colleges, 5, 201
New Kent School, 184–185
New York City
African Free Schools in, 47, 48
and school disciplinary action, 27
Ninth Amendment, 195
Norfolk State University, 126
Norman, Jessye, 264
Norming group, 65
North Carolina, 49, 56, 132
biotechnology in, 158–160, 161
and desegregation, 183, 185–188
free blacks in, schools for, 47–48
and HBCUs, 163–164
Palmer Memorial Institute in, 51
North Carolina A&T University, 120,
158, 171, 262, 265
North Carolina Biotechnology
Center, 158, 161, 162
North Carolina Central University,
121, 158, 162
North Carolina State University, 158
North Central Association of
Colleges and Schools, 5, 201
Northwest Association of Schools
and Colleges, 5, 202
Nunn, Eleanor F.
interview with, 157–165
Nurturing environment, 263

Oakwood College, 111
Oberlin College, 48
OCR. *See* Office of Civil Rights

Office for the Advancement of
Public Black Colleges,
133–134, 206
Office of Civil Rights Elementary
and Secondary School
Compliance Reports, 25
Office of Civil Rights (OCR), 27, 128,
131–133
Office of Economic Opportunity, 7,
8, 54
Office of Minorities in Higher
Education, 55
American Council on Education,
205
Office of Postsecondary Education,
4
Ohio, 56, 132, 133, 270
and HBCUs, funding for, 141–142
higher education reform in,
15–16
public schools in, exclusion of
blacks from, 48
and school disciplinary action,
27
Ohio Department of Education, 15
Ohio State University, 141–142
Oklahoma, 56, 132
and desegregation, 183
and equal educational
opportunity, 179–180
O'Leary, Hazel, 144
Omega Psi Phi Fraternity, Inc., 207
One Florida Initiative, 56–57
100 Black Men of America, Inc., 205
Oppression, 63
*The Origin of Species: The
Preservation of Favored Races
in the Struggle for Life*
(Darwin), 66
*The Other American: Poverty in the
United States* (Harrington), 7

Paine College, 115
Palmer Memorial Institute, 51
Panhellenic organizations, 207–208

Parent
of International Preparatory
Institute student, interview
with, 101–104
Parent Teacher Association (PTA), 86
at International Preparatory
Institute, 98
Parental involvement, 71–72
and economics, 87
at International Preparatory
Institute, 97–98, 102–103
Patterson, Frederick D., 52, 135
Paul Quinn College, 125
Peabody, George Foster, 50
Pennsylvania, 132, 133
The Pennsylvania State University,
133
People of color
and eugenics, 67
population of, increase in, 68
Phi Beta Sigma Fraternity, Inc., 208
Philadelphia
and Abolitionist Society,
establishment of schools by,
47
Philander Smith College, 112
Piaget period, 78
Pierce, Raymond C., 131–133
Plessy v. Ferguson, 50–51, 177–179,
183
*Poems on Various Subjects Religious
and Moral* (Wheatley), 47
Police, 270
assassinations by, 143
Politics, 72–73
and higher education, 13
and school curriculum, 61–62
Poll taxes
and voting rights, 175
Population, minority, 42
increase in, 68
Post-baccalaureate degrees
and HBCUs, 129
Postsecondary degrees, 13–14,
29–31, 30(table)

Postsecondary education, 51
    and teachers, black vs. white,
        39–41
Poverty, 73–74
    and education, 7–9, 23
    and special education, 26
Power, 63, 68, 140
    and racism, 66
Prairie View A&M University, 125
Prejudice
    and ability to learn, 75
Prejudice and Your Child, 52
Preparatory day schools, 51
President(s), college
    of HBCUs, 130, 146–147
    of HBCUs, interview with,
        136–147
President's Advisory Board on
    Historically Black Colleges
    and Universities, 135
Price, Leontyne, 264
Prince George's County, 54
Principal(s), 31, 32(table)
    public school, interview with,
        68–77
Prisons, 270
Private HBCUs, 161
Private school(s), 60
    enrollment in, 23
    headmaster, interview with,
        89–101
    resurgence of, 88–89
Professional organizations, 208–209
Professional racism, 73
Professional staff, 31–32, 33(table)
Propaganda, 34
Proposition 209, 56
Psychology
    and eugenics, 66
Psychology Today, 68
PTAs. *See* Parent Teacher
    Associations
Public funds
    and discriminatory practices, 52
Public school(s)

    and desegregation, 55–56
    enrollment in, 23
    and immigrants, 38
    in Ohio, exclusion of blacks from,
        48
    principal, interview with, 68–89
    and segregation, 38–39
    teacher, interview with, 77–89
Pupil Placement Act, 184

Quality Education for Minorities
    Network, 205
Quality, educational, 1–2, 60, 78, 86,
    88, 197
    and HBCUs, 145–146

"Race-conscious" admissions
    policies, 57
Race-specific programs, 269
Racial diversity, 268
Racial division
    and HBCUs, 108
Racial identification
    and *Plessy v. Ferguson,* 177–178
Racial neutrality, 130, 200
    and *United States v. Fordice,*
        194–197
Racial quotas, 187, 188
Racism, 34, 143–144
    and the bell curve, 66
    and HBCUs, 141–142, 144,
        254–258, 271–273
    professional, 73
Racist white media propaganda, 145
Reading levels, 41
Reading Recovery Program, 76
Reagan, Ronald
    and education funding, cutbacks
        in, 55
Reagan administration, 142
Recognition
    and education, 16
Reconstruction, 258
Redesign. *See* Teacher Education
    Redesign

"Reflections on the Promise of
Brown and Multicultural
Education" (Grant), 62–63
*Regents of the University of
California v. Bakke,* 7,
190–193, 199–200
Regional Accreditation. *See*
Accreditation, regional
Religious orientation
and charter schools, 43
Remediation, 176, 267
Research and Development
and higher education, 13
Research centers, 209–211
Research Focus on Black Education,
Special Interest Group,
American Education Research
Foundation, 205–206
Resegregation, 61
and tracking, 54, 64
Respect
for teachers, 79
Reverse discrimination, 200
and affirmative action, 6–7
and *Regents of the University
of California v. Bakke,*
190–193
Rhodes Scholars, 51
Richardson, Earl, 146
Roberts, Sarah C., 48
Roosevelt, Franklin D.
and Executive Order 8802, 6–7,
174
Rust College, 118

Saint Augustine's College, 121
Saint Paul's College, 126–127
Salaries, teacher, 37
*San Antonio Independent School
District v. Rodriguez,* 188–190,
199
SAT scores, 267
Satcher, David, 144
Savannah State University, 115,
132

Scholarships, 269
Schomburg Center for Research in
Black Culture, 211
School curriculum
and culture, 80
School demographics, 9
School desegregation. *See*
Desegregation
School districts, 3
School segregation. *See* Segregation
Schooling, 59, 60–61, 88–105
Schools
established by Abolitionist
Society, 47
for free blacks, 47–48
as social systems, 59
Sciences, 267
and higher education, 14
Scientific American, 68
Segregation, 34, 38–39
and busing, 54
and constitutional amendments,
174–175
and Kansas, 52–53
and land-grant institutions,
50
in public schools, and
compliance to dismantle,
185–188
See also Desegregation
Self-identity, 63
Self-image, poor
and "doll" study, 52
Seminaries, private, 108
Separate but equal doctrine,
199
and *Brown v. Board of Education*
(1954), 181–182
and *Plessy v. Ferguson,* 178–179
Servicemen's Readjustment Act of
1944. *See* GI Bill
Shaw University, 49, 121
Shockley, William, 67
Sigma Gamma Rho Sorority, Inc.,
208

Slavery, 47, 272
  and constitutional amendments,
    174–175
SLD. *See* Specific Learning
    Disabilities
Slow learners, 82
SMART objectives, 154
Smith, Joshua, 265
Social equality, 63
Social issues
  and higher education, 13
Social justice, 265
Social order
  and U.S. Supreme Court,
    decisions of, 173, 297–300
Social problems
  and teaching, 79
Social systems
  schools as, 59
Socioeconomic background
  and instructional style, 81
Socioeconomic status
  and academic achievement, 6
  and achievement, 37–38
Sociology
  and education, 33–35
The Souls of Black Folks (DuBois), 51
South Boston High School, 54
South Carolina, 49, 132
  and desegregation, 181, 183, 184
  free blacks in, education for, 47,
    48
  people of color in, 42
South Carolina State University, 123
Southern Association of College and
    Schools, 5, 202
Southern Education Foundation,
    206
Southern University and A&M
    College, 116
Southern University at New Orleans,
    117
Spearman, Charles, 67
Special education, 25–26, 61, 75, 199
  and charter schools, 42

Specific Learning Disabilities (SLD),
    78
Spelman College, 56, 115–116
Spikes, Delores, 146
Sports, 265
Standardized tests, 35–36, 65
The Standards for Colleges and
    Universities Preparing
    Teachers. *See* Teacher
    Education Redesign
Stanford-Binet Test, 65, 67
Stanford University, 67
State certification, 37
State constitution, 3
State curriculum, 3
State examinations, 37
States
  and education, control of, 2–4
Steel, Claude M., 21
Stereotypes
  and low expectations, 64
Stillman College, 111
Stokes, Louis, 143
"Strengthening HBCUs," 177
Student outcomes, 2
Students
  changes in, 79–80
Students and Free Enterprise
    Program, 153
Sullivan, Louis, 144
Supplementary programs, 105, 203
Supportive environment, 263
"The Survival of the Black Male,"
    143
Suspension. *See* Disciplinary action
*Swann v. Charlotte-Mecklenburg
    Board of Education,* 185–188,
    200
Sweatt v. Painter, 180–181, 182, 199

"Talented tenth," 51
Talladega College, 111
Teacher Education Redesign, 15–16
Teacher expectations, 63, 64
  and testing, 82–83

Teacher(s), 31–32, 32(table)
    and accountability, 10
    and autonomy, at International
        Preparatory Institute, 95–96
    black vs. white, education of,
        39–41
    during Civil War, 49
    and desegregation, 36
    discrimination against, 53
    in Montessori schools, 76
    public school, interview with,
        77–89
    salaries of, 37
    and state certification, 37
Teaching profession
    changes in, 78–79
    preparation for, 10
    and Teacher Education Redesign,
        15–16
Technical training, 259
Technology, 9, 10, 24, 72
    access to, 36
    and higher education, 14
Ten Percent Law, 56–57
Tennessee, 50, 56, 132
    and HBCUs, closing of, 271
    and school disciplinary action, 27
Tennessee State University, 124–125,
        156
Terman, Lewis, 67
Test administrators, 82
Test scores
    and cultural bias, 66
Testing, 82–83
    and ability grouping, 63–64
    achievement, 10
    and the bell curve, 65–68
    and Florida assessment program,
        11–12
    and instructional style, 81
    at International Preparatory
        Institute, 96–97
    and politics, 72–73
    and tracking, 64–65
    See also particular tests

Texas, 132, 133
    and desegregation, 183
    and equal educational
        opportunity, 180–181
    and funding, school, 188–190
    and school disciplinary action, 27
    and Ten Percent Law, 56–57
Texas Court of Civil Appeals, 180
Texas Minimum Foundation School
        Program, 188
Texas Southern University, 125–126
Texas Supreme Court, 180
Textbooks, 75, 86
Thirteenth Amendment, 49, 50, 174,
        195
Thomas, Arthur E.
    interview with, 136–147
Till, Emmett, 272
*To Strengthen Quality in Higher
        Education,* 14
Tougaloo College, 119
Tracking, 61, 63–64, 199
    and resegregation, 54
    and testing, 64–65
TUI. *See* The Union Institute
Tuskegee Institute, 52, 135
Tuskegee University, 111, 135, 171

UNCF. *See* United Negro College
        Fund
UNCF IBM Doctoral Fellowship, 154
Understanding
    and minority teachers, 85
Uniforms, 95
The Union Institute (TUI), 155–156
    accomplishments and challenges
        of, 169–171
    beginning of, 167
    design of, 168–169
    and doctoral programs, access to,
        167–169, 170
    Entry Colloquium, 170–171
    goal of, 167–168
    HBCU Initiative, 165–171
    impetus of, 165–167

United Negro College Fund (UNCF), 52, 135, 154, 206

United States v. Fordice, 55, 130, 133, 163, 194–197, 200

Universal education, 1–2, 22

University of Alabama, 53

University of Arkansas, Pine Bluff, 112

University of California at Berkeley, 67

University of California at Davis and reverse discrimination, 190–193

University of Delaware, 68

University of Georgia, 53

University of Maryland-Eastern Shore, 118

University of Mississippi, 53, 194, 195

University of North Carolina at Chapel Hill, 158

University of North Carolina at Pembroke, 158

University of Oklahoma, 179–180

University of Southern Mississippi, 194, 195

University of Texas, 180

University of Texas Law School, 180–181

University of the District of Columbia, 113

University of the Virgin Islands, 126

Urban Research Group Grant, 153–154

U.S. Bureau of Refugees, Freedman, and Abandoned Lands, 49

U.S. Bureau of the Census, 7

U.S. Circuit Court of Appeals, 53

U.S. Commission on Civil Rights, 6

U.S. Congress
and Freedman Bureau, 49
and HBCUs, 129
and Morrill Act of 1862, 49
and Morrill Act of 1890, 50
and special education, 26

U.S. Constitution
and education, control of, 3–4

U.S. Department of Defense
and zero tolerance, 28

U.S. Department of Education, 4, 9, 25, 128, 131, 176
and accreditation, regional, 201
and HBCUs, 136

U.S. Department of Health and Human Services, 8

U.S. Department of Health, Education, and Welfare (HEW), 54, 55, 187, 194

U.S. Office of Education, 176

U.S. Supreme Court, 50–51, 52–53, 130, 163, 177–197
and affirmative action, 7
decisions of, and social order, 173, 197–200
and Dred Scott decision, 49
See also particular decisions

Values orientations
and charter schools, 43

Virginia, 132, 133
and desegregation, 181, 183, 184–185

Virginia colony, 47

Virginia State University, 127

Virginia Union University, 127, 171

Visualization, 74

Vocational education, 50

Vonovich, Governor, 142

Voorhees College, 123–124

Voting rights
and constitutional amendments, 175

Voting Rights Acts of 1964 and 1965, 175

W. E. B. DuBois Institute for Afro-American Research, 211

W. E. B. DuBois Learning Center, 105

Walker, Alice, 264

Wallace, George, 53

War on Drugs, 270
War on Poverty, 7
Washington
    and anti-affirmative action
        ballot, 56
Washington, Booker T., 17, 50, 259
Washington, D.C.
    American Negro Academy in, 51
Weekend activities, 105, 203
West Virginia, 132
West Virginia State College, 127, 130
Western Association of Schools and
    Colleges, 5, 202
Western Europeans
    and eugenics, 67
Wheatley, Phillis, 47
White anger, 107
White flight, 55
White House Initiative on HBCUs,
    128, 135–136, 206

and Executive Order 12232, 55
Wilberforce University, 122, 146
Wilder, Douglas, 264
Wiley College, 126
Winston-Salem State University,
    121, 158, 171
Wisconsin, 203
Woodson, Carter G., 18, 34, 35, 51,
    52, 88, 256
Wright, Richard, 272
Wright State University, 139

Xavier University, 117, 146

Young, Andrew, 264
Young, Marion Wright Edelman,
    144

Zero tolerance policies, 28
Zeta Phi Beta Sorority, Inc., 208

⬤⤙ About the Author

Cynthia L. Jackson is originally from New York City. In the early 1960s, her family moved to Atlanta when her father accepted the position of dean of the school of social work at Atlanta University. Her mother was a professor at Morris Brown College in Atlanta. Both institutions are HBCUs.

Jackson received her baccalaureate degree in sociology from Spelman College, a historically black women's institution in Atlanta. Her master's degree in elementary education is from Atlanta University, the first historically black graduate institution in the country. Her Ph.D. degree, from The Ohio State University, is in educational development policy analysis. Jackson is the fourth generation in her family to have graduated from college. Her elementary level education was in public and private schools in New York City. She attended school for two years in Atlanta, when the school system was segregated. She graduated from a white private college preparatory boarding school in western Massachusetts. By her senior year she was the only black female student and one of three black students in the entire school.

Her precollege education experiences afforded her exposure to relatively multiracial and multiethnic private and public educational settings in New York, a segregated educational public school setting in Atlanta, and a token desegregated private high school setting in Williamstown, Massachusetts. From 1973 to 1978, she was an elementary teacher at DeKalb County School System in Georgia. For two years, she taught in a school whose student population was 100 percent white and wealthy. Her third year she taught in a school whose student population was 98 percent white and wealthy, and 2 percent black and poor. The last two years she taught in a school that was 85 percent black and 15 percent white, primarily working class and inner city. Her assignment to the last school came after she made several requests to be transferred to an inner-city school and the school district personnel director kept telling her that she was "one of the few Afro-Americans we can send to white schools." These experiences gave her first hand knowledge of the correlation between economics, race, and access to educational opportunities. It is for this reason that she dedicated her career to providing educational opportunities for blacks, other people of color, and other discriminated groups.

She has twenty-five years of experience as the originator of academic and outreach programs for a variety of educational and community organizations. As graduate college dean for underserved populations, she was the architect of The Union Institute Historically Black Colleges and Universities (HBCU) Initiative. Currently, she is a graduate college core faculty member at The Union Institute in Cincinnati, Ohio.